Child Rights in India

Geeta Chopra

Child Rights in India

Challenges and Social Action

Springer

Geeta Chopra
Department of Human Development
and Childhood Studies,
Institute of Home Economics
University of Delhi
New Delhi
India

ISBN 978-81-322-2445-7 ISBN 978-81-322-2446-4 (eBook)
DOI 10.1007/978-81-322-2446-4

Library of Congress Control Number: 2015944171

Springer New Delhi Heidelberg New York Dordrecht London

Printed on acid-free paper

Springer (India) Pvt. Ltd. is part of Springer Science+Business Media (www.springer.com)

Wherever there is a Human Being, I see God—given rights inherent in that human being, whatever may be the sex or complexion.

William Llyod Garrison

Dedicated to
My heart and my soul, my lovely children,
Arushi and Parth
And
My dear husband Sanjay for his quiet
support!!

Foreword

Having descended on earth, each child is imbued with tremendous potential capable of doing wonders. However, there has been a tradition of sorts of ignoring the voices and wants of children with the result that they did not grow and develop well. Their aspirations and likings were usually sidelined even in matters directly concerning them. It was only after the issue of Child Rights emerged as a vital instrumentality for their development that countries framed pro-child policies, legislations and regulatory mechanisms. In this context the initiative of UNCRC seeking to guarantee the health, well-being and safety of children has been an important milestone for securing for children what is rightfully their due. The UNCRC recognises that certain rights are essential to the proper development of a child and therefore non-negotiable. Child rights are important not for children alone, but for the society and nation at large. With this conviction, it is incumbent on all concerned to make adequate investments in young people for their proper grooming and facilitating development of their abilities. Equally important is ensuring a healthy childhood to them. Studies have shown that rights-based education is an effective tool for promoting good citizenship and the concepts of respect and responsibility.

Most studies outlining the actual status of child rights in India have been scanty and not suitably comprehensive so that different government schemes and programmes like Early Childhood Care and Education (ECCE), Integrated Child Development Services, National Rural Health Mission, Rajiv Gandhi Creche Scheme, Sarva Shiksha Abhiyan, Right to Education and more recently, Beti Bachao Beti Padhao Abhiyan have not been able to adequately address the issue. We are yet to fully understand that knowing our rights empowers us, boosts our self-esteem and we are less likely to infringe on others' rights.

I have known Dr. Geeta, the author of this publication for over 15 years, who has been working in the field of prevention and early detection of childhood disabilities amongst resource-crunched communities. Based on her studies, the educational materials she brought out on infant and child survival and development of young children in the form of sets of books, posters and screening schedule for disabilities, have even used by NIPCCD, presumably by other child development organisations as well. The present book on Child Rights presents yet another facet of her professional commitment as an academician, researcher and a teacher.

This book is a detailed, comprehensive and in-depth account of children in India, their rights and the challenges in achieving them. The range of issues covered is extensive and the information disseminated very interesting and detailed. Her way of writing is well articulated and holistic. In my view, this book fulfils the vacuum in the existing treatise on child rights in India.

I congratulate Dr. Geeta for this much needed endeavour and believe that she shall continue her efforts for the benefit of child development students, policy makers, legislatures and field functionaries.

Dr. Dinesh Paul
Director
National Institute of Public
Cooperation and Child Development
New Delhi

Preface

The genesis of the book lies in the days when my dear daughter left for pursuing her management degree from Indian Institute of Management, Ahmedabad in 2010. I was distraught without her. That is when I first started writing this book, primarily to fill up my time and to divert my attention away from missing her. In the early days of this book, it resembled more like a report and was primarily a collection of relevant material from the Internet. Yet, it did act as a resource to some extent in my classroom teaching. Reading new things on the net and putting them as a compendium was not such a bad activity after all!

By 2012, Delhi University had started working on the semester mode and most of the courses had been overhauled. The subject that I had been teaching for 20 years with a welfare approach, was now called 'Child Rights'. It had an altogether new perspective and meant that the material that I had collected needed to be turned around. In 2013 somewhere in October, I picked up the chapters again and started to relook. The first thing I did was that I wrote a very basic chapter on Introduction to Child Rights. Then a chapter in the previous book had demographic information based on Census 2001. That needed an update as per Census 2011. Please remember, I was using all this for my teaching purposes too. So the information that I was to share with my students had to be the latest and the best. Rework on the book had begun. Concerted effort on completing the book started only after Springer agreed to publish the work. This was in August 2014, and till the submission of the manuscript which was in February 2015, I was on an average devoting 5–6 hours on the book every day. The journey of writing this book has been very pleasurable for me. The research that went into writing the book also contributed immensely to the content of my lectures, and further improved me as a teacher.

The book is a comprehensive compendium on the Child in India, the challenges which the child faces in survival, development, education or by virtue of a disability or lack of care by the society. The book in a simple manner introduces the concept and meaning of child rights and subsequently puts forth measures taken by the government and civil society to help achieve the child rights. The major themes expounded are infant and child survival, early child development, street and working children, children in conflict with law, children with disabilities, child trafficking, child sexual abuse, amongst others. It raises the question of survival, development and participation of these special groups of children and how their chances of achieving full potential is severely compromised. The book also documents the responses of the society for the care and protection of children.

The book presents a commentary on the situation of children in India and the difficulties in living faced by them due to the especially hard conditions that they live in. Each chapter gives the magnitude of the problem and clarifies the major policy framework which the government has adopted. Major legislations providing legal support are included. At certain places, attempt is made to even cite some legal cases in an attempt to emphasise how legislations are providing succour to children facing challenges in development. Relevant newspaper articles are interspersed in the text. Each chapter has a section that presents the innovative and credible work of social organisations, which can suggest ideas to emulate for further action in the field. Efforts of exemplary NGOs working in the field are profiled in the chapters. The topics covered are such that they would generate social awareness amongst the youth.

The broad purpose of the book is to comprehensively discuss the roadblocks which the child in India faces, what the causes of these roadblocks are and what the government and the social sector are doing to help children in India achieve their potential.

The aim of writing this book is to explain the concept of child rights and to highlight the plight of children in India. The book is likely to find readership amongst students pursuing higher education in the universities of India. 'Child Rights', 'Child Welfare', 'Child and the Law' are common courses offered by universities across the country. The book should fit in the various curriculums.

A book on Child Rights is urgently needed as this course is now being offered in undergraduate studies in many Delhi University colleges in the least. This book would be useful for numerous home science colleges and agriculture universities which offer courses in Child Development, Child Welfare, Child and the Laws, NGO Management, Human Development and Family studies across India. This book should also find readership amongst social work students. The NCERT is also proposing to include Child Rights and Human Rights as a course for classes XI and XII. A publication on this subject is much needed and appropriate and this book should come as a sigh of relief for students studying this course.

Geeta Chopra

Acknowledgments

Karya mein parmatamn ho tu aap sahaye
Apana aashish dejiye, mangal kar phairaiye

(Dear Lord, please help me in the work that I am doing, please give me your blessing by placing your hand on my head)

No work is possible without the kind blessings and the command of God. My first acknowledgement is to my God for choosing me to write this book in the important area of Child Rights, for giving me ideas to conceptualise the work and the energy to execute this assignment. I am humbled and feel immense gratitude towards God for giving me this opportunity.

I would like to give credit to my students, whom I love dearly, for being so enthusiastic in class time, for engaging in discussions and for making me strive to do more and more for them. This book is an effort to act as a source book for students of Child Rights and Child welfare (depending on what nomenclature is being used), and attempts to fill a huge void due to lack of books in this field. I sincerely hope that the 'constant' search for finding the 'right material' from the Internet to make notes will now be 'not so constant'. The nagging empty space for a complete book will no longer be there. Thank you my students for creating the need in me to write a book for you all.

I would like to thank the teaching as well as non-teaching staff of my department in college for the constant support and encouragement. I would specifically like to thank my young colleague, Ms. Renu for painstakingly going through each chapter of the book and giving me feedback on it. She also used the book for her teaching and provided valuable comments from time to time. I would also like to thank Ms. Mansi Sethi for critically evaluating each chapter of the book and also editing parts of it. I am grateful to Ms. Bhavana Negi for going through the book in its early days and giving me pointers which helped me firm up the ideology of the book. I would also like to thank Dr. Sheetal Nagpal who was my Ph.D. student and is now a colleague, for going through the contents of the book and for giving invaluable feedback. Thanks all of you for being my sounding boards.

I am grateful to Arushi, my daughter, whom I missed so much in the two years she was away pursuing her management degree, that I picked myself up to write this book. I also want to express my gratitude to my dear son, Parth, for being a very sensitive human being and for being my best critique. He constantly pushes me to achieve. I would like to thank the rock of my life, my husband, Sanjay, for his staunch support in all my endeavours. His calm temperament and all the resources that he makes available to take care of my other responsibilities, helps me to focus with a free mind on my professional work. Thank you.

Lastly, I would like to thank Springer for accepting my manuscript and for giving me the creative and academic freedom to shape my book the way I wanted to.

Geeta Chopra

Contents

Abbreviations

ACA	Adoption Coordination Agency
AIE	Alternative and Innovative Education
ALIMCO	Artificial Limbs Manufacturing Cooperation of India
BBA	Bachpan Bachao Andolan
CAN	Concerned Action Now
CARA	Central Adoption Resource Agency
CBR	Community-Based Rehabilitation
CEDC	Children in Especially Difficult Circumstances
CLPRA	Child Labour Prohibition and Regulation Act
CLR	Child Learning Resources
CMR	Child Mortality Rate
CR	Child Rights
CRPF	Child Rights Protection Forum
CSA	Child Sexual Abuse
CWC	Child Welfare Committee
CWD	Children With Disability
CWSN	Children With Special Needs
DCPS	District Child Protection Society
DDRC	District Disability Rehabilitation Centres
DPEP	District Primary Education Programme
ECCE	Early Childhood Care and Education
ECD	Early Childhood Development
ECE	Early Childhood Education
EFA	Education for All
EGS	Education Guarantee Scheme
EPFO	Employees Provident Fund Organisation
ESIC	Employees State Insurance Corporation
GAWA	Guardians and Wards Act
GOI	Government of India
HAMA	Hindu Adoption Maintenance Act

ICDS	Integrated Child Development Scheme
ICF	International Classification of Functioning, Disability and Health
ICPS	Integrated Child Protection Scheme
IED	Inclusive Education for Disabled
IEDC	Integrated Education for Disabled Children
IMR	Infant Mortality Rate
IPC	Indian Penal Code
ITPA	Immoral Traffic Prevention Act
IYCF	Infant and Young Child Feeding
JJ ACT	Juvenile Justice Act
JJB	Juvenile Justice Board
KGBV	Kasturba Gandhi Balika Vidyalya
MDG	Millenium Development Goal
MDM	Mid-Day Meal
MMR	Maternal Mortality Rate
MWCD	Ministry of Women and Child Development
NAB	National Association for the Blind
NCERT	National Council of Educational Research and Training
NCLP	National Child Labour Project
NCPEDP	National Center for Promotion of Employment for Disabled People
NCRB	National Crime Records Bureau
NFHS	National Family Health Survey
NGO	Non Government Organisation
NHFDC	National Handicapped and Finance Development Corporation
NHM	National Health Mission
NHRC	National Human Rights Commission
NP-NSPE	National Programme of Nutrition Support to Primary Education
NRHM	National Rural Health Mission
NSSO	National Sample Survey Organisation
PAP	Prospective Adoptive Parents
PC&PNDT	Preconception & Prenatal Diagnostic Techniques
PIED	Project Integrated Education for the Disabled
POCSO	Protection of Children Against Sexual Offences
PRI	Panchayat Raj Institute
PWD	Persons with Disability
RAHI	Recovering and Healing from Incest
RCI	Rehabilitation Council of India
RGI	Registrar General of India
RIPA	Recognised Indian Placement Agency
RTE	Right to Education
SAA	Specialised Adoption Agency
SARA	State Adoption Resource Agency
SEN	Special Education Needs
SJPU	Special Juvenile Police Unit
SLL	Special Local Laws

SRS	Sample Registration System
SSA	Sarv Shiksha Abhiyan
THR	Take Home Rations
U5MR	Under 5 Mortality Rate
UGC	University Grants Commision
UNCRC	United Nations Convention on the Rights of the Child
UNCRPD	Un Convention on the Rights of Persons with Disabilities
UNICEF	United Nations Children's Fund
WHO	World Health Organisation

About the Author

Geeta Chopra, Ph.D., is Associate Professor at the Department of Human Development and Childhood Studies, Institute of Home Economics, University of Delhi. She has been teaching for almost 30 years. She is a keen researcher, trainer and an involved academician. She has authored three guidebooks for community workers on Childhood Disability titled "Mother and Child Care: Promoting Health Preventing Disabilities", "Early Detection of Disabilities and Persons with Disabilities in the Community", "Stimulating Development of Young Children with Disabilities: A Practical Guide". She has also co-authored a book 'Child Development: A Practical Manual'. She has been Principal Investigator for research projects which have received funding from government bodies and the World Bank. She is also guiding doctoral research. She is on various government bodies and academic institutes as an expert. Her major areas of interest include Child Rights, Childhood Disability, Early Childhood Care Education and Early Childhood Development.

(Source: Personal collection of author)

UNITED NATIONS CONVENTION ON THE RIGHTS OF THE CHILD

Article 2 (Non-discrimination): The Convention applies to all children, whatever their race, religion or abilities; whatever they think or say, whatever type of family they come from. It doesn't matter where children live, what language they speak, what their parents do, whether they are boys or girls, what their culture is, whether they have a disability or whether they are rich or poor. No child should be treated unfairly on any basis

Chapter 1
Introduction to Child Rights

Abstract The chapter delves into the concept of human rights and then moves on to introduce the notion and concept of child rights. It presents the philosophical underpinnings of human rights and child rights, outlining various theoretical precepts like the Will theory, the Interest theory, the Instrument theory, the Claim theory, the Liberty theory and so on. The historical evolution of human rights and child rights is also given. As the various laws related to children in India give different ages for who is considered a child, 'who is a child', this is discussed in the chapter. India's international commitment and standing on child rights is deliberated though a section on the United Nations Convention on the Rights of the Child, Human Development Index and Millennium Development Goals. The chapter ends with a section on the significance of strengthening families for protecting child rights.

Keywords Child rights · Human rights · Human rights and child rights theories

1.1 Introduction to Child Rights

Children have a mind of their own, so they can dissent. Adults should be ready to let children make up their mind on things that concern them. After all children are not puppets in the hands of adults. Children need freedom. Also, for them to grow and develop physically, socially, emotionally and cognitively, opportunities need to be made available to them. The environment has to be nurturing and stimulating. Children are young, dependent and need care for their well-being and development. The family and society has to provide for food, shelter, clothing, health needs and education. Children should be safeguarded against abuse, so need protection. All children have a claim for those things in a society that would help in their care and provide protection. Children can demand these things from their parents and elders

G. Chopra, *Child Rights in India*, DOI 10.1007/978-81-322-2446-4_1

as their ‘right’. Most children are not aware of their rights. Hence, it is the responsibility of adults to make them aware of their rights. All children have the same rights. It does not matter whether the child is rich or poor, has parents or is an orphan, is strong or weak, sick or healthy, or lives in any part of the world. A Child is a Child.

Child rights are those rights that a person possesses by virtue of being a child. Since children are small, immature, inexperienced and dependent on adults for taking care of them, this makes them vulnerable and easy target for exploitation, hence there is a need to protect them. This makes for a case where conditions are made conducive to protect them. Child rights bring within the ambit every scheme which a child requires, not only to protect their interest, but also to provide them with ample opportunity to grow and develop to the fullest. There are many schemes, policies, legislations and programmes which aim to care and provide protection to children. Yet children are malnourished, exploited, marginalised, neglected, abused, trafficked and are deprived of their basic right to family care, protection, play, shelter, food, health and education. Hence, there is a need to be an advocate of child rights and to create awareness amongst all about concept, salience and ways of achieving child rights.

What is a Right? A ‘right’ is an agreement or contract established between the person who holds a right and a person or an organisation which has the capability and the duty or obligation to fulfil the rights of the person. Rights are entitlements, imply obligations and goals and concerned with social justice, non-discrimination and empowerment. Rights can be called guarantees which an individual can evoke. They are on high priority and compliance with them is mandatory. Human rights aim to secure the basic conditions for leading a minimally good life. Child rights are those special set of privileges which apply to all humans who are younger than 18 years of age. The child rights approach presupposes a change in perspective. Children are no longer seen as needy, but rather as right holders. Also, children are viewed as separate entities. In the child rights approach, child rights are both a goal as well as an instrument for the development of children. This approach does not view situations of poverty simply from the viewpoint of human needs and development practices, but is interpreted as an outcome of unjust practices.

The journey towards achieving child rights is a journey to make sure that children:

- are safe,
- are not discriminated against,
- have their best interests protected,
- have the things they need to survive and develop,
- have a say in decisions that affect their lives.

The concept of child rights has widened and the international will to reinforce and enforce the rights of children has grown over the years with mounting evidence of hardship and abuse suffered by children. Here are some established facts: abandoned by families, some 100 million children submit only by back-bearing work, or turn to petty crime, begging or prostitution. Over 50 million children work under unsafe or unhealthy conditions. Over 120 million children are deprived of schooling in the age group of 6–11 years. Some 32.5 million die every year of disease that could be prevented or cured. Millions, including many in the rich societies are maltreated or neglected, or sexually exploited or become victims of drug abuse (Mythili and Bhagyathara 2007). This clearly underscores the urgent need to save and protect our children using rights as a legal instrument against their exploitation and pitiable plight.

Understanding Child's Rights from the Child's Eyes

All the time I keep hearing instructions. Do this. Do that. Don't do this. Don't do that. Eat This. Play. Sleep. Study. Don't touch this and that. Don't argue. Obey. Serve. Listen !!

You adults always want to decide what we should be doing. But do you know, just as you grown up people have rights, we children too have rights.

One day, nations in the world got together in 1989. They were worried that children were not doing well. People who cared for children had been demanding that children be given their rights. The think tanks of nations sat down and thought; children's rights? What are they?

First they put their minds together. Then they thought let us ask children themselves what they thought that they must have as a definite thing, i.e. a right, a privilege ....they asked many children and this is what children said....

I have a right to be me
I have a right to basic needs of nourishment, housing and clothes
I have a right to be taken to a doctor when sick and health care
I have a right to a loving family
I have a right to education
I have a right to play
I have a right to be involved in family discussions and to express myself
I have a right to be protected against neglect, abuse and exploitation
I have a right to live
I have a right to be wrong, so please don't punish me so hard
I have a right to special care if I have special needs
I have a right to my own culture, religion and language
I have a right to leisure, rest and fun
I have a right to Childhood.

The United Nations wrote down these rights. These are called Convention on the Rights of the Child. Many countries agreed to adopt these rights. So did India commit itself to see that children in India too got these rights.

1.2 The Notion of Human Rights

The doctrine of human rights rests on the belief of moral universalism, a moral universal community of human beings. Moral universalism does not depend on social acceptance or norms. It is accepted universally. It is a natural order. It is based on natural justice. Aristotle writes, 'the natural is that which has the same validity everywhere and does not depend on acceptance' (Nicomachean Ethics 189) (Human Rights, In Internet Encyclopedia of Philosophy). Here, Aristotle unambiguously expounds an argument in support of the existence of a natural moral order. The basis of the doctrine of natural law is the belief in the existence of a natural code based upon the identification of certain fundamental and objectively discernible human goods. Our enjoyment of these goods is to be secured by our possession of equally fundamental and objectively verifiable natural laws. Natural laws are valid irrespective of their having got the approval of the government or not. John Locke took the stand of Aristotle ahead and said that these natural laws came from God and it was duty of each individual to protect themselves and these rights were at the core of protecting human life and helped in self-preservation. Life was a gift from God and human rights helped in the preservation of life. Our duty of self-preservation entails the necessary rights to life, liberty and property.

The eighteenth century German philosopher Immanuel Kant bestowed upon contemporary human rights theory the ideals of equality and moral autonomy of human beings, who determine the moral principles for securing conditions for equality and autonomy (Human Rights, In Internet Encyclopedia of Philosophy). These rights emanate from human reason rather than the supernatural. Ideals such as natural rights, moral autonomy, dignity of human beings and equality became the basis for questioning oppressive regimes and a reason for replacing them with political authorities who understood these emancipatory ideas.

Though the concept of human rights had long been in place, the world sat down to formalise the UN Declaration of Human Rights only in 1948. It was an outcome of the worst human holocausts, the worst human rights violations, an outcome of the world wars. The UNHR consists of a preamble and 30 articles. The UNHR goes beyond the concept of natural rights and makes states responsible for upholding rights. It emphasises the role of family and community in the realisation of these rights. Further, violation of human rights are not merely seen as a state issue, but are a matter of international concern.

Tracing the evolution of Human Rights, many important landmarks may be mentioned such as the Magna Carta (1215), which put forward the idea that no one was above law. Yet by no means were all people considered equal. The American Declaration of Independence was important as a group of people decided to take their destiny in their own hands. Yet, there was slavery and women had an inferior position. The world wars saw human rights violations on a large scale. Hard lessons were learnt including the value of human life and the dignity of every human being. The United Nations was formed in the aftermath of the world wars. One of the first tasks of the UN was to prepare the groundwork for human rights. The Universal Declaration on Human Rights was drafted soon after. UNHR was passed in 1948 and is a broad declaration of the ideals that the world aspires for (Jain 2005).

1.3 Philosophical Analysis of the Concept of Human Rights

Human rights are rights that attach to human beings as moral guarantees for leading a minimally good life. The very fact that you are human, gives you these rights. In conceptual terms, human rights are a derivative of what is considered ‘right’. Let us try understanding the concept of human rights.

Human Rights as Moral Versus Legal Rights Legal rights are those that can be traced in the legal code of conduct of the society or the nation. They are passed by some constitutional body like the legislature or the parliament. These originate within the legal system, whereas moral rights are not rights in the strict sense but are more of moral claims. Moral rights have existed prior to legal rights. Legal rights would change from time to time, but moral rights are more universal. For example, most political movements may not be supported by the laws of that state, but are moral claims of people who are trying to question what they perceive as immoral regimes. India’s fight for freedom from British rule was a moral claim against discrimination on grounds of colour and right to political participation in our own country. Human rights cannot merely be reduced to legal rights. Nor are they just moral rights. Human rights are best thought of as both moral and legal rights. The legitimacy claims of human rights are tied to moral rights, but the practical efficacy comes when they become legal rights. For example, persons with disability have a moral right to equal participation, development opportunities and education. But if this moral right becomes a legal act and instrument, implementation of certain steps for these rights to reach the persons with disability becomes easier and possible.

Human Rights as Claim Rights and Liberty Rights W.N. Hohfeld (1919) was an American jurist. Hohfeld's ambition was to provide a conceptual understanding for our use of right, duty, etc., in practice, thus facilitating a better understanding of the nature of our rights. He identified four categories of rights-claim rights, liberty rights, power rights and immunity rights, which have been clubbed to claim and liberty rights (Human Rights. In *Internet Encyclopedia of Philosophy*). Claim right consists of being owed a duty. It is a claim against another person who has a duty to fulfil the claim of the right holder. Example, Right to free and compulsory elementary Education is a claim right for every child in India between 6 and 14 years, which the government has to provide as a duty to the right holder, whereas liberty rights are not be fulfilled by anyone. Liberty right makes us free to do as one pleases. Example, it is my right to go for a vacation to any part of the world.

The Will Theory and Interest Theory Will theory attempts to establish the validity of human rights on single human attribute-freedom, which is the core of any account of rights. Validity of human rights is tied to personal autonomy. Will theorists make the holder like a sovereign, a monarch. Rights give the person autonomy. Rights give the person power over another's duty. Will theory gives the holder the power to determine what others may or may not do, and so exercise control over certain domains of affairs. So, as per this theory, there can be no such thing over which its holder has no power. The holder of the right has power over the duty bearer. The theory considers those who are incapable of exercising their rights (severely disabled or infirm or very young children) as incapable of having any rights as they are not in a position to exercise their rights.

As per the Interest theory, the basic purpose of human rights is to protect and promote certain essential human interests. They are justifiable as they have an instrumental value in securing conditions of human well-being or for securing basic human good. Some of the rights are life, knowledge, recreation, to practice a religion to name some. Rights allow its holders to improve their life conditions. This theory accepts that not only are the rights unwaivable, but they are for everyone, including for ones who are not so capable. Interest theory coincides with the general view of children and their interests that deserve protection. It also says that it is the adults who should protect their interest.

The philosophical debate related to the Will theory and the Interest theory is specially relevant for Child Rights. The Will theory gives the holder a right, a power, which makes the holder sovereign and powerful. To have a right is to have the power to enforce or waive the duty of which the right is correlative. Do children have the capacity to exercise rights? The Will theory does not answer this question. The Interest theory sees a right as a protector of interest of the holder of the right. So, interest theory coincides with the general view that children's interests need to be protected. It becomes the duty of the adults to protect the interests. So, children have the interest to be protected from abuse, violence, hunger, malnutrition and disease, adults have a duty to protect them.

Status Theory Comes from a tradition which considers that human beings have human rights because of their status of being humans. It rests on the belief that all men are created equal. This is also the reasoning found in the thoughts of Aristotle and Locke and in the American and French revolutions.

Instrumental Theory Believe that rights have been ascribed as they help in providing and promoting overall human welfare. Human rights become the instrument of distributing facilities and privileges across the group.

The major criticism of human rights comes from the concept of moral relativism. The conceptualisation of what is moral or not is decided by the society in which the person lives. There can be no absolute moral codes. Morality is a social and historical phenomenon. Moral beliefs vary widely in the world today. To impose one as being superior to the other would be moral imperialism. Example, child's right to privacy for Indian parents would be alien. Also, for highly marginalised societies, human rights would be so hard to attain. There is increasing awareness to tailor make human rights which are in tune to say, the collective rights of minorities. While the basic philosophy behind human rights is their universal moral doctrine valid for all people everywhere, yet now attempts are being made to adequately address the unique conditions of culturally diverse societies. Example, arranged marriage is a norm in Indian societies. There is great degree of sanction on young people who dare to marry outside of castes and clans by the moral bearers of respective societies (say Khaps, the locally appointed courts, who are known to even kill the youngsters in the name of preserving the honour of the clan). This is in conflict with the right to liberty and freedom to choose your own life partner.

Norway Authorities Take Away Indian Kids for Not Using Spoons and Sharing Bed with Parents

Oslo, Jan 18 (TruthDive): An Indian couple, Anurup and Sagarika Bhattacharya from Kolkata living in Norway is facing the worst part of their lives after their children—a 3 year-old son and 1-year-old daughter—were taken away from them by Norway's child protective services and placed in foster care 8 months ago.

It comes as a shocker to the couple when they were told that their children were not brought up properly because they fed their children with hands and slept with their parents in the same bed.

"My son was sleeping with my husband. They said he should sleep separately from your son," said Mrs. Bhattacharya.

"Feeding a child with the hand is normal in Indian tradition and when the mother is feeding with a spoon there could be phases when she was overfeeding the child. They said it was force-feeding. These are basically cultural differences," said Mr. Bhattacharya.

The matter was reported to Indian authorities and recently the officials of the Indian Embassy in Oslo held talks with the authorities of Norway's Child Protective Service. The Indian officials even met the children. Their innocent parents however were not even allowed to have a glimpse of their beloved children.

Norway's Child Protective Service is a powerful body charged with protecting the rights of children living in difficult family situations. But there are many reports of excesses.

"There has been a report in UN in 2005 which criticized Norway for taking too many children in public care. The number was 12,500 children and Norway is a small country," said Svein Kjetil Lode Svendsen, lawyer

The Bhattacharyas' visas expire in March. If they don't get their children by then, the couple will be forced to stay on (Ramraj 2012).

The case cited above clearly shows a conflict between Indian child rearing practices, and the law of the land of the country in which the family was residing. Ignorance about Indian culture and lack of understanding about the diversity in parent–child relationship made the Norwegian authorities view the parents as cruel and in conflict with law. Child rights here is in conflict with cultural norms. To impose one way of bringing up children as being superior vis-à-vis another is certainly cultural imperialism.

1.4 Scope of Human Rights Duties

Human rights are possessed by everyone. An obvious deduction is that everyone has a duty to protect and promote everyone's rights. National and international institutions bear the responsibility of securing human rights. The realisation of human rights requires establishing conditions for all human beings to lead minimally good lives and thus should not be confused as an attempt to create a morally perfect society. While the object of human rights is modest, the force is ultimate. Ronald Dworkin coined a term 'rights as trumps', to use the game of cards as a simile to denote absolute power to 'rights'. Dworkin argues, considerations of rights claims must trump and take priority over alternative considerations when formulating public policies and when allocating public resources. It prioritises its realisation over alternative political and social considerations. Thus, for example, a minority's possession of rights against discriminatory treatment should trump any and all considerations of the possible benefits that the majority would derive from discriminating against minority group. Similarly, an individual's right to an adequate diet, or safe shelter, should trump the other individual's desire to wear designer clothes, or eat at expensive restaurants. For Dworkin, rights as trumps express the fundamental ideals of equality for all humans, a premise on which the concept and philosophy of human rights is based. Fully realising the aspirations of human rights may not require the provisions of 'state of the art' resources, but this should not detract from the force of human rights as taking priority over alternative social and political considerations.

Findings of a Survey on Children's Conceptualization of Child Rights

A quick survey was conducted by students of B.Sc (Hons) Human Development group (Batch 2012–15) under the guidance of Dr. Geeta Chopra to explore the understanding of 10–18-year-old children about the concept of Child Rights. Initially, an open ended questionnaire was prepared and each student was asked to leave this with 4–5 children in the age group of 10–18 years. Then the information collected by this open ended questionnaire was coded and analysed. Here are the results of the survey:

The sample size of 77 children was taken from urban Delhi, of which 47 % were males and 53 % females. 23 % of children were in the age group 10–12 years, 30 % in the age group 13–15 years and 41 % in the age group of 16–18 years. Of these, 83 % were school going and 17 % were college going.

- The first question that was asked was if they had heard of something called 'Child Rights'? A majority of the respondents said Yes (77 %).
- They were then asked, what are 'rights'? As the questionnaire was open ended, it left scope for a multitude of responses on this question. The responses received were that 'rights' are *'adhikar'* (14 %), facilities/promises (14 %), rules/laws (12 %), power/freedom (21 %), fundamental rights (10 %), moral principles (4 %), provisions (9 %) and so on.
- The next question posed was do children have rights? An overwhelming 83 % said Yes, clearly showing that children were aware that they do have rights.
- Then they were asked what rights children should have? There were multiple responses permitted. More than half of them said Education (58 %), Freedom (32 %), Play (30 %), Right to be heard (12 %), right to equality (12 %), right to health (5 %), protection (8 %), entertainment (6 %)
- When asked if they thought some children were being denied their rights? A large majority (83 %) said Yes.
- With rights also come duty bearers. They were asked who was responsible for fulfilling the rights of children? Whose duty is it to ensure that children's rights reach them? 54 % said government, 49 % said parents, 21 % said society. There were other responses also received like teachers, media, social workers and they themselves were responsible for rights reaching them.

- The last question was a close-ended question. The respondents chose multiple responses. The question was if they were given a chance to give children, rights, what rights would those be? A list was provided and the following answers emerged:
  - Right to Health (81 %)
  - Right to Education (91 %)
  - Right to Marriage (17 %)
  - Right to Live (73 %)
  - Right to Play (71 %)
  - Right to Privacy (45 %)
  - Right to Independence (64 %)
  - Right to Family (57 %)
  - Right to Dance (44 %)
  - Right to Break Rules (19 %)
  - Right to have Fun (62 %)
  - Right to Do what you want (48 %)
  - No child to be discriminated (71 %) Right to be Heard (66 %)

The highest responses were for right to Education and Right to Health. The interesting thing is that the least response was for Right to Marriage as during childhood that is least of concern. Right to break rules was also rejected by the respondents, indicating that children were somewhere aware that rights had to be morally correct too.

1.5 The Emergence of the Idea of Child Rights

The notion of human rights preceded the notion of child rights. It was subsumed that human and child rights would be the same. But gradually, it was realised that children are a specially vulnerable group with a unique set of needs. Though children are humans, so are entitled to Human Rights (which are age appropriate), yet children do have unique needs, hence unique rights and privileges form the back drop of Child Rights.

Despite having 30 articles, many of the specific needs of children for care, protection and dignity were not getting addressed by the UNHR. Historically, this was a time when children were being regarded as separate independent entities. It was only during the 1970s and 1980s that the concept of child rights emerged. This shift came because children were no longer being looked as properties of parents, but individuals who came with their own life forces. There was a recognition that children have interests, requirements, needs and perhaps even rights which should be considered distinctly and separately from those of their parents and adults. Children were now being viewed as autonomous individuals whose rights should be acknowledged and respected.

It was during the twentieth century that the concept of child rights emerged. There was a paradigm shift from a 'welfare' to 'rights' based approach. Two principal schools of thought have contributed to the concept of child rights. The Child Liberationist view considers children as independent, free and individuals who should be treated with dignity. Self-determination is the root of the child liberation view. This view believes that children should have the autonomy to decide in matters that concern them. This could include right to practice a religion of their choice, or live with a parent of their choice in case of divorce or right to information. The Child Protectionist view concedes that children are immature, dependent and their care needs have to be taken up by adults and the society. This is a nurturance model. This advocates the provision of services and environments which provide for contexts where children grow up to be useful productive adults. The UN Convention on the Rights of the Child draws from both the models.

1.6 Should Children Have Rights: The Philosophical Arguments

It has been argued endlessly if children have a moral status and whether they can be regarded as rational beings and if they ought to enjoy rights. It would be worth mentioning that almost all the world nations are today signatory to the UN Convention on the Rights of the Child. So in that sense, children from all the nations have legal rights, though their moral value could be questioned by some.

Liberationist believe that children have all rights that adults have. They are against ageism. Then another view is that children could have some and not all adult rights, as some of the rights are applicable only to adults. Another set of people are of the view that children are too young to understand the value of rights and are not in a position to demand the fulfillment of rights. Children are not competent enough to have rights.

As mentioned in the beginning of this chapter, children for too long have been considered a property of the parents, especially fathers. This is especially true in the Indian context, where parents keep a complete hold over their children even when they become adults. This is the traditional view of philosophers like Locke and Kant, who seemed to espouse the view that since children are not rational beings, they do not have rights. This put them in parental authority. Locke also advocated that parents' control over children should be in proportion to their age, development and experience.

There is also a view that God created children and it is God who is the true owner of the child. But he gave parents the power, the 'trusteeship' for acting in the best interest of the child. So parents were to provide a home, discipline the child, maintain the child, provide for medical treatment, protect against wrong influences, control education, give religious values, beliefs and practices and so on. But do parents always decide in the 'best interest' of the child? For that matter, do parents decide even on the 'basic interest' of children? If it were so, would we have a staggering number of children engaged in child labour, child prostitutes or children who are trafficked?

The paternalistic theory makes no distinction between adults and children. According to this view, children need rights so that they can be protected from negative influences. Example, children engaging in child beggary on road crossings would need to be protected for their good and rights give them the legal protection. The purpose is to guide the child to adulthood with the maximum opportunities to achieve life goals and also allow for making autonomous choices.

According to theory of 'children's need based rights', child rights emerge not because children are autonomous, but from their dependency. This is as per the Interest theory that was discussed earlier. This view is echoed across where it is believed that in case of children, we need to identify the areas where support is needed. It becomes the duty of the parents, state and community to augment those areas. So child rights are more of duties and obligations of the state towards children.

The world is diverse and each society and culture hold its own ethos and moral codes of conduct. With diversity found everywhere, how does one explain a universal set of rights? As the international community is getting integrated towards universal norms, how would cultural diversity be respected? Cultural relativism asserts that human values are far from being universal and vary greatly from culture to culture. In other words, human rights are culturally relative rather than universal. This view sharply contrasts with the universality of moral principles and ethics for human good, the principle on which the human rights debate rests. The developing countries have been pressing the issue of cultural relativism against UNCRC. For the effective implementation of any rights-based convention, societies need to engage constructively with the provisions rather than view these as externally imposed culturally alien documents which threaten the cultural basis of the society. But, this argument poses a danger that human right violations could be then justified in the veil of cultural relativism. For example, can we examine the right of liberty and freedom of expression of women in some Islamic states? Are their rights affected and influenced by cultural and ethnic relativism? Yet at the same time, child rights approach could question age old dictates like child marriage or sati or dalit rights. Universalists have argued that there are universal norms and these need to be promoted through the right-based approach.

Nobel Peace Prize Brings Child Rights Centre Stage

The Nobel, rightly recognises not just his efforts but the continuing plight of children who are either inducted into or born into bondage.

Mr Satyarthi's struggle goes beyond just getting children released, he has pushed their right to education, for rehabilitation and for enforcing child-related laws. Mr Satyarthi's dream of a world without child labour may seem unrealisable at the moment. But the Nobel recognition will mean that this continuing evil will now feature much higher on the development agenda of the Indian government. To that end, the Nobel committee has done the children of South Asia, especially India and Pakistan, a signal service ("Child Rights take Nobel Centre Stage" 2014).

Pandey (2014) writes 'Activists hope Nobel win will help put focus on child rights', opining that activists working for child rights hope that with Kailash Satyarthi winning a Nobel Peace prize for this cause, there will be a spotlight on the issue. NGOs claim it is mostly on their insistence that the police and the government conduct joint raids to rescue minor children working in inhuman conditions. "The award will certainly help in changing the mindset not only of the bureaucracy but the law-enforcement agencies. There is bound to be a wider impact of this award and it will definitely help in creating greater awareness about child rights. So far, a number of bills are pending related to trafficking and child rights—so it will put pressure on the government to act", said Rishi Kant, an activist with NGO Shakti Vahini that works for the welfare of children.

PROFILE: Kailash Satyarthi

Nearly 30 years ago he left a promising career as an electrical engineer to set up Bachpan Bachao Andolan (Save Childhood Movement) and since then, by his own count, he has rescued more than 80,000 children.

He also heads the Global March Against Child Labour, which represents about 2,000 social groups and union organisations in 140 countries.

His campaigns over the years have ensured that India's carpet industry has stopped using child labour.

He also successfully led a movement to bring in a new law in 2012 to make employment of children under the age of 14 illegal—a law he considers his big achievement.

But India still has millions of child labourers—official estimates put the number at five million; Mr Satyarthi says it is as high as 60 million.

Many parents say poverty forces them to send their young children to work, while campaigners say child servitude is a reality in India and that it will continue.

But Mr Satyarthi has described that point of view as "absolutely pessimistic".

"We must all be totally against child labour. I want to see in my lifetime that there is no child slavery in the world," he told the BBC in an earlier interview.

The Nobel Committee made clear that this was why he was selected: "Showing great personal courage, Kailash Satyarthi, maintaining Gandhi's tradition, has headed various forms of protests and demonstrations, all peaceful, focusing on the grave exploitation of children for financial gain".

http://www.bbc.com/news/world-asia-29568634 retrieved 15th April 2015

1.7 Who Is a Child?

The word 'child' is used in various senses. It may be used as a term of relationship: whose child is he? This is recognised as a relationship of parent and child. The term 'child' is also used for a person who, on account of his young age, is considered to be of immature intellect and imperfect discretion and is therefore unable to comprehend the consequences of his own act. The term 'child' is also used in several welfare legislations which accord protection to and confer benefit on the young age (Diwan and Diwan 1994).

All cultures share the view that the younger the children, the more vulnerable they are physically and psychologically and less they are able to fend for themselves. The idea of childhood is governed more by dependence, power relations than by chronology. Age limits are the society's judgment about the children's capabilities and ability to take responsibility. Age limits are also posed by the legal set-up of each society, which in turn determines when a person can vote, when they can marry, what justice system awaits them, at what age or when they can legally take up paid work.

The trouble with child rights begins with the very definition of a child by law. According to the UN Convention on the Rights of the Child, 'a child means every human being below the age of 18 years, unless the law applicable to the child, majority is attained earlier'. The Census of India defines a person below the age of 14 as a child. According to Article 21(a) of the Constitution of India, a child is a person under 14 years of age. Under the 'Child Labour (Prohibition and Regulation) Act 1986, a child means a person who has not attained the age of 14 years. The minimum age at which compulsory education ends as per Article 21 A of the constitution is 14 years and it synchronises with the minimum age for employment. As per the Indian Penal code 1860, nothing is an offence which is done by a child under the age of 7 years (Section 82, IPC). The age of criminal responsibility is raised to 12 years if the child is found to have not attained the ability to understand the nature and consequence of his/her act (Section 83, IPC).

According to National Plan of Action for Children, 2005, the definition of a child is a person up to age of 18 years. According to Juvenile Justice (Care and Protection of Children) Act 2000, the age is 18 for both boys and girls. As per Indian Majority act, 1875, unless a particular personal law specifies otherwise, every person domiciled in India is deemed to have attained majority upon completion of 18 year of age. Thus, persons younger than 18 years are considered minors. According to Hindu, Muslim, Christian and Parsi personal law, a person is supposed to reach the age of majority at 18 years.

According to Child Marriage Restraint act 1929, the legal age for marriage is 21 for boys and 18 for girls. It is interesting to note that the age of marriage in Muslim personal law is the age of puberty (around 14 years). It is held that Muslim girls are not exempt from this law. If the marriage is performed while she is minor, the marriage would not be void, but the persons who participated in this marriage are not immune for legal punishment under the Child Marriage Restraint Act. The age of sexual consent is not mentioned for boys, but for girls it is defined at 16 years. This implies that she cannot marry at 16 years but can consent for sexual intercourse at 16 years. Raising the age of consent for sexual intercourse to 18 years needs to be considered. The legal age for consumption of alcohol is 21 years for both boys and girls (though this varies in different states in India). The voting age is 18 years and the age of majority is also 18 years.

The age of the person is determined by the birth certificate, and if this document is not there, then it is based on the school records. Sometimes, a medical certificate also can come as age proof. On many occasions, accurate means of determining the age may not be possible and could have ramifications, especially in case of Child Labour disputes or in case of children in conflict with law. Some methods of determining the age are signs of puberty, bone ossification and bone age, dental maturity, teeth ossification, X-ray of wrist and assessing skeletal maturity.

As will be amply clear, there is no consensus on who we consider as a child. Though one may like to have uniform age limit legally prescribed for the status of child, it may perhaps not be possible or even desirable (Bajpai 2006).

The question that comes to one's mind is that should there be a uniform definition of the child in Indian laws? The general view is that if India has ratified the UNCRC, then India should adopt across board the definition of child as an individual under 18 years of age. The age specified in various legislations may be outdated and not based on scientific evidence. If this is done, then the age for compulsory education and child labour will go up to 18 years, but the age for marriage or consumption of alcohol will come down to 18 years too. So having one age for all purposes may not work.

1.8 India's International Commitment Towards Children

International Conventions and Declarations Ratified by India

- The United Nations Convention on the Rights of the Child, 1989
- World Conference on Education for All, 1990

- World Fit for Children Declaration, 1990
- World Summit for Children, 1990
- Optional Protocols on involvement of children in armed conflict
- Optional Protocol on the sale of children, child prostitution and child pornography, 2005
- UN Rules for the Protection of the Juveniles Deprived of their Liberty, 1990
- UN Standard Minimum Rules for the Administration of Juvenile Justice (Beijing Rules), 1985
- United Nations Guidelines for the Prevention of Juvenile Delinquency (Riyadh Guidelines) 1990
- Hague Convention on Protection of Children & Cooperation in respect of Inter-country Adoption, 1993
- SAARC Decade on the Rights of the Child 2001–2010
- SAARC Convention on Prevention and Combating Trafficking in Women and Children for Prostitution 2002
- SAARC Convention on Regional Arrangements for the Protection and Welfare of Children, 2002
- Millennium Development Goals (MDGs)

(Ministry of Women and Child Development, (n.d.)

1.8.1 The UN Convention on the Rights of the Child

At the beginning of the twentieth century, France started to look at the protection of children, especially in the medical, social and judicial fields. From France, this movement spread across to Europe and elsewhere.

It was in the early twentieth century, after World War I and then after World War II, when millions of children were orphaned, disabled and rendered homeless and suffered uncountable atrocities, that it was increasingly realised that children required special care and protection. Efforts were made globally to make laws for childcare and protection. In 1919, the international community created *The League of Nations* (later to become the UN), which started giving space and thought to the concept of child protection. In 1924, the League of Nations adopted the 'Declaration of the Rights of the Child', which is the first international treaty concerning children's rights. In five chapters it gives specific rights to the children and responsibilities to the adults.

World War II and its casualties left thousands of children in a dire situation. Consequently, the UN Fund for Urgency for the Children was created in 1947, which became *UNICEF* and was granted the status of a permanent international organisation in 1953. In 1959 the General Assembly of the UN adopted the *UN* Declaration of the Rights of the Child. The *U.N. Declaration of the Rights of the Child* (*DRC*) (1959) reiterated the children's rights stated in the League of Nations Declaration (1924) and called upon voluntary organisations and local authorities across the world to safeguard children's rights. In the declaration, children were entitled to certain rights, viz. to a name and nationality, adequate nutrition, housing, recreation, medical services and education. Specific needs of physically, mentally and socially handicapped children were also taken into account. The declaration also specified that 'children shall be among the first to receive protection and relief in times of distresses'.

The *European Convention on Human Rights (ECHR) (1950)*, the *International Covenant on Economic, Social and Cultural Rights (1966)* the *International Covenant on Civil and Political Rights (1966)*, *Convention of the Elimination of All Forms of Discrimination Against Women (1979)* and most importantly *Hague Conventions (1965; 1980; 1993 and 1996)* also referred to children's rights.

The most landmark achievement in the efforts for children's rights is the *UNCRC (United Nations Convention of the Rights of the Child) (1989)*.

The *1989 UN Convention on the Rights of the Child (UNCRC)* was ratified by 192 nations. The Government of India ratified the CRC on 11 December 1992. The UNCRC is a proactive international effort to draw an agreement between nations to give rights and privileges to children across the world. The UNCRC are the standards to which all governments must aspire for helping children realise these rights. The UNCRC is "the most complete statement of child rights ever made". The UNCRC is guided by the principle of a *first call for children*—a principle that the essential needs of children should, at all times, be given priority in the allocation of resources at all times. The convention is derived from a core set of human values and ethical premises that recognise the inherent dignity and the equal and inalienable rights of all members of the human family as the foundation of freedom, justice and peace in the world. Accordingly, the Convention states that the rights shall be extended to all children without discrimination of any kind, irrespective of the child's or his or her parent's or legal guardian's race, nationality, colour, sex, language, religion, political or other opinion, social origin, property, disability, and birth or other status. It advocates measures for the protection and harmonious development of the child that are consistent with the traditions and cultural values of different peoples. By providing safeguards against economic and other policies that have a negative effect on the well-being of children, the Convention reaffirms a commitment to promote social progress that will ensure a better quality of life and greater freedom for people in general and children in particular. It also underscores the importance and potential of international cooperation for promoting and improving the living conditions of children in every country.

Opportunities for early childhood care and development are both a child's right and a major contributor to development. UNCRC recognises that children are unique, precious and a special part of human existence. It places the child at the centre of all human effort with respect to human resource development and protection of life. The UNCRC is the most accepted treaty in the history of human rights. It has a universally agreed set of non-negotiable standards and obligations. Every right in the convention is inherent to human dignity and is geared for harmonious development of the child. These rights are benchmarks against which progress can be assessed. It is the first legally binding international instrument to incorporate the full range of human rights—civil, political, economic, social and cultural rights.

The fundamental principles of CRC are:

- *Principle of first call for children/Principle of best interest of the child* in all actions concerning children, whether taken by state, courts, disaster management teams, social welfare organisations or administrative offices, the best interest of the child will be the primary consideration.
- *The basic right to survival and development* right to live, right to be educated, right to get opportunities so that they develop well
- *The principle of non-discrimination* all children are equal irrespective of their color, sex, caste, nationality, ability
- *The right of the child to be heard* they should be heard specially if the matter concerns them directly. This would be specially relevant in the context of legal cases concerning children.

The UNCRC contains 54 articles, which can be divided into three groups: protection rights, provision rights and participation rights. They are called the three 'P's'. Children have to be protected against cruelty, abuse, neglect and delinquency. They have to be provided with nutrition, health care, a family, safety of home, name and nationality. They have a right to participate in matters that affect them directly, so they have the freedom of expression and participation.

The CRC vests four sets of rights with the child—Survival, Development, Protection and Participation. By and large, all these rights are interdependent and cannot be dealt in isolation. They have to be applied and implemented simultaneously if at all the rights of every child are to be respected.

The UNCRC devotes article 7, 9, 20, 22, 23, 24, 25, 26, 27, 28, 29, 30, 31, 42 to *Rights to Survival and development* included are rights related to life, health, nutrition, clean water, sanitation, environment, education, support for early childhood development and care, relax and enjoy, help from authorities if poor, adequate standard of living, right to a name from birth, right to acquire nationality, right to know and be cared for by his or her parents, rights of refugee children, rights of children with disabilities; *Rights to Protection* includes articles 19, 32, 36, 35, 11, 34, 37, 40 related to protection of children from all forms of discrimination, exploitation, abuse, sexual abuse, punishment, inhuman or degrading treatment and neglect, disability, right to special protection in situations of emergency and armed conflicts; *Rights to Participation* include article 13, 14, 15, 16, 17 related to respect for the views of the child, right to freedom of expression, right to information from mass media, TV, newspapers, thoughts, conscience and religion; freedom of association and peaceful harmony, right to privacy.

The CRC also gives children their basic human rights—civil, economic, social, cultural, and political—which enable them to achieve their full potential. The *civil rights* of children include the right to a name and a nationality, protection from torture and maltreatment, special rules governing the circumstances and conditions under which children may be deprived of their liberty or separated from their parents, etc. The *economic rights* under the CRC include the right to be benefit from social security, the right to a standard of living adequate to ensure proper development and protection from exploitation at work. The *social rights* include the right to the highest attainable standard of health services, the right to social care for handicapped children, protection from sexual exploitation and abduction, and the regulation of adoption. Rights to education, access to appropriate information, recreation and leisure, and participation in artistic and cultural activities are included in the *cultural rights* of the children under the CRC (Bajpai 2006).

During the 1990s, there was growing awareness of the importance of prompt birth registration as an essential means of protecting child rights. Failure to register births promptly has been linked to the trafficking of babies. The lack of a birth certificate may prevent a child from receiving health care, nutritional supplements and social assistance, and from being enrolled in school. Later in childhood, identity documents help protect children against early marriage, child labour, or, if accused of a crime, prosecution as an adult.

The UNCRC is a pro-family document. It recognises that the child, family and state are the three important corners of the triad on which child rights rest. UNCRC emphasises that the family is the natural environment for the child and holds family as the primary provider and protector for the child. The convention actively protects and tries to preserve the integrity of the family. Child rights are not viewed as antagonistic to parents rights. The rights try to bring forth the 'best interest' of the child, and look at the family to find a way towards this. If the families are found to be incapable of taking care of their child, then the state can take over the custody of the child.

Inspite of international and national efforts to secure the rights of the child and give them a life with 'minimum goods', yet millions of children around the world are still being denied the chance to reach their full potential. Every child must be ensured the best start in life—their future, as indeed the future of their communities, nations and the whole world depends on this.

1.8.2 Human Development Index

The recent human development index estimated for 2009 by UNDP puts India in the 134th position among 177 countries with HDI scores of 0.612. This is a dismal position considering that India is now considered an economic giant. This is much lower compared to the highest HDI scores of 0.971 held by Norway.

The human development index (HDI) is a composite index that measures the average achievements in a country on three basic dimensions of human development

- a long healthy life, as measured by life expectancy at birth;
- knowledge, as measured by the adult literacy rate and the combined gross enrolment ratio from primary, secondary, tertiary school;
- a decent standard of living as measured by GDP per capita in purchasing power parity (PPP) US Dollars (UNDP 2004).

Aristotle argued that "wealth is evidently not the good we are seeking; for it is merely useful and for the sake of something else." It is easier to measure national incomes than human development. Many economists would argue that national income is a good indicator of human well-being. While there is evidently a strong relationship, since economic growth is an important means to human development, human outcomes do not depend on economic growth and levels of national income alone. They also depend on how these resources are used—whether for developing weapons or producing food, building palaces or providing clean water. Human outcomes such as democratic participation in decision-making or equal rights for men and women do not depend on incomes.

1.8.3 Millennium Development Goals (MDGs)

The *Millennium Development Goals* (*MDGs*) are eight international development goals that 192 United Nations member states and at least 23 international organisations have agreed to achieve by the year 2015. They include reducing extreme poverty, reducing child mortality rate, fighting disease epidemics such as AIDS, and developing a global partnership for development. The **Millennium Development Goals (MDGs)** are eight goals with 21 targets, and 60 measurable indicators for each target. Base year for MDG was 1990 and final year 2015. For India, some of the MDGs are achieving infant mortality rate to 28, U5MR to 42 and maternal mortality rate to 109 by the year 2015. India's efforts are still ongoing for reaching the targets set by MDG.

Millennium Development Goals (MDGs) At a Glance

Goal 1: Eradicate extreme poverty and hunger
Goal 2: Achieve universal primary education

Target 2A: By 2015, all children can complete a full course of **primary schooling**, girls and boys

Goal 3: Promote gender equality and empower women

Target 3A: Eliminate gender disparity in primary and secondary education preferably by 2005, and at all levels by 2015

Goal 4: Reduce child mortality

Target 4A: Reduce by two-thirds, between 1990 and 2015,

- *Under-five mortality rate*
- *Infant (under one) mortality rate*
- *Proportion of* 1-*year-old children immunised against measles*

Goal 5: Improve maternal health

Target 5A: Reduce by three-quarters, between 1990 and 2015,

- *Maternal mortality ratio*
- *Proportion of births attended by skilled health personnel*

Target 5B: Achieve, by 2015, universal access to reproductive health

- *Contraceptive prevalence rate*
- *Adolescent birth rate*
- *Antenatal care coverage (at least one visit and at least four visits)*
- *Unmet need for family planning*

Goal 6: Combat HIV/AIDS, malaria, and other diseases
Goal 7: Ensure environmental sustainability
Goal 8: Develop a global partnership for development

1.9 Strengthening Families for Protecting Child Rights

The first line of support for any child is a family. When in distress, it is the family that should have the capacity to support and protect the child. For full development, children should grow in harmonious family environment free from conflict, abuse, poverty and strife. It is common for states to provide support to families 'at risk'. Some examples of state support for families that are disadvantaged in India are, the government has introduced the food security bill to provide for the basic food needs of families. The Mahatma Gandhi Rural Employment Guarantee act (MNREGA) is rural employment guarantee scheme helps families to have a minimum income guarantee to sustain itself. Under MNREGA, a member in a family is provided with 100 days of employment within 5 kms of his residence, within 15 days of applying on a local development project. In urban areas with both parents working, daycare facilities are needed to support families with young children so that both the parents can take up employment with a free mind. There are safety nets for medical help, education, adequate nutrition when families are unable to pay for these basic needs.

Despite the key role in nurturing, supporting and protecting children, families still fail to offer this ideal environment. In extreme cases—such as situations of sexual abuse and child trafficking—they are part of the problem for children, rather than the solution.

According to WHO, each year 40 million children under the age of 15 are victims of family abuse or neglect serious enough to require medical attention. Social mobilisation around child-rights issues during the decade has led to a much greater recognition of the magnitude and urgency of this problem. New initiatives to address physical and sexual abuse have been taken up in many countries. Some of these initiatives protect children, while others protect women and girls. In India, innumerable cases of child abuse within the family are reported. Though data on this is lacking due to the sensitivity of the issue, child sexual abuse within the family is also a frequently occurring problem, where the protector becomes the destroyer. Children being sold as labourers and children, especially girls being sold to traffickers by their own parents, is a harsh reality.

Apart from poverty, children could be affected by abandonment, parents getting AIDS, armed conflicts, civil unrest and terrorism. The number of children afflicted by these is really large. It is so large that it can outstrip the society's capacity to provide alternative care, leaving many children to fend for themselves.

Children deprived of family environment have a right to special protection and alternative care. In abject poverty, parents are found incapable to provide food, clothing and shelter to children. At other times parents feel unable to deal with their child's disability or relinquish the child due to social stigma (like being an unwed mother). This underscores the importance of providing families in difficult circumstances with the adequate support they need to shoulder their responsibilities by state players.

References

Bajpai, A. (2006). *Child rights in India Law policy and practice* (2nd ed.). New Delhi: Oxford University Press.

Child Rights take Nobel Centre Stage (2014, October 11). *The Hindustan Times*.

Diwan, P., & Diwan, P. (1994). *Children and legal protection*. New Delhi: Deep and Deep publications.

Human Rights. In *Internet Encyclopedia of Philosophy*. Retrieved on April 4, 2014 from http://www.iep.utm.edu/hum-rts/.

Jain, M. (Ed.). (2005). *Human rights education for beginners*. New Delhi: National Human Rights Commission.

Ministry of Women and Child Development, Government of India. (n.d.). *A Report of the Working Group on Development of Children for the Eleventh Five Year Plan (2007– 2012)*.Retrieved from http://wcd.nic.in/WG_Report.pdf.

Mythili, D., & Bhagyathara, D. (2007). Rights of the child – A landmark. In R. Ganga & M. Supputhai (Eds.), *Children's rights as basic human rights*. New Delhi: Reference Press.

Pandey, N. (2014, October 12). Activists hope Nobel win will help put focus on child rights. *The Hindustan Times*.

Ramraj, M. (2012, January 18). Norway authorities take away Indian kids for not using spoons and sharing bed with parents. Retrieved from http://truthdive.com/2012/01/18/norway-authorities-take-away-indian-kids-for-not-using-spoons-and-sharing-bed-with-parents.html.
UNDP. (2004). *Human Development Report, 2004*. New Delhi: Oxford University Press.
http://www.bbc.com/news/world-asia-29568634. Retrieved April 15 2015.

(SOURCE: Authors personal collection)

UNITED NATIONS CONVENTION ON THE RIGHTS OF THE CHILD

Article 4 (Protection of rights): Governments have a responsibility to take all available measures to make sure children's rights are respected, protected and fulfilled. When countries ratify the Convention, they agree to review their laws relating to children. This involves assessing their social services, legal, health and educational systems, as well as levels of funding for these services

Chapter 2
The Situation of the Child in India: Quest for Equity

Abstract This chapter profiles the traditional view of childhood as per Indian scriptures. It moves on to then present the demographic profile of children in India, with the current infant mortality rate, under 5 mortality rate, nutrition status, health profile of children, sex ratio and maternal and girl child indicators. Statistics related to diarrhoea, immunisation, breast-feeding, infant and child survival are quoted and discussed. Reasons for falling child sex ratio as well as high IMR amongst others, are put across. NFHS 3 and Census 2011 figures are quoted. The Indian indicators are pitted against Human Development Index and Millennium Development Goals. Various articles related to children in the Constitution of India are put together in this chapter. Policy initiatives by the government of India for the benefit of children are briefly presented. There is one whole section devoted to discuss the role of non-government organisations in social development, wherein NGOs are classified and their merits and demerits are discussed.

Keywords Demography · Childhood in india · NGO role · Policies for children in india

2.1 Childhood in Indian Context

Little is known about the early history of childcare, except through the gleanings of scriptures. It is a pleasure to read the expression of the childhood of *Sri Rama*, where the mothers are shown to be very nurturing, indulgent and caring towards the four sons. The description of *Krishna Leela* is a poetic treat and the details of pranks played by *Sri Krishna* during childhood days speak generously of joyful abundance with which children where indulged in as well as valued.

G. Chopra, *Child Rights in India*, DOI 10.1007/978-81-322-2446-4_2

The best reference that one can get of the conceptualisation of the stages of child development in Hindu scriptures is through the *Grihyasutras* (700–300 B.C.), which put across various rituals which correspond to the developmental stage of early childhood. The rituals are:

(a) *Nama-karna* or the naming ceremony held in the first or third month of life—giving a name to the child
(b) *Annaprasana,* the introduction of solid food in the infant's diet performed around the sixth month
(c) *Chudha-Karma* or *Mundan* i.e. tonsure, first head shaving, signifying broadly introduction to personal hygiene, in the third year
(d) *Akarsharabhyase* introducing the child to first alphabets, around the fifth year
(e) *Upanayana*, the formal introduction to one's caste in the eighth year.

A child up to 7–8 years is considered too young to be given training, but after *upanayana,* he is considered to have entered the stage of *brahamacharya,* when he will primarily spend his time in learning. The next stage, *grihastashrama,* is when an individual is expected to marry and procreate. Here one sees that the progeny were valued and cherished, and parents were expected to nurture the child as a matter of duty. Children were essentially the responsibility of the family, kin group and the caste. Orphaned children were rarely abandoned. The belief that what we face in this birth is an outcome of our *karma* of the previous birth, made it easy to accept a handicapped child. Institutional educational care was represented by *gurukuls.* Children by the age of 7–8 were placed under *gurus,* and learned skills appropriate to their own caste. One's *gurus* and parents were considered sacred and treated as such.

Ayurveda, like any other Indian tradition considered the total life span of an individual to be over 100 years. The *Rig Veda*, the first of the four *Vedas*, considered to be the earliest recorded book of wisdom in human civilisation, wishes every individual to lead a healthy life of 100 years: "*jeevem sárdah satam*". In the earlier phase of ayurveda, the total life span was divided into the following three categories: *balyavasth* (childhood): 24 years; *yuvavastha* (young): 44 years and *vaidhavastha* (old age): 48 years. Thus the total life span was considered to be 116 years. However, later Susruta gave an elaborate and systematic classification of age of childhood as follows:

Balyavayya (childhood): 0–16 years. The *balyavaya* further constituted three stages of *ksirpa* (milkfed), *ksirannada* (weanlings) and *annad* (fed on cereals).

According to classical texts like *Manu,* the child belonged to the bottom of the social order along with the old and sick, newly married and pregnant women and slaves and servants. But all at the bottom were not to be dealt alike. While lower castes and servants who violated caste rules and norms were meted out harsh punishments, children, women, the old and sick were to be protected. The traditional Hindu texts and scriptures hardly have a reference to a female child, or for that matter to a brother–sister relationship. It seemed, women got an identity only after they married—as a wife or as a mother.

Traditional and Contemporary View on Child Rearing

There is no formal theory of child rearing in the Indian perspective, certain prescriptions are laid down in traditional teaching regarding the qualities to be nurtured in children and the ideal parental attitudes to be adopted in order to ensure the development of desired qualities in children. All these aspects are embedded in the spiritual context of *dharma and neeti.* The emphasis does not seem to be on specific parental behaviour but more on imbibing values and attitudes. In the contemporary view, there seems to be a general awareness of the relationship between child rearing practices and child's personality and social behaviour. Also, the element of spiritualism is not very strong in the contemporary view.

The traditional view of the child is that of a pure, innocent, amoral, asocial being with a set of *samskaras* which represent inherent dispositions presumably carried over from the previous birth. There is a belief that the child needs love and protection and yet needs to be disciplined, which according to Manu's code is more punishment than love.

In spite of a special relationship which is focal in the parent–child discourses, the traditional view warns against too deep an attachment in the interest of spiritual growth. The parent is reminded that getting too involved in this relationship might become an obstacle in the way of *dharma and moksha,* because intense attachment to the child can be a source of *moah.*

As per contemporary Indian view, the parent–child relationship is 'symbiotic', i.e., mutually beneficial. Parents are often indulgent. Sons continue to be important (for ritualistic reasons as well as for carrying the family name forward). Children are also seen as old age security, as a way of enhancing parents' sense of personal power, status and pleasure or as a potential earning member. The last mentioned attitude is discordant with the generally overindulgent and protective parental attitude. Yet in the current scenario, with increased instances of child bonded labour and servitude, the exploitative role played by parents in certain Indian contexts cannot be brushed under the carpet. It would not be entirely incorrect to say that parents could be having children with a utilitarian attitude. It could amount to expecting the children to support, albeit at the cost of their own childhood, which is further justified by the economic condition of the family.

According to the traditional view, both father and mother are treated as equally important. But in certain situations, either of the two could be glorified more. The mother primarily has the nurturing role taking care of physical and emotional needs, while the father fulfils the protective, advisory and authoritative role, taking care of moral, economic and intellectual needs.

In today's times, the parental role is completely mother centric, as the majority of studies on child rearing practices focus on the mother–child relation. There seems to be an assumption that the availability of the mother at home is necessary for child rearing.

2.2 Status of Children in India

Every year, tens of millions of infants around the world begin an extraordinary sprint—from defenseless newborns to becoming proactive young children ready for school. And every year, countless numbers of them are stopped in their tracks—deprived, in one way or another, of the love, care, nurturance, health, nutrition and protection that they need to survive, grow and develop. Poor, malnourished and unhealthy children make for poor and powerless states which are at the mercy of stronger states. Not providing for good health, nutrition, psycho-social care and cognitive stimulation of young children is a truly missed opportunity, which no nation can afford to let go. Investing in children is among the most far-sighted decisions leaders can make. A country's position in the global economy depends on the competencies of its people and those competencies are set very early in life. In this chapter, we will examine how India is doing as far as children and their development is concerned.

India stands at the crossroads of history. India is home to more than one billion people, of which 40 % are children, defined as a person under 18 years of age. We have the demographic advantage of a large young population, while the rest of the population of the world is ageing. But the challenges that we are continuing to face in education, child survival, health, malnutrition, we need to urgently address these, or the demographic advantage may soon turn into a liability. The fate of many of our children is still determined by caste, religion and gender. Many are denied basic rights, opportunities and a secure childhood. Children in India are trapped in a maze of imbalances that deprive, exclude and exploit. Investment in children is not only a desirable societal investment for the nation's future but also a step towards fulfilment of the rights of every child. In this context, India faces the immense challenge to provide to every child her rights to survival, protection and development.

Census 2011: Highlights with Respect to Children (http://censusindia.gov.in/)

- The total number of children in the age group 0–6 is 158.8 million (5 million less since 2001)
- The proportion of child population in the age group of 0–6 years to total population is 13.1 %, while the corresponding figure in 2001 was 15.9 %. The decline has been to the extent of 2.8 points.
- Uttar Pradesh (29.7 million), Bihar (18.6 million), Maharashtra (12.8 million), Madhya Pradesh (10.5 million) and Rajasthan (10.5 million) constitute 52 % children in the age group of 0–6 years.
- Overall sex ratio at the national level has increased by 7 points to reach 940 at Census 2011 as against 933 in Census 2001. This is the highest sex ratio recorded since Census 1971 and a shade lower than 1961. Increase in sex ratio is observed in 29 States/UTs.

- Three major States (Jammu and Kashmir, Bihar and Gujarat) have shown decline in sex ratio compared to Census 2001.
- Kerala with 1084 has the highest sex ratio followed by Puducherry with 1038; Daman and Diu has the lowest sex ratio of 618.
- Child sex ratio (0–6 years) is 914. Increasing trend in the child sex ratio (0–6) seen in Punjab, Haryana, Himachal Pradesh, Gujarat, Tamil Nadu, Mizoram and A&N Islands. In all remaining 27 States/UTs, the child sex ratio shows decline over Census 2001.
- Mizoram has the highest child sex ratio (0–6 years) of 971 followed by Meghalaya with 970. Haryana is at the bottom with ratio of 830 followed by Punjab with 846.

It is estimated that around 40 % of India's children are vulnerable to or experiencing difficult circumstances like children without family support, children forced into labour, abused/trafficked children, children on the streets, vulnerable children, children affected by substance abuse, by armed conflict/civil unrest/natural calamity, etc., as well as children, who due to circumstances have committed offences and come into conflict with law. Survival, growth, development and protection of these very large numbers therefore need priority focus and attention (Ministry of Women and Child Development 2011).

In international comparisons of the status and condition of children, India continues to rank poorly on several key counts. Human Development Index (HDI) measures the achievement of countries on three basic dimensions of human development: a long and healthy life, knowledge and decent standard of living. It includes indicators about children like the IMR, status of education and child labour. The world's tenth largest economy unfortunately ranks 136 out of 187 on the HDI. Denmark is 15, Mexico 81 and Japan 10 on HDI. The population of children aged 0–6 years has declined from 164 million (16 % of the total population) as per Census 2001 to 159 million (13.1 % of the total population) in Census 2011. In Kerala and Tamil Nadu, children constitute less than 10 % of the population. This decline is due to decline in the fertility rate from 3.1 children in 2001 to 2.7 as per Census 2011.

In India, of every 1000 children born, 42 (SRS Bulletin 2013) die before they see their first birthday—most of which are avoidable. About 22 % of newborn infants have low birth weight. Only 23.4 % of children are reported to have started breast-feeding within 1 h of birth. 46 % of infants receive exclusive breast-feeding till 6 months of age. Timely complementary feeding is introduced to only about 55.8 % infants. As many as 45 % of our children are stunted (too short for age), 23 % wasted (too thin for height) and 40 % are under weight (too thin for age). Despite regular immunisation programmes, only 44 % of 12–23-month-old infants are fully immunised against vaccine preventable diseases. A whooping 7 out of 10 children between 6 and 59 months of age suffer from anaemia (NFHS 3, 2005–2006).

We have the world's largest child labour force. There is a gross disregard for the girl child which is reflected by the skewed child sex ratio—914 females for 1000 males (Census India 2011, http://censusindia.gov.in/)

Critical concerns:
India population 1.21 billion
Child population (0–6 years): 158.8 million (Census 2011)
Total child population (0–18 years): 430 million (Census 2011)
IMR: 42 per thousand live births (SRS, Sept, 2013)
U5MR: 35 urban, 61 rural (Census 2011)
Children born with low birth weight: 22 % (NFHS-3)
Children under 3 with anemia: 79 % (NFHS-3)
Exclusive breast-feeding till 6 months: 46 % (NFHS-3)
Malnourished children: 45 % stunted, 22 % wasted, 40 % underweight (NFHS-3)
Children fully immunized: 44 % (NFHS-3)
Sex ratio: 1000:940 (Census 2011)
Child sex ratio: 1000: 914 (Census 2011)
Every second new born has reduced learning capacity due to iodine deficiency
Third largest crime in India after drug and guns smuggling is child trafficking.
45,000 children go missing in India every year.

Infant mortality rate and the under 5 mortality rate are widely accepted indicators of the state of children of any nation. While IMR is the number of children who die before the first birthday per 1000 live births, under five mortality rate is the number of deaths of children under 5 years of age for a live 1000 births. High IMR is an indication of the lack of health care and environmental conditions, while high U5MR is an outcome of cumulative conditions which lead to disadvantage and death. Looking at the trends in IMR, there has been a consistent lowering of IMR in the past 10 years. In 2006, IMR was 57, in 2008 it was 53, in 2009 it was 50, in 2010 it was 47 and as per SRS (Sept, 2013) IMR is 42 (46 rural and 28 urban). The Millennium Development Goal of IMR to be achieved by 2015 for India was 28, which looks to have been achieved for urban India, which stands at 28 (SRS Bulletin 2013). The MDG for U5MR is 42. The U5MR was 55 in 2009. Urban U5MR is 35, so MDG has already been achieved, while the rural U5MR is 61 (Census 2011). Six states in India which are likely to achieve the MDG targets of IMR and U5MR are Kerala, Tamil Nadu, Maharashtra, West Bengal, Punjab and Himachal Pradesh.

Analysis of the determinants of child survival in India clearly shows that IMR and U5MR among children born to illiterate mothers is higher than those born to mothers with some education. The relationship between education and mortality becomes significant when the education of mother is more than 8 years of schooling. IMR and U5MR is highest among children of mothers younger than 20 years of age. Also, children born less than 2 years after the previous delivery are less likely to survive. Mortality among children of mothers who are malnourished, anaemic and obese is also higher.

The Census 2011 threw up the most disturbing finding of a falling Child Sex Ratio (CSR). The female literacy has risen from 53 % (Census India 2001. http://www.censusindia.net/) to 65 % (Census 2011). The corresponding figure for male literacy was 75 % in 2001 and 82 % in 2011, but the CSR has dropped showing a rising son preference and unwelcoming trend for the female child. Clearly, the legislation for sex selection of foetus is not working and there is a need to rethink more effective strategies in this regard.

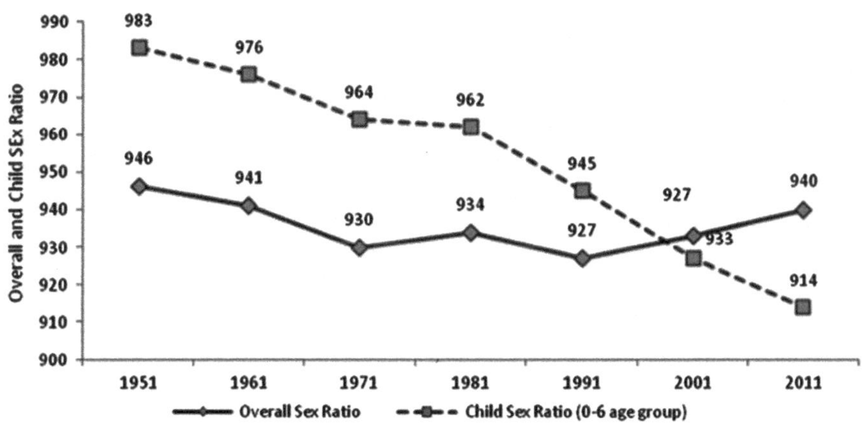

Source: (1) Data taken from Office of Registrar General of India and Census Commissioner (1951-2001); (2) data taken from Office of Registrar General of India and Census Commissioner (2011)

NFHS 3 (2005–2006) found that the family size was now getting restricted. If the firstborn was a daughter, then when the woman conceived a second time, chances of sex determination and aborting a female fetus were high. Small families, yes. But daughters, no! SRS 2008 data showed that the death rate among girls aged 1–4 years was 40 % higher compared to boys. With higher female child mortality, coupled with sex selection, the deficit would increase at a fast pace. Women suffer a persistent disadvantage from before birth, early infancy well into reproductive years. It seems that sex selection is spreading even to smaller cities, contributing to a declining CSR. There are social and cultural factors that underlie the declining numbers of girl children in India. No legislation would work in our conditions.

Some of the reasons for alarmingly low sex ratio are son preference and burden to protect the 'honour' of the female child; low value of girl child due to evils like dowry; death rituals of parents which are recommended to be performed by sons; female foeticide and infanticide; neglect of girl child resulting in high girl child mortality; patriarchal structure; and sons viewed as old age security and girls as belonging to some other family.

There is a gap of 16.6 % in female literacy. As per Census 2011, male literacy is 82.1 %, whereas female literacy is 65.5 %. Compared to Census 2001, this gap has come down from 21.6 % (Census 2001, Female literacy was 53.7 % and male literacy was 75.3 %), clearly showing a jump of almost 12 % points in female literacy in the past decade. Yet India has a long way to go towards achieving total literacy.

Reviewing maternal health indicators, antenatal care (ANC) refers to pregnancy-related health care, which is usually provided by a doctor, an ANM or another health professional. Ideally, antenatal care should monitor a pregnancy for signs of complications, detect and treat pre-existing and concurrent problems of pregnancy, and provide advice and counselling on preventive care, diet during pregnancy, delivery care, postnatal care and related issues. In India, the Reproductive and Child Health Programme aims at providing at least three antenatal check-ups which should include a weight and blood pressure check, abdominal examination, immunisation against tetanus, iron and folic acid prophylaxis, as well as anaemia management.

Maternal Mortality Ratio (MMR) refers to the number of women who die as a result of complications of pregnancy or childbearing in a given year per 100,000 live births in that year. Although the MMR dropped from 212 deaths per 100,000 live births in 2007–09 to 178 in 2010–12 (www.censusindia.gov.in/vital_statistics/.../MMR_Bulletin-2010-12.pdf), India is behind the target of 103 deaths per live births to be achieved by 2015 under the United Nations mandated Millennium Development Goals.

According to NFHS 3, 2005–2006 data, 50.7 % women got at least three ANC checkups done. 22.3 % took iron-folic acid tablets for 90 days or more. 48.8 % had assisted childbirth and 40 % delivered in institutes. 36.8 % availed post-natal care within 2 days of childbirth. NFHS 3, 2005–2006 also reported that the percentage of mothers who received antenatal care from a doctor increases sharply with education, from 29 % for women with no education to 88 % for women who have completed 12 years of education or more. NFHS 3 data also showed that 58 % of pregnant women were anemic. Also, of the women in the age group of 20–24 years, 47 % had got married by 18 years of age.

Universal immunisation of children against the six vaccine-preventable diseases (namely, tuberculosis, diphtheria, whooping cough, tetanus, polio and measles) is crucial to reducing infant and child mortality. NFHS 3 collected information on vaccination coverage for all living children born in the 5 years preceding the survey. According to the guidelines developed by the World Health Organisation, children are considered fully vaccinated when they have received a vaccination against tuberculosis (BCG), three doses of the diphtheria, whooping cough (pertusis) and tetanus (DPT) vaccine; three doses of the poliomyelitis (polio) vaccine; and one dose of the measles vaccine by the age of 12 months. BCG should be given at birth or at first clinical contact, DPT and polio require three vaccinations at approximately 4, 8 and 12 weeks of age and measles should be given at or soon after reaching 9 months of age. Considering the immunisation status, NFHS 3, 2005–2006 indicated that 43 % children between 12 and 23 months were completely immunised, which included BCG, measles, 3 doses of DPT and Polio. For each of the vaccines, the status was BCG-78 %, measles-58 %, 3 Polio-78 %, 3 DPT-55 %. Only 24 % of 12–23 months old had received Vitamin A dose in the past 6 months.

As many newborn infants cannot be weighed right after birth, hence obtaining a record of birth weight of all infants at the time of birth is a challenge. The NFHS 3, 2005–2006 could obtain the weight of 34 % infants at birth, 5 years before the survey. It reported 22 % newborns as being low birth weight, i.e. weighing less than 2500 g at the time of birth. The proportion of births with low birth weight decreases with the increasing education level of the mother and increase in the income level.

Diarrhoea is the single most common cause of death among children younger than 5 years. Children who get diarrhoea die due to dehydration, which happens due to loss of fluids from the body. It is important to restore the fluids in the body if the child is having diarrhoea. The government of India started the Oral Redydration Therapy programme as one of the priority measures for survival of young children. The major aim of this programme is to inform the mothers and the community about the causes and management of diarrhoea. ORS is widely available and can be easily used by the mothers. NFHS 3, 2005–2006 collected information on ORS usage and found that children who had had episodes of diarrhoea in the past 2 weeks and received ORS were a mere 26 %. Only 61 % having diarrhoea were taken to a health facility. While suffering from diarrhoea, children should continue to be fed as they normally are, and this occurs for only a small number of children when they had suffered from diarrhoea. NFHS 3, 2005–2006 data showed that only 37 % of children were given the same food to eat after having recently suffered from diarrhoea.

Three standard indices of physical growth that describe the nutritional status of children are height-for-age (stunting), weight-for-height (wasting) and weight-for-age (underweight). Stunting index is an indicator of linear growth retardation and cumulative growth deficits. Stunting reflects failure to receive adequate nutrition over a long period of time and is also affected by recurrent and chronic illness. It, therefore, represents the long-term effects of malnutrition in a population and does not vary according to recent dietary intake. Wasting index measures body mass in relation to body length and describes current nutritional status. Wasting represents the failure to receive adequate nutrition in the period immediately preceding the survey and may be the result of inadequate food intake or a recent episode of illness causing loss of weight and the onset of malnutrition. Underweight is a composite index of height-for-age and weight-for-height. It takes into account both acute and chronic malnutrition. Children whose weight-for-age is below minus two standard deviations from the median of the reference population are classified as underweight. According to NFHS-3, 45 % children are stunted, 23 % wasted and 40 % underweight.

Infant feeding practices have significant effects on both mothers and children. Mothers are affected through the influence of breast-feeding on the period of postpartum infertility and hence on fertility levels and the length of birth intervals. These effects vary by the duration and intensity of breast-feeding. Proper infant feeding, starting from the time of birth, is important for the physical and mental development of children. Breast-feeding improves the nutritional status of young children and reduces morbidity and mortality. Breast milk not only provides important nutrients but also protects the child against infection. The timing and type of supplementary foods introduced in an infant's diet also have significant effects on the child's nutritional status.

According to NHFS-3, only 23 % infants were breast-fed in the first hour after birth. It is recommended that infants should be breast-fed exclusively till 6 months of age. As per NFHS-3, only 46 % infants were exclusively breast-fed between 0 and 5 months. Moreover, only half of the infants (55 %) were receiving complementary weaning foods between 6 and 9 months of age. Adoption of appropriate infant and young child feeding practices (IYCF) are salient for child survival and development. The discussion clearly shows that a large percentage of our infants are not being fed appropriately.

Certain indicators in social development in India cause a sense of satisfaction, while others continue to be reminders that our efforts in this direction must be intensified to bear more concrete results. India's shortfall may not be because of lack of political or administrative will, but mostly on account of the magnitude of the problem, the size of the numbers involved, financial constraints, the complexity of the vicious cycle of poverty, and India's determination to rely mostly on the democratic tools of sensitisation, advocacy and motivation rather than on coercive and regulatory measures. While India accounts for a meagre 2.4 % of the world surface area, it supports and sustains a whooping 17.5 % of world population. In contrast, the United States occupies 7.2 % of the world surface area and supports 4.5 % of the world population. So, the challenges that come with a burgeoning population are mammoth and these challenges are going to be discussed in this book.

Have you ever wondered why child death (IMR) and mother death (MMR) are going down so slowly in India? Part of the answer can be found in a recent survey report put out by the census office. The eight most poor states where this survey was done are home to half the country's population. And, it is in these states that 71 % of infant deaths, 72 % of deaths of children under 5 years, and 62 % of maternal deaths take place. More than three-quarters of pregnant women in any of these states do not get the full ante-natal checkup. In UP, Bihar and Rajasthan, over 90 % women did not get the full ANC. So, the foundation for something going wrong at delivery time is laid. A very large proportion of mothers did not get a check-up within 48 h of delivery. They could be suffering from bleeding or infections and the risk is highest at this time. In Odisha, this proportion was low at 17 % but it went up to nearly 40 % in Bihar. The reason for children's vulnerability to diseases and death is revealed by two key statistics. From one-third to nearly half the infants aged 12–23 months do not get fully immunised. In UP, 47 % infants remain unvaccinated, in Assam 36 %. This is despite a huge immunisation programme conducted by the government. The states covered in the survey are: UP, Bihar, Rajasthan, MP, Chhattisgarh, Jharkhand, Odisha, Uttarakhand and Assam. The survey covered a large sample of nearly 21 million people spread over 284 districts of these states. Maternal death rate averages 265 in these nine states compared to 178 for India. Infant death rates average between 46 and 68 in these states except Uttarakhand which has 40. India's average infant mortality rate is 42 (Varma 2014).

2.3 Constitution Framework Supporting Children in India

India's commitment to children is clearly manifested in its constitution wherein several articles are dedicated to children, viz.:

Article 14—The State shall not deny to any person equality before the law or the equal protection of laws within the territory of India.
Article 15(3)—Nothing in this article shall prevent the State from making any special provision for women and children.
Article 21—No person shall be deprived of his life or personal liberty except according to procedure established by law.
Article 21A—The State shall provide free and compulsory education to all children of the age of 6–14 years in such manner as the State may, by law, determine.
Article 23— Prohibition of traffic in human beings and forced labour—(1) Traffic in human beings and *begar* and other similar forms of forced labour are prohibited and any contravention of this provision shall be an offence punishable in accordance with law. This article clearly highlights the commitment of the Constitution prohibiting trafficking in human beings. However, there is a need for a comprehensive law on anti-trafficking, which will take into account the provisions of the Optional Protocol on the Sale of Children, Child Prostitution and Child Pornography (Ministry of Women and Child Development, n.d.)
Article 24—No child below the age of 14 years shall be employed to work in any factory or mine or engaged in any other hazardous employment.
Article 39(e)—Provides that the health and strength of workers, men and women, and the tender age of children are not abused and that citizens are not forced by economic necessity to enter avocations unsuited to their age or strength (Ministry of Women and Child Development, n.d.)
Article 39(f)—Provides that children are given opportunities and facilities to develop in a healthy manner and in conditions of freedom and dignity and that childhood and youth are protected against exploitation and against moral and material abandonment
Article 45—The State shall endeavour to provide early childhood care and education for all children until they complete the age of 6 years.

Article 47—State shall regard the raising of the level of nutrition and the standard of living of its people and the improvement of public health as among its primary duties (Ministry of Women and Child Development, n.d.)

The 86th Amendment Act of 2001 of the Constitution of India has once again drawn our attention to the component of Early childhood development. With this amendment, Article 45 of the constitution which earlier pledged to provide free and compulsory education to all children between 6 and 14 years now talks about providing free and compulsory early childhood education to all children between birth and 6 years of age.

2.4 Policies for Children in India

1974	National Policy for Children
1975	Integrated Child Development Services Scheme
1983	National Health Policy
1986	National Policy on Education
1987	National Policy on Child Labour
1991–2000	National Plan for SAARC Decade of the Girl Child
1992	National Plan of Action for Children
1993	National Nutrition Policy
1996	Communication Strategy for Child Development
1996	Reproductive and Child Health policy
2000	National Population Policy
2001	National Policy for the Empowerment of Women
2006	Integrated Child Protection Scheme
2005	National Commission for Protection of Child Rights
2010	Right to Education Act

Is childhood disappearing from India today? Working children, urbanisation, high infant and child mortality rates, pressure on young children to study, poverty and economic necessities which compel parents to sell their children into servitude are reasons more than enough to make us ponder if childhood is really as carefree a stage as it should be. Dismal conditions in which children are growing, the outcomes of which are reflected in the child-related indicators, are major developmental challenges we face today. There is a growing need for collaboration between early childhood professionals, government policy makers and community agencies if we want to restore some glory to childhood days.

A number of policy initiatives have been prepared for the benefit of children in India. Policy documents are reference points while planning interventions and programmes for any group. Some of the major policies for children are briefly presented in this section.

1. National Policy for Children, 1974 India is one of the few states that has written a National Policy for Children. This policy provides the conceptual basis for an integrated approach to address the whole child and commits the State to provide adequate services to children, both before and after birth and through the period of growth, to ensure their full physical, mental and social development. It declares that children are the nation's supreme assets and that children's programmes should find a prominent place in our national plans for development of human resources. The salient features of the National Policy for Children are:

- To provide for a comprehensive health programme covering all children
- To provide nutrition services with the objective to remove deficiencies in diet of children
- Free and compulsory education for children up to age of 14 years
- Non-formal education facilities
- Facilities for education, training and rehabilitation of socially disadvantaged and physically, emotionally and mentally retarded children will be provided.
- Equality of opportunity to all children will be ensured
- Children to be protected against neglect, cruelty and exploitation
- No children under fourteen to be engaged in hazardous occupation
- Children a priority in natural calamities or disasters
- Special programmes will be taken up to encourage and assist gifted children
- Family ties are to be strengthened
- Laws to be amended so that in matters of legal disputes, the interests of the child are given paramount importance.

The above policy is now old and we now have new policies which conform to the standards laid down by the UN Convention on the Rights of the Child.

2. National Policy on Education, 1986 (modified in 1992) and its National Plan of Action, which has a whole section on Early Childhood Development. It clearly recognises the holistic nature of child development, and that early childhood is the crucial foundation for human resource development and cumulative lifelong learning. ECCE is viewed as a feeder and support programme for universal elementary education—especially for first-generation learners, and an important support service for working mothers and girls (Ministry of Women and Child Development, n.d.).

3. National Health Policy, 2002 accords primacy to preventive and first line curative care, and emphasises convergence, and strategies to change care behaviours in families and communities.

4. National Charter for Children, 2003 intends to secure for every child her inherent right to be a child and enjoy a healthy and happy childhood, to address the root causes that negate the healthy growth and development of children, and to awaken the conscience of the community in the wider societal context to protect children from all forms of abuse, while strengthening the family, society and the nation. However, it does not declare India's acceptance of children's entitlements as their rights. With India's accession to the UNCRC and its two Optional Protocols rights-based framework has been accepted as the guiding frame for policy measures and programming for children (Ministry of Women and Child Development, n.d.).

5. National Plan of Action for Children, 2005 For the first time in the history of planning for children, India has adopted a clear understanding and definition of the child in the NPAC 2005. The NPAC definition of the child as a person up to the age of 18 years and its clear declaration that '*all rights apply to all age-groups, including before birth*' reiterates the 1974 National Policy mandate that the State takes responsibility for children 'both before and after birth', and the child's interests are to receive paramount attention. This national reaffirmation must set the frame for future planning and intervention to secure the well-being of all children of the country and provide them a caring and protective environment (Ministry of Women and Child Development, n.d.).

The National Plan of Action for Children, 2005 (http://www.wcd.nic.in/NAPAug16A.pdf, accessed on 11th Nov, 2014) has identified twelve key areas keeping in mind priorities and the intensity of the challenges that require utmost and sustained attention in terms of outreach, programme interventions and resource allocation, so as to achieve the necessary targets and ensure the rights and entitlements of children at each stage of childhood. These are:

- Reducing infant mortality rate
- Reducing maternal mortality rate
- Reducing malnutrition among children
- Achieving 100 % civil registration of births
- Universalisation of early childhood care and development and quality education for all children achieving 100 % access and retention in schools, including pre-schools
- Complete abolition of female foeticide, female infanticide and child marriage and ensuring the survival, development and protection of the girl child
- Improving water and sanitation coverage both in rural and urban areas
- Addressing and upholding the rights of children in difficult circumstances
- Securing for all children all legal and social protection from all kinds of abuse, exploitation and neglect
- Complete abolition of child labour with the aim of progressively eliminating all forms of economic exploitation of children
- Monitoring, review and reform of policies, programmes and laws to ensure protection of children's interests and rights
- Ensuring child participation and choice in matters and decisions affecting their lives

6. The National Commission for Protection of Child Rights (NCPCR) was set up in March 2007 under the Commission for Protection of Child Rights Act, 2005, an Act of Parliament. The commission's mandate is to ensure that all laws, policies, programmes and administrative mechanisms are in consonance with the Child Rights perspective as enshrined in the constitution of India and also the UN

Convention on the Rights of the Child. The child is defined as a person in the birth to 18 years age group (http://ncpcr.gov.in/, retrieved on 12 Nov, 2014).

The National Commission for Protection of Child Rights (NCPCR) emphasises the principle of universality and inviolability of child rights and recognises the tone of urgency in all the child related policies of the country. For the commission, protection of all children in the 0–18 years age group is of great importance. Policies define priority actions for the most vulnerable children. This includes focus on regions that are backward or on communities or children under certain circumstances, and so on. The NCPCR believes that while in addressing only some children, there could be a fallacy of exclusion of many vulnerable children who may not fall under the defined or targeted categories. For the Commission, every right the child enjoys is seen as mutually-reinforcing and interdependent and all the rights of children are of equal importance (http://ncpcr.gov.in/, retrieved on 12 Nov, 2014).

2.5 Non-Government Organisations: Role in Social Development

A non-government organisation (NGO) is an integral part of any civil society in today's world. Primarily, an NGO is a non-profit making organisation with voluntary service towards social and community development as its prime motto. NGOs are relatively free from the laws of the society. In fact, their functioning is governed by rules formulated and agreed upon by those very people who have decided to form it. An NGO is characterised by its voluntary spirit, flexibility of operation, grass-root contact, self-reliance and ease of operation which is free from red-tapism. NGOs are omnipresent in today's world. They work directly with people. They stimulate voluntary action among the target community and also involve the active members of that community. The freedom and flexibility that they enjoy, along with personal contact with the beneficiary, gives them opportunities to innovate as well as constantly monitor their programmes and make their programmes more and more need based. NGOs have the ability to communicate with people at all levels, from community to the top government officials and decision-makers.

NGOs have become increasingly important for global development. But, for the developing world, their contribution can often be critical. NGOs often provide essential services to the communities which, at times, the resource crunched governments cannot afford. The contribution of NGOs in healthcare services, childcare, women's development, social justice and empowerment and attainment of basic human rights cannot be overemphasised. NGOs play a vital role in shaping and implementing participatory democracy.

Development practitioners, government officials and foreign donors consider the NGOs by virtue of being small scale, flexible, innovative and participatory as more successful in reaching the poor and in poverty alleviation. This consideration has resulted in rapid growth of NGOs in initiating and implementing development programmes (Padmavathi 2009).

The functioning of NGOs is charactertised by the following features:

1. *More action oriented*: NGOs can undertake need-based activities as they are in direct touch with the people to whom services are being provided. Most NGOs focus on the pressing needs of the community and develop strategies and programmes to address those needs.
2. *Flexible methods and practices*: as the NGOs are small organisations, it is easy for them to take quick decisions and constantly keep reviewing their programmes. The flexibility that they enjoy is a truly unique feature of NGOs.
3. *More focused on development work*: NGOs are mostly goal focused, hence the achievements made by them are more tangible. The 'goal confusion' is one of the important contributory factors for the limited success of government programmes.
4. *Relative independence*: As the functioning of NGOs is governed by their own rules, this autonomy of function allows them to choose their target group, goals, approach and strategies to be adopted, etc., and they function relatively independently of local power structures.

Classification of NGOs

NGOs can broadly be classified on the basis of functions that they perform:

1. *Grass root organisation*—these NGOs work directly with the community. These organisations undertake health and nutrition intervention, education programmes for the disadvantaged sections, rehabilitative services for children with disabilities and so on.
2. *Advocacy*—chiefly work on raising awareness in the community on issues which can affect the lives of people. Includes taking up publicity campaigns and developing IEC material. For example, organisations raising awareness on female foeticide or child rights, disability rights. These NGOs also liaison with government departments to undertake policy changes or change budgetary provisions for their target group.
3. *Research and training*—primarily engaged in capacity building. Also engage themselves in researching issues of functional importance. For example, identifying within the community best practices in infant and childcare. Or enumerating anemic children in the under 6 age group.
4. *Networking organisations*—these NGOs gather other NGOs working in related fields under one umbrella. Together, they can act as pressure groups for bringing about changes in government policies and programme initiatives. For example, NGOs working for child adoption.
5. *Mother organisations*—these organisations collect funds as well as disburse funds to other NGOs. They do not run their own programmes. Instead, they identify programmes of other NGOs which fall in their area of interest and provide financial support to those organisations.
6. *International organisations*—these organisations have their base in other countries but have interest in funding programmes of other organisations elsewhere.

7. *Self help groups*—typically, ten or more persons can get together to make a self-help group. In most cases, the objective is to promote enterprise and generate income. Women's groups are popular self-help groups.

Role of NGOs in Developmental Activities

NGOs are expected to play a role in all conceivable aspects of development. People as well as policy makers alike attribute innumerable roles to NGOs and presume that NGO activity is a remedy to a number of problems in society. Before independence, NGOs confined their role to charity, relief and welfare activities. By the second half of the 1970s, the scope of NGOs work changed due to changes in the function and philosophy of other development organisations. The role of the government has changed from a police state to a welfare state and subsequently to a development state. Correspondingly, the NGO role has undergone modifications such as that of welfare, development and empowerment (Padmavathi 2009).

The objectives of the NGO reflect the scope of activities and the goal of the NGO. Most NGOs have multiple contributions to make. The most important role of NGOs is to deliver basic services to the underprivileged. The activities could include education, immunisation, sanitation, hygiene, health issues, maternal health, running old age homes, etc. NGOs could also work on providing low-cost housing to poor, construct tube wells, set up community owned micro-hydro projects, drinking water, public toilets, etc.

NGOs can act as the eye and ears for the government. They could convey the problems, constraints, potentialities and aspirations of people. They could also act as the arm of the government by making sure that the benefits of the government schemes reach the masses. They act as catalysts of social change as they could make the communities aware of their rights and empower them enough to raise their voice to ask their rights. Through capacity building of community and self-help groups, NGOs help the communities to generate income and develop economic independence.

NGOs also run consumer protection forums, literacy programmes and advocacy groups. Some engage in training, research, awareness generation, information dissemination and developing IEC material. NGOs also help the government to attain its goals of say 'education for all' through its total literacy mission by running the non-formal literacy centres. Foreign agencies also allocate funds to NGOs to undertake projects on issues of global concern, say AIDS or infant survival or breast-feeding promotion.

According to Bajpai (2006), NGOs have played a significant role and have been at the forefront providing services to children, showing a shift from the welfare approach to thrust on development and empowerment in the interventions for the children. The NGOs have developed several strategies based on child rights perspective to intervene on behalf of children and protect their rights. Many NGO and grass-roots organisations have intervened with various approaches. Some of the interventions have been in the following kinds of activities:

- Research and documentation.
- Advocacy of all level to bring about structural and policy changes.

- Preparing alternative reports on status of child rights.
- Promoting networking and coordination among NGOs to jointly advocate on issues which affect the rights of the child.
- Awareness building.
- Mobilisation of public opinion.
- Intervening in special cases of violations.
- Providing a platform for expression of children's concerns.
- Direct action like raids and liberation of children in servitude.
- Building pressure groups.
- Capacity building (building in the necessary skills, structures, attitudes, and knowledge) required to work better.
- Lobbying with the government to review existing schemes towards being more child-oriented.
- Running field action projects to reach out to children.
- Direct work with children and their communities.

Demerits of NGOs

- Operate at a very small level. The scope and the ability to reach to large population is restricted.
- Dependence on outside financial resources.
- Resource crunch always there. So the replicability of innovative ideas becomes very difficult.
- Some NGOs could be 'suitcase NGOs'. i.e., they operate from suitcases, the only objective being to collect funds from the government and other agencies on the name of being a registered NGO.
- May not be willing to share their ideas with other organisations out of fear of competition.

This book will present the work of some of the NGOs working in the area of Child Survival, Education, Child Protection and Disability in the following chapters. The NGO effort is a part of social action that is being taken to meet the challenges which children in our country face in the form of child rights violations. The focus in this book is on Indian NGOs, though international NGOs like CARE, Agha Khan foundation, Plan International, Oxfam, Action Aid (to name some) are also active in India. Mostly, the main role of these NGOs is to act as funding agency for development projects which fall in their purview of work.

References

Bajpai, A. (2006). *Child rights in India Law policy and practice* (2nd ed.). New Delhi: Oxford University Press.

Census India (2001). Retrieved Jan 12, 2009 from www.censusindia.net.

Census India (2011). Retrieved from http://censusindia.gov.in/.

Ministry of Women and Child Development, Government of India (2011). Report of the working group on Child Rights (2012–2017). For the twelfth five year plan. New Delhi. Retrieved from http://planningcommission.nic.in/aboutus/committee/wrkgrp12/wcd/wgrep_child.pdf.

Ministry of Women and Child Development, Government of India. (n.d.). *A Report of the Working Group on Development of Children for the Eleventh Five Year Plan (2007–2012).* Retrieved from http://wcd.nic.in/WG_Report.pdf.

National Family Health Survey (NFHS 3) India 2005–2006. Ministry of Health and Family Welfare. Retrieved from http://www.rchiips.org/nfhs/nutrition_report_for_website_18sep09.pdf.

Padmavathi, K. (2009) Role of NGOs in the empowerment of women. In P.V. Reddy (Ed.), *Development issues*. Jaipur: Rawat Publications.

SRS Bulletin (2013, September) Volume 48 no. 2. Retrieved from http://censusindia.gov.in/vital_statistics/SRS_Bulletins/SRS_Bulletin-September_2013.pdf.

Varma, S. (2014, August 19). 8 states report 71 per cent of total infant deaths. *The Times of India.*

(Source: Personal collection of author)

UNITED NATIONS CONVENTION ON THE RIGHTS OF THE CHILD

Article 6 (Survival and development): Children have the right to live. Governments should ensure that children survive and develop healthily

Chapter 3
Early Childhood Care and Education: Right to Survival and Development

Abstract This chapter reiterates the significance of early childcare in promoting survival, development and participation of children. The salience of ECCE and ECD is underscored in the chapter by quoting brain research. The UNICEF model of care is presented which highlights the determinants of child survival and development. Linkages between infant care practices and its impact on survival are also explored. Objectives of ECCE programmes for the birth–6 years age group are discussed. Status of ECCE in India is cited. Then the chapter moves on to profile the governmental initiatives like Integrated Child Development Services (ICDS), National Rural Health Mission, Reproductive and Child Health Scheme, Rajiv Gandhi Creche Scheme, Midday Meal programme, Sarva Shiksha Abhiyan (SSA), Right to Education (RTE), which target infant survival, preschool education, elementary education and child health. The chapter winds up with a brief description of NGOs working for ECD like Mobile Creches, FORCES, Centre for Learning Resources (CLR), KATHA and Pratham

Keywords Early childhood care and education (ECCE) · Integrated child development services · National rural health mission · Rajiv Gandhi creche scheme · Sarva shiksha abhiyan · Right to education

Is it enough to be alive and to survive? Or it is as important, or perhaps more important to develop your faculties to the fullest, enjoy a reasonable state of health and education, strive and contribute to nation development. Survival alone is not enough. It is the quality of life that is important.

Living is a process, the end of which is not just survival, but physical, mental and social well-being. Thus, child survival can be defined more positively, being thought of as something more than simply avoiding death. Surviving children fall along a continuum running from near death through sickness to a healthy state. The further a child is along that continuum towards a healthy state, the better the chances are of continued survival. The process of surviving, then, can be thought of as actively seeking a healthy state, of moving towards the healthy end of the

G. Chopra, *Child Rights in India*, DOI 10.1007/978-81-322-2446-4_3

death-sickness-health spectrum rather than simply preventing or arresting the process of dying (Myers 1992).

Accepting this positive reconceptualisation of child survival—as a process of seeking a healthy state at birth and in the early months and years of life—requires looking beyond the analysis of causes of mortality and beyond programmes that reduce mortality. It means examining where children are along a health-growth-development continuum. It means searching for programmes that will improve their health. This requires clarity about what, in a positive sense, constitutes moving towards a healthy state which necessarily include seeking mental and social health as well as physical well-being for young children (Myers 1992).

3.1 Salience of Early Childhood Years

Early childhood sets the foundation for life. What happens—or does not happen—to children in the earliest years of their lives is of critical importance, both to their immediate well-being and to their future. Ensuring that young children have positive experiences and their needs for health, nutrition and stimulation are met is crucial for their development and well-being. If the child has received the best start in the earliest years of life, she is more likely to have grown healthy, developed language and learning capacities, gone to school and led a productive, rewarding life.

Research in the field of neuroscience, particularly on the brain, has provided very convincing evidence of the 'critical periods' located within these early years, particularly the first 3 years, for the formation of synaptic connections in the brain and for the full development of the brain's potential. Research has also indicated that if these early years are not supported by, or embedded in, a stimulating and enriching physical and psychosocial environment, the chances of the child's brain developing to its full potential are considerably, and often irreversibly, reduced. What follows logically is the crucial importance of investing in these early years to ensure an enabling environment for every child, and thereby a sound foundation for life, which is not only the right of every child but also something that will impact, in the long term, on the quality of human capital available to a country (National Council of Educational Research and Training 2006).

Brain architecture is constructed through an ongoing process that begins before birth and continues into adulthood. It is impossible to say that a certain percentage of brain development occurs before a certain age—it is not that simple. It is true that the early years are the most active period for establishing the neural connections that comprise our brain architecture—700 new connections form every second in the first 3 years of life. As it emerges, the quality of that architecture establishes either a sturdy or a fragile foundation for all the capabilities and behaviour that follow. Skill begets skill as brains are built in a hierarchical fashion, from the bottom up. Increasingly complex circuits and skills build on simpler circuits and skills over time. The interaction of genes and experience shapes the circuitry of the developing brain. Young children serve up frequent invitations to engage with adults, who are either responsive or unresponsive to their needs. This 'serve and return' process is fundamental to the wiring of the brain, especially in the early years. Although manageable levels of stress are normative and growth-promoting, toxic stress in the early years can damage developing brain architecture and lead to problems in learning and behaviour, as well as increased susceptibility to physical and mental illness. Precipitants of toxic stress may include severe poverty, serious parental mental health impairments, child maltreatment and/or exposure to violence, in the absence of stable, nurturing relationships with the adults in a child's life (http://developingchild.harvard.edu/ retrieved 10 March 2014).

Early childhood is quoted by some as between birth and 6 years of age and by others between birth and 8 years (also includes early primary years along with pre-primary years). This period of life is characterised by most rapid growth and some of the most significant achievements—including talking, walking, forming attachments, encountering fear and pleasure and discovering oneself and the world beyond home. During this time, children learn to be autonomous and experiment with objects in the surrounding environment. They show a lively curiosity at what is going on around them, enjoy the company of other children and seek to imitate adult behaviour. At this stage, children play all the time. Play provides opportunities for the body to grow and chance to reflect, empathise, emote, discover, count, acquire self discipline, communicate and socialise. Play fosters creativity and develops higher order intellectual structures.

Early years are the golden years of learning and are also called as 'windows of opportunity'. Very young infants need stimulation and active interactive initiatives from adults in their environment to develop their faculties. Early years are critical for the development of brain of the child. Most brain development happens before a child reaches 36 months of age. By 36 months of age, children develop their abilities to think and speak, learn and reason and lay the foundation for their values and social behaviour as adults. Factors such as adequate nutrition, good health, freedom from diseases, clean water and a safe environment free from violence, abuse, exploitation and discrimination, all contribute to how the child grows and develops.

Early childhood is a period in life when the individual is particularly open to new experiences and especially able to take advantage of them. When children do not get the care they need during developmental prime times, or if they experience starvation, abuse or neglect, their survival, growth and development may be compromised. Early care and nurture have a decisive and lasting impact on how children grow to adulthood and how they develop their ability to learn and their capacity to regulate their emotions. The love, care and nurturance children receive in their first years—or the lack of these critical experiences—leave lasting imprints on young minds, hence underscoring the importance of early years in determining the life of an individual.

When the key ingredients for healthy, positive development are not present, the early years become a time of vulnerability rather than promise. Persistent environmental stress from unstable housing, an absence of adequate nutrition and high parental stress, coupled with few opportunities for rich early learning experiences, can be toxic to early brain development. Children with risk factors, such as living in low-income households, abuse or neglect, prenatal exposure to alcohol or other substances and low parental education, have a higher incidence of developmental delays and disabilities than the general population. Disparities emerge as early as 9 months and widen by 24 months of age (Halle et al. 2009). Divergence in language abilities begins to emerge before a child's first birthday and widens by age 3 (Hart and Risley 1995). Infants and toddlers who experience or are at risk for maltreatment are most vulnerable. More than half of children under age 2 who have any contact with the child welfare system—regardless of substantiation of abuse or neglect—are considered at high risk for developmental delays or neurological impairment (U.S. Department of Health and Human Services 2007).

In this context, it is important to consider if children in India are having a stimulating and enriching early childhood experience or is the childhood in India embedded in deprivation, distress and disease.

3.2 Early Childhood Development

Arguments in favour of providing enriched opportunities for Early Childhood Development (ECD) are varied and numerous. They range from the economic argument of greater productivity, and the ethical argument of the right to live and develop potential to the fullest, to the social argument of greater equality between classes and sexes, to the scientific argument of greater intelligence and more balanced social behaviour and to the political argument of greater participation in society. The CRC focuses on four sets of rights—survival, development, protection and participation. By and large, all these rights are interdependent and cannot be dealt in isolation. They have to be applied and implemented simultaneously if at all the rights of every child are to be respected. ECCE is a child's right. It is a major contributor to the survival, growth and development of children. Building on the CRC, the World Declaration on 'Education for All' was adopted at Jomtien, Thailand, in 1990. It highlights that 'learning begins at birth' and encourages providing for ECCE. Children being naive and young cannot take action on their own, they have to be dependent on the actions of others for realising their rights.

The question in point is what are the programmes which would foster early childhood development?

It has been demonstrated that the most effective programmes are those which 'integrate' health, education, nutrition, social and economic development, and that younger children benefit from such interventions more than older children. The latest research on the relationship between health, nutrition and stimulation argues convincingly that an adequate food supply is not enough to ensure a child's survival, neither is access to micro-nutrients, neither is education, nor absence of disease. Children's growth and development is fostered when all these variables are present, within a caring environment.

UNICEF Model of Care

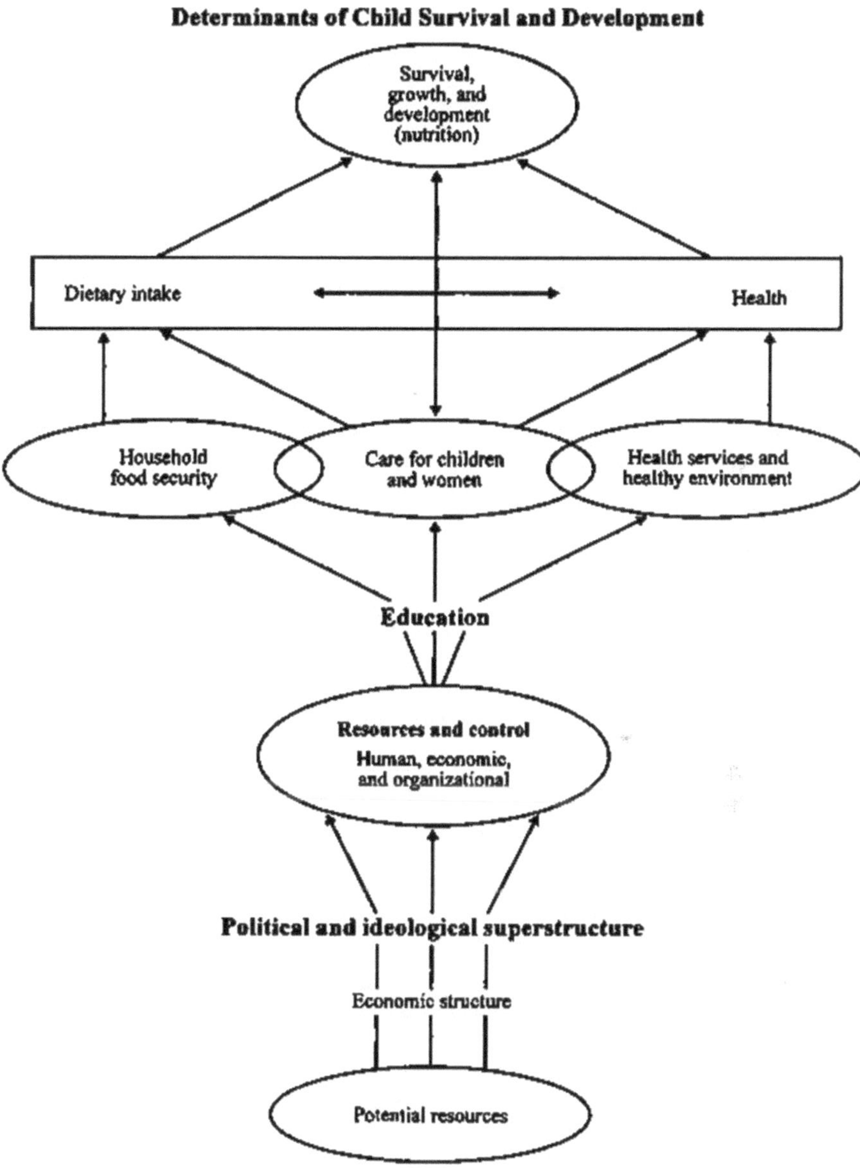

(*Source* Engle et al. 1997)

The UNICEF model for care which presents the determinants of child survival and development can now be examined in the context of the above discussion. It draws a direct relationship between survival, growth and development of children with the care of the infant and the mother. Further it points to a give and take between dietary intake and health of children. Causal relationship between community resources, health environment and education and the impact of economic resources and political ideology is also drawn.

There is an intricate and implicit relationship between the quality and nature of care received by the pregnant mother, infant and the young child and the chances of survival and proper development of the child. When the practices are examined, these day to day activities which look quite simple can make the life of the child.

Feeding Practices

- Initiate breast feeding within 1 h of birth
- Exclusively breast feed till 6 months
- Do not give pre-lacteals (Say, giving honey to the baby immediately after birth)
- Give colostrum to the new born
- Introduce complementary feeding at 6 months
- Increase breast feeding when sick
- Give one seasonal fruit/vegetable daily.

Hygiene Practices

- Clean the baby soon after s/he passes stool
- Wash hands before feeding
- Teach children to wash hands before and after eating food
- Children to wash hands with soap after defecating
- Take bath daily, cut nails regularly
- Keeping surroundings clean
- Drinking clean water
- Wash fruits before eating and wash vegetables before eating/cooking
- Keeping food and water covered.

Psychosocial Care

- Look at infant/make eye contact while breast feeding
- Touch, caress, stroke the baby
- Play with child, and allow child to play
- Point out objects in the child's environment
- Talk to the child
- Massage the infant
- Answer child's questions.

Health Practices

- Weigh infant once a month till she is 3 months of age and every 3 months subsequently
- Immunise infants and children

- If high fever, keep wet cloth on child's fore head to bring down temperature
- Give more liquids during diarrhoea
- Regular health check up.

It is obvious that the care of children directly affects the infant health and well-being. Good feeding practices, immunisation and clean environment all impact the infant. Further, provision of childcare and health services is paramount to the child's health. These services are directly impacted by the government of that time and its concern for children, i.e. its political ideology and programmes. Education opportunities and the resources allocated for it are a decision which the political bosses take. How safe the children are is also affected by the laws, which are enacted by the government. So, the infant survival, growth and development are not a product of the immediate family, but is affected by the society, government and other forces around the child.

Early childhood development approach are a range of activities and commitment on part of the parents, family, community and nation with an aim of providing a healthy physical, social, emotional and stimulating environment to children in very early years of life. It enables them to blossom and realise their best potential, laying a strong foundation for them to grow as a useful member of the family and the society, and a valuable human resource for the country.

ECD activities generally cover children between birth to the time that they join a formal school, which is normally 6 years. It also includes care of pregnant woman, because safe prenatal beginnings are the first sure steps towards healthy newborns. ECD also includes improving community awareness on infant care, mother care and childcare. Thus, ECD programmes include:

- Early stimulation and care of 0–2-year-old infants and toddlers at home, in crèches and in *balwadis.*
- Preschool education for 3–6 year olds fostering development of body, intellect, social-emotional skills and language and communication abilities.
- Care of pregnant women in the family and community.
- Parent education and improving awareness in community on positive childcare practices (Chopra n.d.).

As mentioned, Early Childhood Development includes infant care. Although developmentally most critical, the under-3 age group is the most neglected age group. Infant care includes infant feeding, weaning, immunisation, health and nutrition care, psychosocial care and protection from diseases among others. ECD also encompasses preschool education. In the preschool programme, children learn through manipulating objects and learn by doing. They acquire the concept of shapes, sizes, numbers, space and relationships. Their body grows and muscles strengthen. The finger muscles also gain strength which help them to colour, scribble and then write. Preschool experience provides tremendous developmental opportunities to young children and also lays the foundation for the rigours of formal schooling. Good quality ECD programmes necessarily address both care and education of children. Pregnant women, families and communities are also part of ECD as their skills and knowledge about safe motherhood and childcare practices determines what the children will receive from them.

The ECCE programme should ensure 'holistic development' of the child and reflect the inseparable nature of care and education by comprehensively addressing the need for care, nutrition, health and well-being of young children and parent counselling along with supporting the development of all domains.

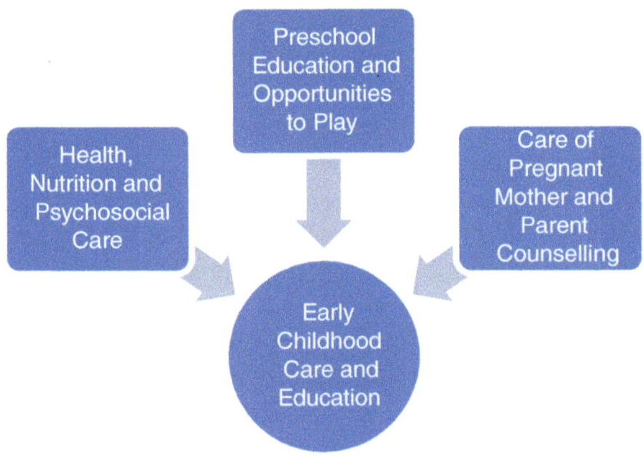

Objectives and Components of ECCE

The general objective of Early Childhood Care and Education is to facilitate optimum development of the child's full potential and lay the foundation for all round development and lifelong learning. ECCE compensates for environmental deprivations that children face in the early years. ECCE experiences are to be provided to ALL children, including the children with disabilities, who have a right to equitable opportunities. The specific *objectives* of ECCE are:

- Establish a sound foundation for a good physique, adequate muscular coordination and basic motor skills.
- Imbibe good health habits and independence.
- Enhance language and communication skills: improve vocabulary and expression of thoughts and feelings in fluent, correct, clear speech.
- Develop the five senses and cognitive skills and concepts which are foundation for higher order thinking and reasoning.
- Provide opportunities for play, active exploration, investigation and experimentation.
- Develop emotional maturity by guiding the child to express, understand, accept and control feelings and emotions.
- Develop independence, aesthetic appreciation and creativity by providing child with sufficient opportunities for self-expression.

- Make a smooth transition from preschool to primary through development of emergent literacy and school readiness.

As mentioned, ECCE focuses on programmes for children between birth and 6 years. But is a 1-month-old infant same as a 4-years old? The answer off course, is NO! As the infant and the preschooler are developmentally different, the related programmes for children of these age groups also have to be different.

Components of the programme for 0–3 years olds People everywhere feel that the care of the infant is the responsibility of the parents and is naturally happening. This kind of expectation is not really wrong as that is how it should be. But in poor families or where mothers are working with tenuous childcare arrangements in her absence, families may not be able to take adequate care of the infants. In such a case, it becomes important on the part of the state to assume the responsibility of childcare and have alternative childcare programmes. The broad objectives and components of ECCE programme for 0–3 years olds are as follows:

- Adopt age appropriate feeding practices, that is, start breast feeding within 1 h of birth, exclusive breast feeding till 6 months and continue to breast feed till 2 years. Introduction of complementary feeding at 6 months and making available nutritious and balanced food to the child;
- Monitor the growth of the child, identifying malnourished children and providing them necessary help;
- Keep the surroundings and the child clean;
- Immunise the child against vaccine preventable diseases;
- Protect the child from physical dangers and accidents;
- Interact with infants, nurture them and provide warmth and psychosocial care;
- Provide for ample sleep and rest;
- Talk and play with the child and give opportunities to explore and discover;
- Provide crèche services, especially if the parents are working;
- Strengthen the knowledge and skills of parents and community on better infant and childcare practices and beliefs.

Components of programme for 3–6 years olds The broad objectives and components of programme for 3–6 years olds include the following:

- Ensure that 3–6 years old children are attending a preschool;
- Provide proper nutrition and health care;
- Provide opportunities for the child to develop good physique and muscular coordination;
- Provide opportunities to play, as play gives unlimited possibilities to learn about the world and the people;
- Give them a suitable environment where children can socialise and interact with peers;
- Enable them to develop desirable habits, discipline and self help skills;

- Foster cognitive development and encourage intellectual curiosity and creativity;
- Encourage language and communication skills;
- Provide an environment where the child is allowed to express, understand and control emotions;
- Offer daycare facilities for children who have working parents;
- Strengthen parents and communities through regular contact with them by organising community meetings, *bal melas* etc;
- Lay the foundation for formal schooling through improved concentration, physical and emotional independence, alert mind, fit body and a desire to learn.

Young children with different abilities should also be reached by ECCE. Children with disabilities should be a part of the AWC's attending the preschool programme. Inclusion of children with disabilities at such an early age would lay the foundation for lifelong inclusion, develop social and communication skills in children and develop acceptance of diversity. With minor adaptations, it is possible for children with disabilities to be a part of the preschool programme of AWC. Legally also, it is unlawful to deny admission to any child on the basis of a disability.

Early Childhood Education: Basic Activity Ideas

1. For development of the physique: running, jumping, skipping, climbing, throwing—catching ball, skipping, dancing, jumping on the spot, swimming, etc.
2. Small muscle coordination: scribbling, colouring, tracing, sketching, pasting, sorting of pebbles/beads, buttoning, paper folding, playing with clay and plasticine, etc.
3. For language and communication: listening to stories, free conversation, making up stories, role play, riddles, free play.
4. For cognitive development: recognising colours, shapes, counting, learning about things in ones surroundings, information about vegetables, fruits, animals, people who constitute society (family, teacher, tailor, farmer, cobbler, police, shop keeper, etc.)
5. Social-emotional: playing group games, interacting with peer mates, role play, waiting for turn, sharing play things/food, learning rules of fair play, learning not to hit friends, saying please/sorry, learning to manage independently while away to preschool, etc.

3.3 Status of Early Childhood Care and Education Services in India

- There are 1.18 million anganwadi centres in the country catering to 346 lakh preschool children (Sheeranjan and Awathi 2010).
- Integrated Child Development Services (ICDS) has 1.18 million AWCs. But these centres have no provision of crèches for the 0–3 age group, nor are daycare facilities included for 0–6 years old children of working mothers. ICDS leaves the care of under 3's largely with the family.
- Census 2001 declares that there are 120 million working mothers, 90 % of whom work in the unorganised sector. As per current estimates, 60 million children under 3 are in need of crèches. Crèches are needed at work places to facilitate continued breast feeding, complementary feeding, to provide a safe environment and to cater to the psychosocial and learning needs of under 3's.
- The Rajiv Gandhi Crèche Scheme has sanctioned 22,038 crèches for children of working mothers as against a requirement of 800,000. This programme covers only 0.55 million children in the age group 0–5 years.
- District Primary Education Programme (DPEP) has opened 10,000 ECE centres in non-ICDS areas.
- Sarv Shiksha Abhiyan: 73,860 ECCE centres and 254,179 schools have pre-primary wing (Sheeranjan and Awathi 2010).
- It is estimated that the private sector provides preschool education services to more children than the ICDS. The quality of services provided by privately run preschools needs to be regulated as there is a wide variability in services provided by them. NGO services for ECCE are reaching to a varying number from 3 to 20 million (National Council of Educational Research and Training 2006).

3.4 ECCE as Per Costitution and the Legal Framework

- As per the Constitution of India, Article 45 'The State shall endeavour to provide ECCE for all children until they complete the age of 6 years'.
- Though the Right to Education Act, 2009 is for children of age 6–14 years, Section 11 pertains to ECCE 'With a view to prepare children above the age of 3 years for elementary education and to provide ECCE for all children until they complete the age of 6 years, the appropriate government may take necessary arrangement for providing free pre-primary education for such children'.
- The National Early Childhood Care and Education (ECCE) Policy, 2013 reaffirms the commitment of the Government of India to provide integrated services for holistic development of all children, along the continuum, from the prenatal period to 6 years of age. The Policy lays down the way forward for a comprehensive approach towards ensuring a sound foundation, with focus on early learning for every Indian child.

3.5 Linking Early Childhood Care with Child Protection

Unarguably, early childhood constitutes the most vulnerable stage of life. Deprivation and neglect in this stage can lead to development retardation. ECCE has mostly been linked to 'right to development'. But when we examine closely, ECCE contributes clearly to child protection. Proper care in early years reduces neglect. A child who in the absence of parents (due to jobs or otherwise incapacity to care), is in the safe environments of a ECCE programme, is protected from abuse of many forms which could arise due to violence by known persons, neighbours or strangers. With joint families breaking and families migrating to bigger cities for livelihood, both parents working, this is posing a threat to children. Child abuse by relatives and neighbours is on the rise. Home is at times, not the safest haven. The relationship of ECCE with child protection cannot be ignored.

Hence, the need of the hour is of more crèches and daycare centres. ICDS can also include crèches for children under 3. There should be more trained manpower of ECCE workers, which is a serious concern to be addressed. The salaries offered to ECCE workers and the status accorded to them is so abysmal that this is not viewed as an attractive job option by young people. Being an early childhood care worker is a low paid job. This reflects the society's apathy and lack of concern for our children. It seems we are happy to pay people who work in technology or finance. But when it comes to professionals who have to take care of our most prized possession, our children, we do not consider them worthy to be paid well! Planning for and investing in quality childcare professionals and facilities is imperative to prevent more and more young children from falling out of the safety and protective net.

3.6 Government Programmes for Children

- Integrated Child Development Services (ICDS)
- Health Services of Government of India
- Rajiv Gandhi Creche Scheme
- Sarva Shiksha Abhiyan (SSA)
- Midday Meals
- Right to Education Act

3.6.1 Integrated Child Development Services (ICDS)

ICDS is the only major national programme in India that addresses the health, nutrition and ECCE needs of children under the age of 6 years. As the needs of a child cannot be addressed in isolation from those of their mother, the programme also extends to pregnant women and nursing mothers. ICDS provides a comprehensive set of services, all aimed at improving the survival, growth and development of children.

All the services of the ICDS scheme are disseminated from the *anganwadi* centre (AWC). The Anganwadi is operated by an Anganwadi Worker (AWW) who is the back bone of the programme. She surveys all the families in the neighbourhood, enrols eligible children, ensures that food is served on time every day, conducts the preschool education activities, is assisted by health functionaries to organise immunisation sessions, makes home visits to pregnant mothers and so on. The AWW is assisted by an *Anganwadi* Helper (AWH) or *Sahayika*. Her main duties are to bring children to the Anganwadi, cook food for them and help with the maintenance of the AWC.

An Anganwadi covers a population of about 1000 persons (say 200 families) in rural and urban areas and 700 persons in tribal areas. In sparsely populated regions of the country like hilly or desert areas, an Anganwadi may cover a population of around 300 persons. The ICDS programme is organised as a collection of 'Projects'. Normally, an ICDS project covers a population of around 100,000, and has within it about 100 Anganwadis. The in-charge of each project is Child Development Project Officer (CDPO). The CDPO is assisted by 'Supervisors', who make regular visits to the Anganwadis, check the registers, inspect the premises, advise the Anganwadi worker, enquire about any problems she may have and so on.

The services provided under ICDS fall under three broad headings: *nutrition*; *health*; *early childhood care and preschool education* which are briefly presented:

(i) Nutrition

- *Supplementary Nutrition (SNP)*: Supplementary Nutrition is provided for 300 days in a year in the AWC to children and expectant and nursing mothers. The objective is to bridge the gap between the average food eaten by children from low-income disadvantaged families and the recommended national intake. The food provided at the AW is supposed to add-on the food eaten at home, and not substitute it. The food given at the AWC varies from state to state but usually consists of a hot meal cooked at the Anganwadi, based on a mix of pulses, cereals, oil, vegetables, sugar, iodised salt, etc. Sometimes 'take-home rations' (THR) are provided for children under the age of 3 years. Vitamin A doses are also given to children at the AWC.
- *Growth Monitoring and Promotion*: Children under three are weighed once a month, to keep a check on their health and nutrition status. Children between 3 and 6 years are weighed once in 3 months. Growth charts are kept to detect any sudden drop in weight (growth faltering) and steps are taken to control slipping down of weight. Growth monitoring also helps identify malnourished children, who are then provided with special supplementary food which could be therapeutic in nature or at times double the ration. The severely malnourished children may even be referred to district health centres.

- *Nutrition and Health Education* (*NHEd*): The aim of NHEd is to help women aged 15–45 years to look after their own and their families health and nutrition needs. NHEd is imparted through counselling sessions, home visits and demonstrations. It covers issues such as infant feeding, family planning, sanitation, utilisation of health services, diarrhoea management, etc.

(ii) Health

- *Immunisation*: Children under six are immunised against polio, diphtheria, pertusis, tetanus, measles and tuberculosis, while pregnant women are immunised against tetanus. This is a joint responsibility of ICDS and the Health Department. The main role of the Anganwadi worker is to assist health staff (such as the Auxillary Nurse Midwife) to conduct immunisation, to maintain records of the same and motivate the parents to get their children immunised.
- *Health services*: A range of health services are supposed to be provided through the Anganwadi Worker including health checkups of children under six, ante-natal care of expectant mothers, post-natal care of nursing mothers, recording of weight, management of undernutrition and treatment of minor ailments. Here again, the ANM and LHV (Lady Health Visitor) of the health department help with service delivery.
- *Referral Services*: This service attempts to link sick or undernourished children, those with disabilities and other children requiring medical attention with the public healthcare system. Complicated cases are referred by the Anganwadi worker to the medical officers of the Primary Health Centres (PHCs).

(iii) Early Childhood Care and Preschool Education

ECCE as planned out in ICDS, focuses on total development of children up to 6 years from underprivileged families. It includes promotion of early stimulation of the under 3's through intervention with the mothers as part of the programme. But this is hardly happening. The under-3 component of the ICDS is very weak. The programme for 3–6 years olds at the AW is directed towards providing and ensuring a natural, joyful and stimulating environment. Child-centred play-way activities which build on local culture and practices are used. Preschool Education aims to promote the social, emotional, cognitive, physical and aesthetic development of the child and lays foundation for primary schooling.

ICDS has been in the process of being restructured. The major reorganisational ideas for restructuring are being summarised here:

- Repositioning the AWC as a 'vibrant ECD centre' to become the first village outpost for health, nutrition and early learning with adequate infrastructure and human resources for ensuring a continuum of care in a life-cycle approach to early childhood care and development, emphasising the child's physical, cognitive, emotional and social development until the age of 6 years. AWCs would be equipped as a child-friendly centre with adequate infrastructure, facilities (kitchen, safe drinking water and child-friendly toilets), wall painting, play space and joyful learning environment. The activities of AWC would be expanded to include extended hours (minimum of 6 h), provide flexibility to state for running of crèches and daycare centres.

- The provision of daycare and crèches is essential for care and development of children in 6 months–6 years of age, specially when mothers go for work and there are no adult care givers at home. To begin with, 5 % of the AWCs would be converted into AWC-cum-crèche.
- Special focus on the under 3's by developing strategies to promote infant and young child feeding practices, early stimulation, early screening and referral, monthly monitoring of child growth and development milestones.
- Home-based counselling for essential newborn care, lactation support and child spacing.
- Promotion of local foods, food demonstrations, celebration of nutrition week, breast feeding week and ICDS day.

Community participation is an important element in the design of ICDS. The community can be mobilised to provide the Anganwadis with better facilities (e.g. a fan, place for running of Anganwadi, helpers, etc.), to ensure that they open on time every day, or to encourage mothers to participate in counselling sessions. Unfortunately, community participation in ICDS is quite weak.

With the gradual passage of time, the coverage of ICDS has steadily increased since its inception way back in 1975 when it started with 33 projects. As in year 2012, ICDS has 6908 operational projects. It has a network of more than 13 lakh anganwadi workers. More than 7.9 crore children between the age of 6 months–6 years are receiving supplementary nutrition. More than 1.8 crore pregnant and lactating women are availing services under the ICDS scheme. Preschool education is reaching almost 3.6 crore 3–6-year-old children (http://wcd.nic.in/icdsimg/ICDS-March%202012.pdf retrieved March 2014). Today, the programme is operational in almost every block. However, its services have still to reach all parts of the country.

Over 25 lakh Anganwadi Workers and Anganwadi Helpers constitute the core of these services and have the potential to be prime movers for social change—along with ASHAs, ANMs, teachers and women members of panchayati raj institutions. ICDS is the critical link between children and women and with the primary health care and elementary education systems. It also provides a protective environment for young children—including care and protection of the young and adolescent girl child (Report of the Inter Ministerial Group on ICDS Restructuring 2011).

3.6.2 *Government Health Programmes for the Mother and the Child*

Reproductive and Child Health Program: Reproductive and Child Health (RCH) was launched in 1997 by the Ministry of Health and Family Welfare, Government of India to supplement the MCH program. RCH can be explained as a state in which 'People have the ability to reproduce and regulate their fertility; women are able to go through pregnancy and childbirth safely, the outcome of pregnancy is successful in terms of maternal and infant survival and well-being; and couples are able to have sexual relations free of the fear of pregnancy and contracting diseases'. This means that every couple should be able to have child when they want, that the pregnancy is uneventful, that safe delivery services are available, that at the end of the pregnancy the mother and the child are safe, well and that contraceptives by choice are available to prevent pregnancy and there is protection from contracting diseases.

The RCH has envisaged to provide an integrated package of services, which will include the following:

- Services for mothers during pregnancy, childbirth and post-natal period and
- also safe abortion services, whenever required.
- Services for children like newborn care, immunisation, Vitamin A prophylaxis, Oral Rehydration Therapy (ORT) for diarrhoea, management of Acute Respiratory Infections (ARI), anaemia control, etc.
- Services for eligible couples through availability and promotion of use of contraceptive methods, and infertility services when required.
- Prevention and management of Reproductive Tract Infections (RTIs) and Sexually Transmitted Infections (STIs).
- Adolescent health services including counselling of family life and reproductive health.

National Rural Health Mission (NHRM): Given the particular challenges, risks and opportunities associated with pregnancy, childbirth and early childhood, the promotion of maternal and child health has been one of the most important objectives of the ministry of health and Family Welfare. The ministry is actively pursuing the goal of reduction of maternal, neonatal and infant mortality rates by focusing on interventions (Ministry of Women and Child Development, Government of India 2011). The (NHRM) was launched in 2005 by the Ministry of Health and Family Welfare with an aim to provide accessible, affordable health care to rural poor. Further to this, The Janani Shishu Suraksha Karyakram was launched in 2011 under the NHM to provide cashless delivery services to pregnant women to newborn till they were 30 days old. Pregnant women are provided with free institutional deliveries by skilled attendants aimed at reducing maternal mortality and neonatal mortality. Every year, 13 lakh infants die before they reach their first birthday and out of these, 9 lakh die within the first 4 weeks of life (2/3rd) out of these, 7 lakh deaths happen in the first week itself, accounting for 75 % of IMR. (www.NHRM.gov.in retrieved on 14 March, 2014). So, focusing the services in a mission mode for deliveries and survival of the neonate would be a huge step in reducing IMR.

The following are the Free Entitlements for pregnant women:

Free and cashless delivery
Free C-Section
Free drugs and consumables
Free diagnostics
Free diet during stay in the health institutions
Free provision of blood
Free transport from home to health institutions
Free transport between facilities in case of referral
Free drop back from institutions to home after 48 h stay.

The following are the Free Entitlements for sick newborns till 30 days after birth. This has now been expanded to cover sick infants:

Free treatment
Free drugs and consumables
Free diagnostics
Free provision of blood
Free transport from home to health institutions
Free transport between facilities in case of referral
Free drop back from institutions to home (www.NHRM.gov.in retrieved on 14 March, 2014).

Janani Shishu Suraksha Karyakram has resulted in phenomenal growth in institutional deliveries. More than one crore women are benefiting from the scheme (www.NHRM.gov.in retrieved on 14 March, 2014).

This information was given by Minister for Health and Family Welfare Shri Ghulam Nabi Azad in written reply to a question in the Rajya Sabha. (Source Press Information Bureau New Delhi, Dec 11 2013)

Under the National Rural Health Mission, the key steps being taken by the Government of India to reduce MMR and IMR in the country are:

- Promotion of institutional deliveries through Janani Suraksha Yojana (JSY).
- Capacity building of health care providers in basic and comprehensive obstetric care, Integrated Management of Neonatal and Childhood Illness (IMINCI) and Navjaat Shishu Surakshta Karyakaram (NSSK), etc.
- Operationalisation of sub-centres, primary health centres, community health centres and district hospitals for providing 24 × 7 basic and comprehensive obstetric care and childcare services.

- Strengthening of facility-based newborn care by setting up Newborn care corners (NBCC) in all health facilities where deliveries take place to provide essential newborn care at birth; and Special New Born Care Units (SNCUs) at District Hospitals and New Born Stabilization Units (NBSUs) at First Referral Units for the care of sick newborn.
- Name-based web enabled tracking of pregnant women and children has been introduced to ensure antenatal and post-natal care to pregnant women and care to newborns, infants and children.
- Mother and Child Protection Card in collaboration with the Ministry of Women and Child Development to monitor service delivery for mothers and children.
- Iron and folic acid supplementation to pregnant and lactating women and children for prevention and treatment of anaemia.
- Weekly iron and folic acid supplementation to adolescent girls.
- Engagement of 8.71 lakhs Accredited Social Health Activists (ASHAs) to generate demand and facilitate accessing of health care services by the community.
- Home-Based Newborn Care (HBNC) through ASHA has been initiated to improve new born care practices at the community level and for early detection and referral of sick new born babies.
- Village Health and Nutrition Days in rural areas as an outreach activity, for provision of maternal and child health services.
- Janani Shishu Suraksha Karyakaram (JSSK) has been launched on 1st June, 2011, to eliminate any out of pocket expense for pregnant women delivering in public health institutions and sick newborns accessing public health institutions for treatment till 30 days after birth.
- Management of Malnutrition particularly Severe Acute Malnutrition (SAM) by establishing Nutritional Rehabilitation Centres (NRCs). As breastfeeding reduces infant mortality, exclusive breastfeeding for first 6 months and appropriate infant and young child feeding practices are being promoted in convergence with Ministry of Woman and Child Development.
- Universal Immunization Program (UIP) against seven diseases for all children. Government of India supports the vaccine programme by supply of vaccines and syringes, cold chain equipments and provision of operational costs.

3.6.3 Rajiv Gandhi Creche Scheme

The *Rajiv Gandhi Creche Scheme* has been launched by the government for children of working mothers. The scheme has been designed by merging the National Creche Fund and Scheme of Assistance to Voluntary Organisations for running crèches for children of working and ailing mothers. In today's economy, there is a rising need for women to contribute to the household incomes. Working women require support with regard to the care of their younger children especially infants. Creches are essential for the mother as well as the infants.

Under the scheme, crèches are being allocated to states and union territories on the basis of child population. Every crèche unit would provide services to 25 babies for 8 h, i.e. from 9 a.m. to 5 p.m. The services being provided include sleeping facilities, health care, supplementary nutrition and immunisation. Currently, 22,038 creches have been sanctioned to run across the country.

According to the scheme, crèche should have a minimum of 6–8 sq feet per child. It should be well lit, with proper ventilation and fan should be provided. The crèche should have a play area, toilet facilities and sleep arrangement (mattresses, cot, cradles, pillows, sheets) suited for infants and young children. The crèche must have a source for getting clean drinking water. Food provided to the children must have adequate nutritional value and there should be variety in the food that is given to the children every day. The food should be acceptable to the babies and children. For this, the workers should know what are the nutritious preparations suitable for babies and children and they must cook food with due care and cleanliness.

Basic cooking equipment like stoves, pots and pans should be made available. Cooking area should be monitored and be separate from children area.

The component of Training has been added to the Scheme to orient the Crèche Workers as well as the Implementing Agencies to provide better services and to build up child-friendly environment in the Centre. A short-term training will be provided to every crèche worker and helper. The trained worker will be able to do the following:

- Organise preschool education activities for children between 3 and 6 years of age based on the ECE guidelines provided during training.
- Organise stimulation activities for children below 3 years.
- Prepare low-cost teaching–learning aids.
- Teach Personal hygiene Habits to the Children.
- Prepare Nutritious food for children attending the crèche centre.
- Keep the centre and its surroundings neat and clean.
- Motivate parents for immunisation and obtain assistance of health staff in ensuring immunisation of children.
- Provide proper arrangements for sleep and rest of children.
- Ensure regular home visits and mothers meetings to elicit community participation.
- Create awareness about better childcare in the community.
- Ensure weekly visits by doctors/healthworkers.

The crèche may charge Rs. 20 from BPL families and Rs. 60 from others. BPL families should be given priority. Weekly visits by doctors should be carried out for treatment and checkup.

3.6.4 *Sarva Shiksha Abhiyan (SSA)*

The role of education and literacy in bringing about social change and mobility is well recognised. It opens up opportunities for attaining both personal and social goals. Education also improves the quality of life. Universalisation of Elementary Education (UEE) has been guided by five parameters: (i) universal access, (ii) universal enrolment, (iii) universal retention, (iv) universal achievement and (v) equity. The major programmes of elementary education included Sarva Shiksha Abhiyan, District Primary Education Programme (DPEP) and Midday Meal Programme.

SSA is the principal programme for UEE and is a culmination of all previous endeavours in implementing educational programmes. Reviewing the previous programmes, 'operation blackboard' focused on improving physical infrastructures of schools; DPEP on primary education; 'shikha karmi' on teacher absenteeism; 'lok jumbish' on girls education—SSA has been the single largest holistic programme addressing all aspects of elementary education.

Elementary education consists of primary (class I–V) and upper primary education (VI–VIII) is the foundation of the pillar of education system and has received a major push through the Sarva Shiksha Abhiyan.

Sarva Shiksha Abhiyan (SSA) is Government of India's flagship programme for achievement of Universalisation of Elementary Education (UEE) in a time bound manner, as mandated by 86th amendment to the Constitution of India making free and compulsory education to the children of 6–14 years age group, a Fundamental Right. SSA is being implemented in partnership with State Governments to cover the entire country and address the needs of 192 million children in 1.1 million habitations. The programme seeks to open new schools in those habitations which do not have schooling facilities and strengthen existing school infrastructure through provision of additional class rooms, toilets, drinking water, maintenance grant and school improvement grants. Existing schools with inadequate teacher strength are provided with additional teachers, while the capacity of existing teachers is being strengthened by extensive training, grants for developing teaching–learning materials and strengthening of the academic support structure at a cluster, block and district level. SSA seeks to provide quality elementary education including life skills. SSA has a special focus on girl's education and children with special needs. SSA also seeks to provide computer education to bridge the digital gap.

SSA adopts, 'the bottom-up' process of planning, wherein the felt needs of the served communities and educational needs of learners are well taken care of and the plan fits into the broad framework of SSA. In view of the fact that the desired improvement and sustenance of the improved efficiency level cannot be achieved without the active involvement of the community in the schooling system, SSA has emphasised the involvement of local people and stakeholders in planning. This also ensures reflection of local needs, which is essential for achieving the goals of the programme.

Aims and Objectives of SSA

The Sarva Shiksha Abhiyan aims to provide useful and relevant elementary education for all children in the 6–14 age group by 2010. There is also another goal to bridge social, regional and gender gaps, with the active participation of the community in the management of schools.

Following are the main objectives of SSA:

- All children in school, Education Guarantee Centre, Alternate School, 'Back-to-School' camp by 2003.
- All children complete 5 years of primary schooling by 2007.
- All children complete 8 years of elementary schooling by 2010.
- Focus on elementary education of satisfactory quality with emphasis on education for life.
- Bridge all gender and social category gaps at primary stage by 2007 and at elementary education level by 2010.
- Universal retention by 2010.

Universal Access SSA has brought primary schools at the door steps of millions of children, including the first generation learners, reaching even to the remote unreached areas of the country. *Universal Enrolment* with the launch of SSA, there has been a significant reduction of out-of-school children. Innovative strategies have been used to make education reach the children of minority communities by strengthening the madarsas/maktabs. Village Education Committees have been set up and a number of context-specific strategies adopted to increase the elementary school enrolment. *Universal Retention* school retention has been a big challenge. The fact that children drop out of school early or fail to acquire basic literacy numeracy skills partially reflects poor quality of education. Poor teacher training, teacher absenteeism, lack of early childhood education, gender barriers in education, learning by rote are some of the very many stumbling blocks in universal retention. *Universal Achievement and Equity* SSA has tried to strengthen inputs that impact on quality viz., recruitment of additional teachers, improving teacher-student ratio, regular inservice training to teachers, curriculum renewal, textbook development, free distribution of text books to SCs, STs, girl students, computer aided learning, setting up residential schools for girls under the Kasturba Gandhi Balika Vidyalya scheme among some.

Sarva Shiksha Abhiyan Interventions include:

- Special Training for Out of School Children: specific provision for special training for age appropriate admission for out –of-school children. A majority of out–of-school children belong to disadvantaged communities: scheduled caste, scheduled tribes, Muslims, migrants children with special needs, urban deprived children, working children, children in other difficult circumstances, for example, those living in difficult terrain, children from displaced families and areas affected by civil strife, etc.

- Neighbourhood Schools: establishment of a school by the appropriate government or local authority with in the prescribed area or limits of the neighbourhood with in the period of 3 years from the commencement of the Act to ensure that every child in the 6–14 age group pursues and completes elementary education.
- Bridging Social Categories Gaps: makes specific effort for social inclusion both explicitly and implicitly. Some of the relevant provisions are: no discrimination against children from disadvantaged groups and weaker sections on any grounds; inclusion of women in school monitoring committees; provision of good quality education that includes equity issues, curriculum development in conformity with constitutional stipulations; training, enrolment in age appropriate classes.
- Kasturba Gandhi Balika Vidyalya Scheme launched in 2004 takes up setting up of residential schools at upper primary level for girls, predominantly belonging to SC, ST, minorities, OBCs and BPL communities.
- Special interventions for disadvantaged groups—young learners from socially marginalised face rejection in schooling. SSA prioritises education of these groups by setting up additional KGBV in blocks with higher concentration of SC, ST, OBC, muslims. It also provides for remedial coaching, special interventions for migrating children and creating capacities in schools for dealing with children lagging in studies.
- Preschool Education: The PSE component of ICDS is very weak, which turns away parents and children from continuing their education. SSA has in some areas a component of 1 year of pre-primary education which will gradually be universalised to cover all children. This is critical for school readiness that improves school retention. Beside, this will free the girl child from sibling care. Primary schools within the habitations are ideal for such ECCE. In other habitations, ICDS-Anganwadis will be supported.
- Madarsas/maktabs will be supported for modernisation under the AIE component and the aim is to cover all madarsas in a phased manner.
- In the case of Children with Special Needs (CWSN), the key priority areas are strengthening the identification system of CWSN, ensuring full coverage of CWSN by preparing schools to address the diverse needs that different categories of CWSN have, especially children with Autism Spectrum Disorders, cerebral palsy, deaf-blindness, etc. Strengthening the resource support team for regular and effective academic support to the CWSN. Sensitisation of teachers, parents, community and peers to create an inclusive school environment, coordination with special schools and barrier-free access through the availability of ramps with handrails and barrier-free toilets.

3.6.5 *Midday Meal Programme*

The Midday Meal is the world's largest school feeding programme reaching out to about 12 crore school going children across the country. With a view to enhancing enrollment, retention and attendance and simultaneously improving nutritional levels among children, the National Programme of Nutritional Support to Primary Education (NP-NSPE) was launched as a Centrally Sponsored Scheme on 15th August 1995, initially in 2408 blocks in the country. By the year 1997–1998, the NP-NSPE was introduced in all blocks of the country. It was further extended in 2002 to cover not only children in classes I–V of Government, Government aided and local body schools, but also children studying in EGS (Education Guarantee Scheme) and AIE (alternative and innovative education) centres of SSA. In order to ensure balanced and nutritious diet to children of upper primary group the quantity of pulses provided in the scheme is 25–30 g, vegetables 65–75 g. A Separate component for Payment of honorarium @ Rs. 1000 per month per cook-cum-helper was introduced from 1.12.2009. Following norms for engagement of cook-cum-helper have been made: (i) One cook-cum-helper for schools up to 25 students. (ii) Two cooks-cum-helpers for schools with 26–100 students. (iii) One additional cook-cum-helper for every addition of up to 100 students. More than 26 lakhs cook-cum-helper at present are engaged by the State/UTs during 2010–2011 for preparation and serving of Midday Meal to Children in Elementary Classes.

Today, Midday Meal scheme is serving primary and upper primary school children in entire country. Besides being provided food grains, cooking cost and transport subsidy, schools are also sanctioned kitchen sheds and kitchen equipment. The scheme has had its short comings, which are being addressed by these action points:

- MDM to be managed by the local community and NGOs/PRI
- Sensitise the teachers and others involved in nutrition, hygiene, cleanliness and safety norms
- Promote locally grown foods through kitchen gardens
- Display information on supplies, weekly menu, funds, coverage in schools to ensure transparency.

3.6.6 *Right to Education: Elementary Education Is Now a Right of Every Child*

As per the Constitution (Eighty-sixth Amendment) Act, in which Article 21-A was inserted, RTE act came into being. The Right of Children to Free and Compulsory Education (RTE) Act 2009, means that every child in the age group 6–14 years has a fundamental right to free and compulsory elementary education of satisfactory and equitable quality in a formal school which satisfies certain essential norms and standards.

The title of the RTE Act incorporates the words 'free and compulsory'. 'Free education' means that no child shall be liable to pay any kind of fee or charges or expenses which may prevent him or her from pursuing and completing elementary education. 'Compulsory education' casts an obligation on the appropriate Government and local authorities to provide and ensure admission, attendance and completion of elementary education by all children in the 6–14 age group.

RTE provides for appointment of appropriately trained teachers, i.e. teachers with the requisite entry and academic qualifications. It prohibits physical punishment and mental harassment; screening procedures for admission of children; capitation fee; private tuition by teachers and running of schools without recognition.

The highlights of the RTE Act are:

- The Bill provides that children between the ages of 6 and 14 years have the right to free and compulsory education in a neighbourhood school. The government shall ensure that all children have this right. Children with disabilities including mental illness, mental retardation, blindness and hearing loss, shall also have this right.
- A child above 6 years of age who is not enrolled in school or was unable to complete his education shall be enrolled in an age appropriate class. Furthermore, these children have a right to receive special training in order to reach their peer group level. Elementary education shall be free until completion, even if the child is older than 14 years.
- No child shall be held back, expelled or required to pass a board examination until the completion of elementary education. A child who completes elementary education shall be awarded a certificate as prescribed.
- No child shall be subject to physical punishment or mental harassment. Those officials that contravene this provision shall be liable for disciplinary action under the applicable service rules.
- Kendriya Vidyalayas, Navodaya Vidyalayas, Sainik Schools and unaided schools shall admit at least 25 % of students from disadvantaged and economically weaker groups.

On Curriculum and Recognition

- The appropriate government (central or state government) shall specify an academic authority to develop the curriculum and evaluation procedure for elementary education. The academic authority shall consider constitutional values, child-centred and trauma-free learning and instruction in the mother tongue when developing the curriculum.
- The Bill requires all schools to comply with pupil–teacher ratio norms. All private schools must also comply with infrastructure and teacher norms, failing which, they shall lose their recognition (and need to shut down).

Responsibilities of Schools and Teachers

- The Bill states that government schools shall provide free and compulsory education to all admitted children. Similarly, aided schools shall provide free and compulsory education proportionate to the funding received, subject to a minimum of 25 %.
- Kendriya Vidyalayas, Navodaya Vidyalayas, Sainik Schools and unaided schools shall admit at least 25 % of the students from SCs, STs, low-income and other disadvantaged or weaker groups. Unaided schools shall be reimbursed for either their tuition charge or the per-student expenditure in government schools, whichever is lower.
- The Bill requires teachers to attend regularly and punctually, complete curriculum instruction, assess learning abilities, hold regular parent–teacher meetings and any other duties as prescribed. Teachers are prohibited from giving private tuitions.

Admissions and Transfers

- For admissions purposes, a child's age shall be determined by a birth certificate or another document as specified. But if the child does not have age proof, a child shall not be denied admission for lack of it. Furthermore, a child shall not be denied admission even if it is requested after the start of the academic year.
- The Bill prohibits schools from using a screening process for admissions or from charging a capitation fee. Both offences are punishable with a fine.
- A child required to move shall have the right to transfer admission to any state or local government or aided school. Lack of a transfer certification shall not be grounds for denying or delaying admissions.

Key Issues and Analysis of RTE act

- The objective is that all children should receive elementary education with the passage of RTE act. But the act does not specify any penalty for the violation of this right.
- The act places the responsibility on both central, state government and local authorities to make children receive education. But this division of responsibility makes none of the governments accountable.
- How do children on streets and child labour reach school, especially in the cases where children are not with their families. There is no answer in the act on this.
- The bill provides for right to schooling and physical infrastructure. It does not guarantee quality of education. Even the duties of the teacher are related to punctuality, attendance, etc., and not to learning outcomes of students.
- As no child can be held back until the completion of elementary education, it is quite possible for students to reach grade VIII without even having acquired minimum levels of learning. The bill neither addresses this, nor does it direct schools to provide remedial classes to students who are lagging behind. If parents want their child to repeat a class, the bill does not even permit that.

There are many challenges in the implementation of the RTE act. It is reported that only 19 Indian states have notified the RTE rules. Among them are Rajasthan, Tamil Nadu, Madhya Pradesh, Karnataka, Andhra Pradesh and Maharashtra. Nine states are yet to notify the rules. A major obstacle behind implementation of the RTE Act, as put forward by the states, is paucity of funds. It has been observed that the Hindi-speaking states of Uttar Pradesh, Rajasthan, Madhya Pradesh and Bihar have been the most half-hearted when it comes to implementation of the RTE Act, despite the fact that 67 % of out-of-school children are from these states. Uttar Pradesh has, in fact, gone to the extent of claiming that funds given by the Centre would be utilised to provide free and compulsory education to all children in the age group 6–14. In other words, the state has no intention of contributing towards implementation of the Act and will depend wholly on the Centre. It is clearly not lack of funds that is a hindrance in implementation of the RTE Act but lack of intent and political will. It is a strange irony that even as the states express concern over the financial burden of this ambitious Act, the government has been encouraging the corporate sector by offering major subsidies every year. The government has also favoured the growth of private educational institutions under the public private partnership (PPP) concept (Rai 2015). The government has also put an education cess of 2 % on income tax payers to foot the bills for the implementation of the RTE act.

Non-availability of teachers and setting up of neighbourhood schools is another challenge in the implementation of the act. A very big hurdle is trying to reach a vast number of out of school children, and bringing them into the fold of education, and then retaining them. How to reach out to school drop-outs is another test to pass in the implementation of the act.

As per Article 21A of the Constitution, India has moved forward to a rights-based framework that puts a legal obligation on the Central and State Governments to implement this fundamental child right as enshrined in the provisions of the RTE Act.

3.7 Interventions and Strategies by Non-Government Organisations in Early Childhood Development

Briefly reviewing some of the NGOs working in the area of ECCE, Forum for Crèche and Childcare Services (FORCES) was set up in 1989. FORCES is a network of over a hundred organisations involved in the provision of childcare services. Many of these groups provide daycare services for marginalised sections like construction workers, whereas others are trade unions and workers associations involved in policy issues concerning the child. The issue is the lack of childcare support as a critical factor which impacts the health and development of children and increases poverty and social hardships. FORCES believe that every child has the right to early childcare and development including crèche and childcare services. Special care and benefits during pregnancy, birth, early childcare and maternity benefits to mothers are all intrinsic to the development of the young child. Daycare and childcare services have a direct bearing on not just child survival and development but also on women's health their increased economic productivity and empowerment. FORCES is also engaged in grassroots mobilisations, campaigning and lobbying, policy intervention, research and surveys, dialogue and consultation.

FORCES has nine regional networks which are in Delhi, Uttar Pradesh, Bihar, Tamil Nadu, Karnataka, Gujarat, Maharashtra, Rajasthan and Orissa. It has a rounded membership of child rights groups, trade unions, women's organisations, research and academic institutions, trainers, lawyers, educationists and doctors.

Rendering yeomen services for children of the most marginalised groups—the construction labourers, MOBILE CRECHES was set up in 1969 to support children who live on construction sites, so that they have a safe, healthy and happy childhood. Creche-cum-daycare centres would be set up on the building sites by taking space from the contractors so that the mothers who work as construction labourers can leave their children here, while they go and work. Once the construction at one site gets completed, the crèche-cum-daycare centre would move to the next construction site, hence the name 'Mobile' crèches. On an average this organisation reaches out to 15,000 children in a year, through their 65 plus centres in Delhi, Mumbai and Pune, and an equivalent number through their community outreach program which includes education, nutrition and health campaigns, community meetings and grass root advocacy on the criticality of early care and crèches.

Every year, they reach out to 5,500 families to change attitudes and put the well-being of the child on the agenda of the community through meetings, street theatre, melas, surveys and community campaigns. They have so far reached out to 7,50,000 children, trained 6500 women as childcare workers, run 650 daycare centres and partnered with 200 builders (www.mobilecreches.org retrieved on 3rd December 2014).

The Mobile Crèches runs Childcare program which includes Crèches (0–3 years), Balwadis (3–5 years) and non-formal education classes (6–12 years). The teaching methodology is creative, using art, craft, games, educational visits, etc. Other services provided at the Mobile Crèches daycare centres include health care for the children, prenatal and post-natal care for mothers, midday meals and special diet for undernourished children, recreational facilities—which include stimulating games, educational visits, cultural celebrations, sports days, etc. Mobile Creches also establishes Community Outreach Programmes in which issue-based meetings are held with parents on childcare, hygiene, nutrition, health care, family planning, AIDS, substance abuse, etc.

It runs a creative unit to evolve suitable teaching methodologies and develop appropriate low-cost teaching aids.

Lok-Doot is an innovative street play unit of Mobile Crèches which conducts street plays in the community on social and health issues. It also trains early childhood teachers through the Bal Palika programme to meet the huge unmet need of trained childcare workers.

Centre for Learning Resources is yet another unique NGO working for ECCE. Established in 1984, located in Pune, the CLR undertakes projects to develop relevant programmes and materials in Early Childhood Care and Development and Elementary Education. It contributes uniquely to the body of knowledge in ECCE by developing training and teaching–learning materials, conducting manpower training, offering consultancy to organisations working for ECCE and elementary education and through research in this field. As a technical support organisation, they also provide on request a variety of inputs to government agencies and NGOs running pre-primary centres or elementary schools or alternative education programmes for out-of-school and working children. CLR also raises public awareness about the educational needs of disadvantaged children and their right to a good education. CLR also works to meet the educational needs of post-secondary youth.

CLR has made a name for itself for its training material. Many organisations are developing teaching—learning materials, but the unique part about the CLR teaching-learning Material is that it is tailor made as per the requirements of the user organisation. Rather than providing a fixed material, CLR interacts with the organisation which is asking for support, assesses their needs and then develops special material/programme which is suited to their specific context. The CLR guides teachers in the preparation of their own low-cost teaching–learning materials, as part of its inservice training programmes. They also develop and publish a variety of teaching–learning materials based on the needs expressed by preschool centres, schools and non-formal education programmes. Prototypes are tried out in classrooms and the feedback from this process is incorporated into the final design of the published materials. All the materials are low-cost and promote active learning. They help to develop important early concepts, thinking and reasoning abilities, as also reading and mathematical skills. They are designed for use in pre-primary, elementary and supplementary education programmes—both rural and urban—and lend themselves to multi-grade, multi-level classes as self-learning or group-learning materials. Many teachers and parents are also using them with slow learners and children who need step-by-step remedial help.

KATHA is a 'profit-for-all' voluntary organisation established in 1988. KATHA adopts an unusual approach to education—using story pedagogy to encourage children to come voluntarily into the learning process and foster in them love for life long learning. It runs early childhood education centres, elementary schools and provides vocational skill training. Katha's holistic approach carefully nurtures the child at all three levels to see that she/he does not drop out of school and learning. The three E's are enjoyment, engagement and employment. Katha's Schools are at the centre of poverty alleviation and economic resurgence for the communities. Story pedagogy is a classroom methodology that is patented to Katha. Along with other services, Katha supports a number of self help groups formed by women collectives and imparts IT literacy to adolescent girls.

KATHA recruits and trains teachers who are women from the community. Each community school is headed by women from that slum community. *Balika Mandal* is the adolescent girls group which focuses on empowerment issues, actively encouraging education for girls and emphasising how education and empowerment means fewer maternal deaths at childbirth, lower infant mortality rate, fewer but healthier children who live longer. Katha, through its innovative *School on Wheels* programme, takes learning to children who live on the streets, children, who live outside of our lives, whom we pass everyday but never come to know. It is giving into their hands the skills, the know-how and therefore the possibility of self-reliance leading to development. The School on Wheels, with its brightly painted RTV van, carries the *Tamasha Roadshow* (TRS) from one traffic signal to the next. Filled with fun learning material based on chubby mascot *Tamasha* and her friends, the road show attracts children to a learning environment through theatre, songs, dance, puppetry and even computers.

To date, through its many programmes, Katha has brought schooling to 162,500 children, trained 17,000 of them in IT, taught 90,000 women in income-generation and social activism skills, and brought the joy of reading to more than 6,000,000 children (www.katha.org retrieved on 3rd December 2014).

PRATHAM is a network of non-governmental organisations that promote education for disadvantaged children. Unlike most other NGOs which are born out of the enterprise of only a few individuals, Pratham was established as a Public Charitable Trust in 1994 by the Commissioner of the Municipal Corporation of Greater Mumbai, UNICEF and several prominent citizens of the country. Pratham's work has been a whole new way of approaching the education problem in India and a new way of implementing programmes to create a national impact. Pratham's mission is to ensure 'Every Child in School and Learning well'. The organisation is founded on the firm belief that education is the fundamental right of every child and no child should be deprived of this basic right simply because he/she does not have access to it or does not have the resources to realise his/her dreams.

PRATHAM runs direct programmes where the Pratham team directly plans, conducts and monitors the programmes. The programmes are typically conducted within the community spaces—in people's houses, temples, open spaces, etc. Pratham's direct programs have traditionally been conducted in the urban areas to increase the enrollment and learning levels of children living in urban slums. The programmes conducted under the direct intervention approach include Balwadis (preschool education), learning support programs, libraries and mainstreaming of out of school children.

Pratham's flagship program, Read India, helps to improve the reading, writing and basic arithmetic skills of the children in the age group of 6–14 years. Even though India has made significant strides in improving the enrollment levels of the children, a lot still needs to be done as far as the learning levels are concerned. Read India was therefore launched on a national scale in 2007 to help achieve the following objectives:

- All Std I children know at least alphabets and numbers
- All Std II children can read at least words and do simple sums
- All Std III-V children can at least read simple texts fluently and confidently solve arithmetic problems (http://www.pratham.org/programmes/read-india).

In 2008–2009, the campaign reached 33 million children across 19 states. It covered more than half of the 6,00,000 villages in the country and mobilised over 4,50,000 volunteers problems (http://www.pratham.org/programmes/read-india).

Read India seeks to catalyse existing resources and energise structures to strengthen children's learning. The campaign is being executed with the help of school teachers, anganwadi workers and volunteers, who are mobilised and trained by Pratham teams. While the school teachers work inside their schools, volunteers and anganwadi workers work with children and their mothers outside school. Partnerships have been forged with 11 state governments for the implementation of the programme.

Over the next 3 years, Read India will move to its next level Read India II which will focus on higher levels of academic content, focusing on subject-specific and grade-specific content for Std V–VIII. The campaign will also assist children aged 14–16 years complete their secondary school certification exam by providing them with the required academic support. Facilitated by Pratham, Annual Status of Education Report (ASER-meaning impact in Hindi) is the largest household survey undertaken in India by people outside the government on status of education. It annually measures the enrollment as well as the reading and arithmetic levels of children in the age group of 6–14 years.

Pratam also runs the English Program targets children in the age group of 8–14 years and helps build their basic conversational skills and their ability to read simple texts with comprehension. Computer Aided Literacy, which is a school-based programme which caters to school going children from 6 to 18 age group with about 40 % children in secondary school age. The objective of this programme is to impact childrens basic learning levels using IT and to give them relevant IT knowledge and skills. Pratham's Skills Training Program tries to train youth in market relevant skills such as banking, agriculture, hospitality, etc., and help them start their own businesses.

The Pratham Council for Vunerable Children (PCVC) set up in 2001, plays a key role in influencing polices related to vulnerable children in disadvantaged communities, trafficked children and working children. PCVC has become a key partner with state governments in drafting official protocol in dealing with rescued children and advising legislation concerning child labour. In addition, they are working on replicable task force models with the government and advocacy and policy changes to ensure that the cities that they are working in are child labour free.

Today, the PCVC is operational in 7 states and reaches close to 60,000 children annually in urban and rural areas. Direct programmes include drop-in centres, educational support classes, residential shelters, child rights desks, focused city-block interventions and health and disability initiatives. Additionally, the PCVC reaches about 1,20,000 children annually through child rights awareness sessions in schools, communities and villages. To date, PCVC has rescued and rehabilitated of over 50,000 children in Mumbai city (http://www.pratham.org/programmes/pcvc retrieved on 4th December 2014).

As a nation, we have a commitment to fulfill; that of taking on the responsibility of care of children so as to improve their survival, growth and development; therefore, the need for strengthening the programmes for young children. The fact that children are dependent on others for satisfaction of their requirements creates an even greater obligation to help and protect them.

References

Chopra, G. (ed.). (n.d.). *Module for early childhood care and education for caregivers*. NIPCCD-UNESCO. Unpublished.

Engle, P.L., Menon, P., & Haddad, L. (1997). Nutrition concepts and measurements. International Food Policy Research Institute: Washington, DC.

Halle, T., Forry, N., Hair, E., et al. (2009). *Disparities in early learning and development: Lessons from the early childhood longitudinal study—birth cohort (ECLS-B)*. Washington, DC: Child Trends.

Hart, B., & Risley, T. R. (1995). *Meaningful differences in the everyday experience of young American children*. Baltimore, MD: Paul H. Brookes.

Retrieved December 4, 2014, from http://www.pratham.org/programmes/read-india.

Ministry of Women and Child Development, Government of India (2011). Report of the working group on Child Rights (2012–2017) For the twelfth 5 years plan. New Delhi Retrieved from http://planningcommission.nic.in/aboutus/committee/wrkgrp12/wcd/wgrep_child.pdf.

Myers, R. G. (1992). *The twelve who survive*. London: Routledge.

National Council of Educational Research and Training (2006). *Position Paper National focus group on early childhood education*. Retrieved from http://www.ncert.nic.in/new_ncert/ncert/rightside/links/pdf/focus_group/early_childhood_education.pdf.

Rai, R. (2015). *Challenges in implementing the RTE act*. Retrieved from http://infochangeindia.org/education/backgrounders/challenges-in-implementing-the-rte-act.html.

Report of the Inter Ministerial Group on ICDS Restructuring. Retrieved September, 2011, from http://planningcommission.gov.in/reports/genrep/rep_icds2704.pdf.

Sheeranjan, & Awathi, A. S. (2010, September) *Early childhood care and education*: *Indian perspective*. Paper presented at the world conference on early childhood care and education, Moscow. Retrieved from http://www.unesco.org/education/WCECCE/presentations/Sheeranjan-Awathi.pdf.

U.S. Department of Health and Human Services (2007). *National survey of child and adolescent well-being, research brief no. 4*: *Infants and toddlers in the child welfare system*. Retrieved from http://www.acf.hhs.gov/sites/default/files/opre/infants_todd.pdf.

http://developingchild.harvard.edu/. Retrieved March 12, 2013.

(Source: Authors personal collection)

UNITED NATIONS CONVENTION ON THE RIGHTS OF THE CHILD

Article 19 (Protection from all forms of violence): Children have the right to be protected from being hurt and mistreated, physically or mentally. Governments should ensure that children are properly cared for and protect them from violence, abuse and neglect

Chapter 4
Children in Especially Difficult Circumstances: Right to Protection and Participation

Abstract This chapter introduces all the categories of children in India who are in difficult circumstances. A brief description of the categories included are homeless children, migrant children, orphaned children, child workers, bonded children, street children, child beggars, child sex workers, children affected by AIDS, abused children, children in conflict with law and children with disabilities. Concept of child protection is put forth, followed by a discussion on child protection mechanism offered by the Government of India, the Integrated Child Protection Scheme (ICPS) is deliberated. The reader also learns about the child line service. A brief overview of legislations for children like the Hindu Adoption and Maintenance act 1956, Juvenile Justice act 1986 and 2000, Prevention of Children against Sexual Offences act 2012, Prenatal Diagnostic Technique act 1994, Immoral Traffic (Prevention) act 1956, Child Marriage Restraint act 1929 and 2006, are some of the many acts introduced in this chapter.

Keywords Children in especially difficult circumstances · Child Protection · Integrated Child Protection Scheme (ICPS) · Outline of laws for children in India

4.1 Children in Especially Difficult Circumstances

All children are not fortunate enough to receive an environment which is conducive to provide appropriate development opportunities. The need to protect some children is certainly greater than others due to their specific socio-economic and political circumstances and geographical location. They are more vulnerable in terms of the risk to their right to survival, development, protection and participation. These are the children in especially difficult circumstances.

Children in especially difficult circumstances (CEDC) is a worldwide problem. They suffer from deprivation, exploitation and neglect for no fault of their own and for reasons beyond their control. It is an enormous global social concern that has attracted the attention of the entire world community, ranging from professionals in

G. Chopra, *Child Rights in India*, DOI 10.1007/978-81-322-2446-4_4

the various fields of paediatrics, social work, psychology and psychiatry, to legislators, administrators and politicians.

CEDC are those children whose basic needs are not met. Children in difficult circumstances represent a large and diverse group. Some form of social disruption is common to their lives. All of these children have special needs, specially the need for psychosocial support. The needs vary greatly, especially as the circumstances and reasons for difficulties in existence vary and are ever changing. Some of these children live with their families, while some do not or could be orphans. Some are working or are found vagrant on the streets, while others could be in conflict with law or affected by armed conflicts or natural calamities. Children could be sexually exploited, trafficked or forced to work in bondage hence taking away from them the delights and the innocence of childhood. The health and well-being of CEDC are severely compromised. It could largely depend on the social interventions, moral values and sensitivity of civil society and legal system and the nature of rehabilitative services provided so as to restore to them their childhood. Outcomes depend on the intensity and duration of the adversity, the child's age and gender, and availability of support and protection.

Over the years, based on the social conditions, economic involvement, familial situation and conditions of living, children have been categorised as those in difficult circumstances. The categorisation done by the Ministry of Women and Child Development (n.d.(a)) on Children in Especially Difficult Circumstances includes:

- Homeless children (pavement dwellers, displaced/evicted, etc.)
- Orphaned or abandoned children
- Children whose parents cannot or are not able to take care of them
- Children separated from parents
- Migrant and refugee children
- Street children
- Working children
- Trafficked children
- Children in bondage
- Children in prostitution
- Children of sex workers/prostitutes/sexual minorities/Children of prisoners
- Children affected by wars and conflict
- Children affected by natural disasters
- Children affected by HIV/AIDS
- Children suffering from terminal diseases
- The girl child
- Children with disabilities and related special needs
- Children belonging to the ethnic and religious minorities, and other minority communities, and those belonging to the Scheduled Castes and Scheduled Tribes;
- Children in institutional care, be it in state-run institutions or religious and other charitable institutions
- Children in conflict with law
- Children who are victims of crime

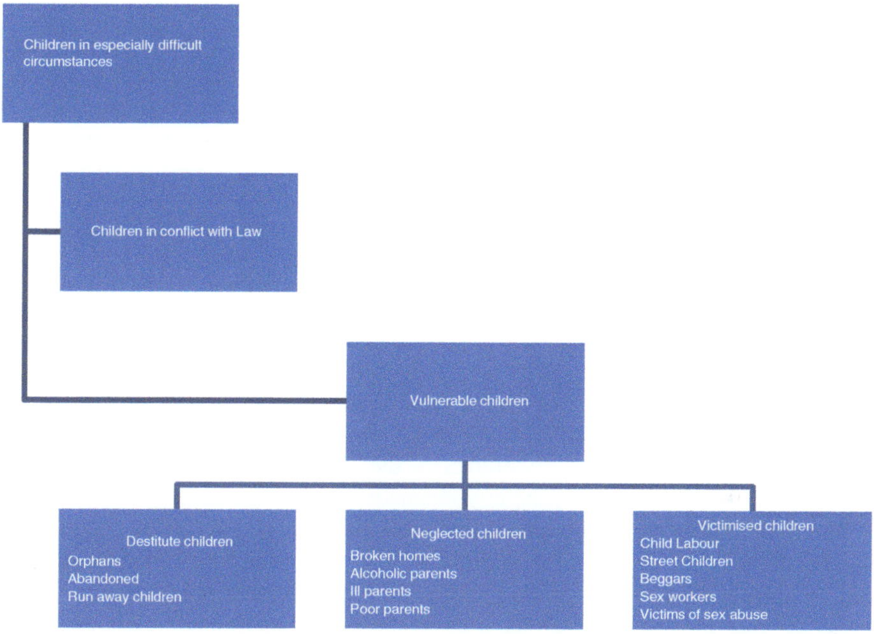

The special conditions that put children in especially difficult circumstances are now being briefly discussed in the paragraphs that follow.

4.1.1 *Homeless Children*

Homelessness is not a condition unknown to children in India. Migration to cities in search of livelihood and dreams of a better life is one of the major causes of homelessness, which is more of an urban phenomenon. Globalisation has also de-stabilised rural livelihoods. Pressures of infrastructure development like construction of high rise buildings, or SEZs (special economic zones) or even dams and highways have taken away the lands of farmers, and shanties and hutments of urban slum dwellers. Situations like natural disasters and conflicts render many homeless or force them to live in unsafe housing conditions. Living on the streets or in urban slum dwellings, lack of basic facilities and unhygienic living conditions become a way of life. The UNCRC has recognised right to adequate housing as a right of every child.

4.1.2 *Orphaned and Abandoned Child*

Death of biological parents or abandonment by them leads to a child becoming an orphan. Death could be due to natural reasons like illness or due to accidents or natural calamity. Abandonment could be due to poverty, illness of parents, gender of the child, being an unwed mother, being an unattractive child or even disability in the child. With caring practices moving more towards non-institutional services, adoption of the orphaned or abandoned child provides to the child a family and to the parents a child. Currently, the state of adoption in India is very dismal. There are far more number of children who are orphaned, abandoned and destitute and far few who have been given a home through adoption.

4.1.3 Migrant Children

Large-scale migration of families from rural to urban areas has resulted in severe overcrowding, degrading work conditions, homelessness, deprivation of basic services and appalling living conditions in the city. Yet, to return to the village means starvation: to remain in the city means possible survival at least physically.

The major reason for migration to the cities is that the traditional occupations in villages do not provide sufficient income. So, the basic need for survival pushes the migration from rural to urban areas. The influx of people creates housing problems, sanitation and hygiene issues along with creating an alienation and marginalisation of people. The migrants are faceless, mostly both parents are working, leaving children at home with no adult supervision, low self-esteem and no sense of belongingness. This puts the migrant child at great risk of becoming vagrant, taking to loitering on streets or being exposed to anti-social elements. With the National Rural Employment Guarantee Scheme in place, it is hoped that the migration of village dwellers to cities should decrease, as this scheme guarantees the employment in rural areas. Under this scheme, a person has a right to 100 days of employment for each family within 5 km of their residence and within 15 days of applying on a local development project.

4.1.4 Child Labour

The total number of working children in the country has declined from 12.6 million as per the Census 2001 to 4.35 million as per Census 2011 which shows 65 % reduction. The number of child labourers in the country was 11.28 million in 1991. Of 12.59 million in 2001, out of the total child population of 210 million (5–14 years), 5.77 million are classified as 'main' workers and 6.88 million as 'marginal' workers. The share of workers of the country aged 5–14 years to the total workforce is 3.15 %. The analysis of the 2001 census data shows that there are 6.8 million boys and 5.8 million girls who are child labourers. In addition, it is found that the majority of 'main' workers are boys, whereas the majority of 'marginal' workers are girls. Main workers are those who have worked for more than 6 months and marginal workers are those who have worked for less than 6 months. Unofficial figures on number of child labour in India vary significantly from the official figures.

Many children are engaged in occupations and processes classified as 'hazardous labour', i.e. harmful to the physical, emotional or moral well-being of children. The factors that contribute to child taking to labour force, and hazardous child labour in particular, include parental poverty and illiteracy; social and economic circumstances; lack of awareness; lack of access to basic and meaningful quality education and skills; high rates of adult unemployment and under-employment and cultural values of the family and society.

Working children are exploited economically and often physically, including sexually. They are forced to do heavy work, work overtime, are often deprived of food, schooling, play and rest, and work in unhealthy and unsafe conditions. Crucial early years when the child should be attending school and acquiring skills for a productive and fruitful adult life are lost in the toil of earning, often in most unconducive conditions, to feed their own mouths and those of their family. A child labour also throws out the adult from productive employment.

4.1.5 Bonded Child Labour

The primitive practice of bonded child labour is prevalent in India. Recent reports are indicating that India has highest numbers of humans who have been enslaved in the entire world. Bondage is a traditional worker–employer relationship when the parents borrowed money for their needs, which could have been for medicine or food or marriage of daughter, mostly on astronomical interest rates which they could not repay with their meagre earnings. Hence, the child is pledged to lifelong bondage to the lender. As long as the poor in India remain so poor, parent's indebtedness, poverty and unethical trade practices will make it very difficult to abolish pledging of children into bondage and many such cruel practices which have put to shame India's image as a nation that cannot take care of her children.

4.1.6 Domestic Child Worker

Domestic child workers are commonly seen in cities and metropolis. A systematic exploitation is found, wherein the children are made to work for long hours, with meagre food, meagre wages and at times physical and sexual torture.

Till recently, domestic child labour was not one of the prohibited occupations in the Child Labour (Prohibition and Regulation) Act, 1986. But recently it has been notified by the Ministry of labour, prohibiting employment of children below 14 years as domestic servants or in dhabas, tea stalls and restaurants. This is a much needed amendment but, as a result of this notification, there is a likelihood of a large number of children being laid off, especially in metropolitan cities and big towns.

Therefore, there is a need to address the rehabilitation of these children including shelter, education, food, health and other needs and to restore them to their families. It is possible that the families of these children are not in position to take care of them. In such a scenario, an alternative action plan will need to be in place; otherwise, these children are likely to be recycled as child labours.

4.1.7 Street Children

Street children or children living and working on the streets are a common phenomenon in urban India. Often treated as an eyesore and nuisance, their presence in everyday urban life is difficult to ignore. In spite of the relative high visibility of street children, there is very little information available on their exact numbers. An official figure available from a 1997 report of the DWCD, Ministry of HRD, Government of India stated that 11 million children lived on the street at that time, of which 420,000 lived in the six metropolitan cities of the country. Even these figures are 8–12 years old and almost no effort has been made to update these figures (Ministry of Women and Child Development n.d.(a)).

Street children have to fight for survival day after day. From finding food, looking for a safe place to spend the night to protecting themselves against the violence that constantly threatens them, life is a constant struggle. Victims of discrimination and revulsion stemming from societal apathy, their needs are seldom considered, forget being met. They are the most marginalised of all categories of children in especially difficult circumstances. They live on the fringes of the society, sometimes with their families and sometimes without. They are exposed to harsh life on the streets fighting for their subsistence. Poverty, broken homes, migration, breakdown of social networks, crime and conflict, street children are exposed to all the risks and abuses: substance abuse, physical and moral violence, sexual abuse, health risks like STD/HIV-AIDS, promiscuity and prostitution. Some live in gangs, thus taking up the laws of the group as their own and are in danger of developing risk behaviours in their everyday lives. These children too have the right to adequate housing/shelter, proper nutrition, education, health care and above all protection from all forms of abuse and violence. This is a group of children neglected completely by legislatures and programme planners.

4.1.8 Child Beggars

No accurate data is available on the number of beggars especially child beggars, but the magnitude of the problem can be appreciated by some old statistics from different parts of the country: According to the statement made by the Minister of State for Social Justice, Government of Maharashtra in State Assembly, the number of beggars in Mumbai, which was 20,000 in 1963, rose to 3 lakh in 2004. Many children are being exploited by organised mafia-style groups; the more serious being, begging, prostitution and drug trafficking (Ministry of Women and Child Development n.d.(a)). These children are not in need of alms to satisfy hunger and basic survival needs. Rather, most of these children are a part of organised beggar groups. Child beggars are at great risk of engaging in petty crime, subjected to sexual and physical abuse, substance abuse and developing health problems like skin ailments and STDs. These children are victims of abuse of different forms and are living on the edge.

4.1.9 Child Sex Workers

In India, a large number of children are trafficked for various reasons such as labour, begging and sexual exploitation. Many girls who are trafficked become a part of the sex trade and are forced into prostitution. Though most of the trafficking occurs within the country, there is also a significant number of children trafficked from Nepal and Bangladesh. Global trafficking of children and women is considered to be more profitable than arms or drugs smuggling.

It is estimated that there are 4,00,000 child prostitutes in the country. Commercial child prostitution is increasing at the rate of 8–10 % per annum. Child victims of commercial sexual exploitation are deprived of basic necessities and suffer the dangers of unwanted pregnancies, maternal mortality, torture, physical injury, mental trauma and disorders and sexually transmitted diseases (http://nipccd.nic.in/pub_coop_div_3.html).

4.1.10 Child Suffering from Abuse

Child abuse can take several forms, i.e. physical, psychological or emotional, sexual abuse and neglect. What would fall in the category of physical abuse varies from culture to culture. In USA and European countries, physical punishment of the child by the parents is considered as a form of physical abuse. It is common knowledge that if you hit or beat your child in the US, the child can call the police. However, in India, our culture is such that physical punishment by parents or other senior members of the family is considered as essential at times to discipline children. It is categorised as abuse only when it leads to bruises or injuries. What is considered abuse in the western countries does not even raise an eyebrow in India and goes virtually un-noticed. The Human Rights Committee of United Nations has stated that the prohibition of degrading treatment or punishment extends to corporal punishment of children. Humiliations, spankings and beatings, slaps in the face, etc. are all considered as forms of physical abuse of children, because they injure the integrity and dignity of a child. Child sexual abuse occurs when an adult or older adolescent abuses a child for sexual activities such as sexual intercourse, indecent exposure of the genitals to a child or viewing child's genitals forcefully, making physical contact with the child's genitals, showing porn films to the child or using a child to produce pornography. Effects of child sexual abuse on the victim(s) include guilt and self-blame, nightmares, insomnia, fear of the abuser or things associated with the abuse (including objects, smells, places etc.), lower self-esteem, sexually transmitted diseases, chronic pain, self-injurious or suicidal tendencies, depression, stress disorders, personality disorders or other psychiatric problems etc.

Unfortunately, in most of the child sexual abuse cases, offenders are people on whom the child had placed trust and are mostly known to the child. The offender in many instances could be a family member, neighbours etc. Hence, it is very essential for parents to develop in the child trust in them so that they can comfortably report to the parent such instances of sexual abuse. It is also important to tell the child the difference between 'good touch' and 'bad touch' so that the child is intolerant to sexual abuse in any form.

4.1.11 Children with AIDS

The first case of HIV/AIDS was reported in India in Tamil Nadu in 1986. Since then the virus has spread from the high-risk groups to the general population very fast. Today, there are 5.7 million people living with HIV/AIDS in India. Women and children are increasingly becoming vulnerable to HIV/AIDS. The new findings conclude that 38 % of the infected persons in India are women. This indicates the increasing feminisation of HIV/AIDS in India. This alarming trend is being observed closely as more HIV-positive mothers will unknowingly pass the virus on to their children. India has an estimated 220,000 children infected by HIV/AIDS. It is estimated that 55,000–60,000 children are born every year to mothers who are HIV positive. Without treatment, these newborns stand an estimated 30 % chance of becoming infected during the mother's pregnancy, labour or through breastfeeding after 6 months. There is effective treatment available, but this is not reaching all women and children who need it (http://www.unicef.org/india/children_2358.htm retrieved on 12 August 2014).

Of all the AIDS infections, 4.36 % are through peri-natal transmission. The HIV prevalence among high-risk groups continues to be nearly 6–8 times greater than that among the general population (National AIDS Control Programme). Child sex workers are a high-risk group. Sexual experimentation among the youth could be another high-risk areas. Using youth-friendly interventions like the education, information, tools and services would help young people make healthy decisions and enable them to adopt protective practices. Working with influential adults such as parents, teachers and traditional and religious leaders would contribute to a more supportive environment that ensures that young people can get the help they need from their communities and remove barriers to accessing services.

The major concern is for millions of children who are becoming orphans due to parents loosing out to AIDS. Such children face gross discrimination by their extended families and have to be often placed in institutions. Sometimes, children live with HIV-positive parents. And sometimes, children are affected by AIDS. These children need long-term care to prolong and improve their quality of life.

4.1.12 Children in Conflict with Law

The term 'children in conflict with the law' refers to anyone under 18 years of age who comes into contact with the justice system as a result of being suspected or accused of committing an offence. Children who come in conflict with law cannot be treated in the same way as an adult offender. The system needs to understand what circumstances lead to the child committing a crime and then help the child to come out of the situation. Being a child, there is always hope that the child with proper guidance and support can be rehabilitated into the main stream rather than becoming a hardened criminal. The entire juvenile justice system rests on this belief and ideology.

It is important to ensure that the child is not being victimised by the system. As reported by the Ministry of Women and Child Development (n.d.(a)), most children in conflict with the law have committed petty crimes or minor offences of which most are not considered criminal when committed by adults. In addition, some children who engage in criminal behaviour have been used or coerced by adults. Too often, prejudice related to social and economic status may bring a child into conflict with the law even when no crime has been committed, or result in harsh treatment by law enforcement officials. In the area of juvenile justice, there is need to reduce incarceration while protecting children from violence, abuse and exploitation. Options that promote rehabilitation that involves families and communities are safer, more appropriate and effective approach than punitive measures.

Justice systems designed for adults often lack the capacity to adequately address these issues and are more likely to harm than improve a child's chances for reintegration into society. For all these reasons, a just juvenile justice system needs to evolve which would strongly advocate directing children away from judicial proceedings and towards community solutions which promote reconciliation, restitution, restoration, rehabilitation and responsibility through the involvement of the child, family members, victims and communities. It also looks for alternatives to custody or sentencing, like counselling and community service.

4.1.13 Children with Disabilities

In India, both prevention of childhood disabilities and protection from the effects of disabilities are mandated as the right of every child. Yet, according to the 2011 Census findings, India's disability population is 26.8 million or 2.21 % of the total population. Of the total population, 5 million are people with visual disabilities, 1.9 million are people with speech disabilities, 5 million are people with hearing disabilities, 5.4 million are people with locomotor disabilities, and 1.5 million are people with mental retardation, 0.72 million with mental illness and 2.1 million with multiple disabilities. In India, different authorities use various estimates, a leading disability NGO, the National Center for Promotion of Employment for Disabled People (NCPEDP) argues that 5–6 % of the population has a disability (Laha 2009). According to World Bank (2007), it is estimated that people with disabilities comprise between 4 and 8 % of the Indian population (around 40–90 million individuals).

Although, 75 % of childhood disabilities can be prevented through primary health care, yet every year 1.5–2 million persons are added to the category of disabled due to neglect of primary prevention services. Utilisation and reach of services during pregnancy and infancy is poor leading to impairments. Out of 4.5 million disabled children who should be availing school facilities, 90 % are not enrolled or have dropped out of the education system (http://nipccd.nic.in/pub_coop_div_3.html).

National Plan of Action for Children, 2005
FOCUS—Children in Difficult Circumstances

Goals

- To ensure that the best interest of the child is upheld in all policies, plans, programmes, interventions and in strategies for children in difficult circumstances.
- To create and uphold a safe, supportive and protective environment for all children within and outside the home.

Objectives

- To protect all children against neglect, maltreatment, injury, trafficking, sexual and physical abuse of all kinds, pornography, corporal punishment, torture, exploitation, violence, and degrading treatment
- To address the survival, development, protection and participation rights of children in difficult circumstances, such as, orphans, street children, beggar children, migrant children, children affected by man made and natural disasters, drug addicts, children of nomads, refugee children, slum and migrant children, children of commercial sex workers, children of prisoners, children affected by/in armed conflict, displaced children, evicted children, young children in charge of siblings, children born as eunuchs or brought up by eunuchs
- To give priority for non-institutional services for the rehabilitation of children
- To prevent children from falling into distress and vulnerability by developing strategies for food and livelihood security for families

- To provide a home for every orphan or destitute child
- To promote in-country adoption of all children with emphasis on the girl child
- To create a system for foster care ensuring the best interest of the child
- To address the needs of shelter, education, health, rehabilitation and prevention from exploitation of children affected by disasters (natural or manmade) and displaced children
- To address needs of education, shelter and reintegration of children in need of care and protection and children of migrant and nomadic parents and refugee children, and for children of commercial sex workers and children of prisoners
- To develop a system of constant and authentic data collection about the extent, magnitude and nature of children in especially difficult circumstances and vulnerable children and also put in place a system of tracking and monitoring of all interventions made for the benefit of such children.

(National Plan of Action for Children 2005)

4.2 Child Protection

According to United Nations Convention on the Rights of the Child (UNCRC), every child has a right to protection. The approach so far of the government has been that only those children who are in difficult circumstances and have suffered violence, abuse and exploitation need child protection. But this is not true. Now it is believed that all children need protection so that they remain within the social security and protective net.

'Child Protection' refers to protection from violence, exploitation, abuse and neglect. Violations of the child's right to protection, in addition to being human rights violations, are also massive, under-recognised and under-reported barriers to child survival and development. Children subjected to violence, exploitation, abuse and neglect are at risk of shortened lives, poor physical and mental health, educational problems (including dropping out of school), poor parenting skills later in life, homelessness, vagrancy and displacement. Conversely, successful protection increases a child's chances to grow up physically and mentally healthy, confident and self-respecting, and he or she is less likely to abuse or exploit others, including his or her own children (Ministry of Women and Child Development n.d.(b)).

'Child Protection' is about protecting children from or against any perceived or real danger or risk to their life, their personhood and childhood. It is about reducing their vulnerability to any kind of harm and protecting them in harmful situations. It is about ensuring that no child falls out of the social security and safety net and, those who do receive necessary care, protection and support so as to bring them back into the safety net. While protection is a right of every child, some children are more vulnerable than others and need special attention. The government recognises these children as ‘children in difficult circumstances’, characterised by their specific social, economic and geo-political situations. In addition to providing a safe environment for these children, it is imperative to ensure that all other children also remain protected. Child protection is integrally linked to every other right of the child (Ministry of Women and Child Development n.d.(c)).

When we take all children in the ambit of child protection, it is a step towards building a comprehensive approach towards child protection, as there is a clear adoption of both a preventive and a protective approach. A preventive approach would include advocacy of child rights issues, like stopping corporal punishment in school, preventing sexual abuse in families and need to speak up or lending support to families on the brink or families with risky behaviour. It would mean involvement of civil society, families, school teachers and administrators and PRI to create awareness among them, to be proactive on issues which affect children. It would include laws for children, child welfare services, media involvement in broaching child protection issues. The protective approach comes in when the child has already suffered violence, discrimination or exploitation. It is post-harm. The effort is to step in for immediate relief as well as work out long-term strategies for rehabilitation, building self-confidence and self-esteem, training, providing legal aid and justice and reintegration.

In India, we face the added uniqueness of diversity of caste, creed and religion, which becomes a child’s identity. The opportunities, whether they are reaching the child or not, are determined by the ‘identity’ of the child. The ‘identity’ would largely determine if the child will be excluded or not. ‘Gender’ is an identity. ‘Caste’ is an identity. ‘Colour’ is an identity. ‘Religion’ is an identity. ‘Disability’ is also a marker of whether a person is going to be excluded. As a society, we need to question if entitlement to rights should be determined by these ‘markers’ which have been assigned to us, mostly by virtue of our being born as a girl or into a certain family.

Child Protection Strengthens Human Development: All rights are related to one another. And all rights feed into one another. No right is superior to another. If India wants to, say, eradicate poverty, we will have to provide a protective net to all children, more so those from the marginalised families. If we want to achieve universal primary education, we cannot do it till all children with disabilities become a part of the education system or the child who is toiling in the factories also joins school. If we cannot help the vulnerable families, they are likely to abandon children or may have to make them work on the streets. Sexual harassment and abuse of girls in schools is a major reason for girls dropping out from schools. So is the non-availability of toilets which are a deterrent to girls going to school. Corporal punishments are another impediment in children from attending school. The Right to Education would be far from being realised if providing safe environments for children in schools is ignored. The right to participation of girls and women is severely compromised when they are married off at tender age and have no say in matters involving their lives (ex. When to have a baby?). Trafficking of children and women makes them slaves with no rights whatsoever. They are taken away from their families, their milieus and are under the control of traffickers with absolutely no one to fall back on. So, preventive child protection strategies are required in equal measure. Failing to protect children from such issues like violence in school, sexual abuse, trafficking, harmful traditional practices and the absence of parental care certainly restricts the opportunities for human development and restricts the quality of human resource available to the country.

Components of a Protective Environment Here are some protective components which can augur a safer world for children.

1. Families, communities and societies which value children and are intolerant to any kind of violence or abuse against children.
2. Community leaders who are committed to promote positive social norms.
3. Families which can look into the eyes of the perpetrators and bring them to justice. There is no culture of silence.
4. The media brings in open light and to public discourse and scrutiny child protection issues and cases.
5. There are protective laws for children which are in line with the international standards for child rights. There is speedy prosecution of offenders and quick enforcement of laws.
6. Children have access to legal aid.
7. Supportive mechanisms are in place for victims of abuse and violence.

Failure to ensure children's right to protection adversely affects all other rights of the child. Thus, the Millennium Development Goals (MDGs) cannot be achieved unless child protection is an integral part of programmes, strategies and plans for their achievement. Failure to protect children from issues such as violence in schools, child labour, harmful traditional practices, child marriage, child abuse, the absence of parental care and commercial sexual exploitation among others, means failure in fulfilling both the Constitutional and International commitments towards children (Ministry of Women and Child Development n.d.(c)).

4.2.1 Existing Child Protection Mechanisms and the Gaps

The constitution of India through its Articles 14, 15, 16, 17, 21, 23 and 24 guarantee special attention to children through various laws and also protect them from exploitation and provide for liberty and equality. India is a signatory to UNCRC and also has ratified various international conventions like the Hague convention on inter-country adoption, the Beijing rules for the administration of Juveniles in conflict with law and the commitment to achieve millennium development goals. India has many legislations to protect children from abuse and exploitation like the

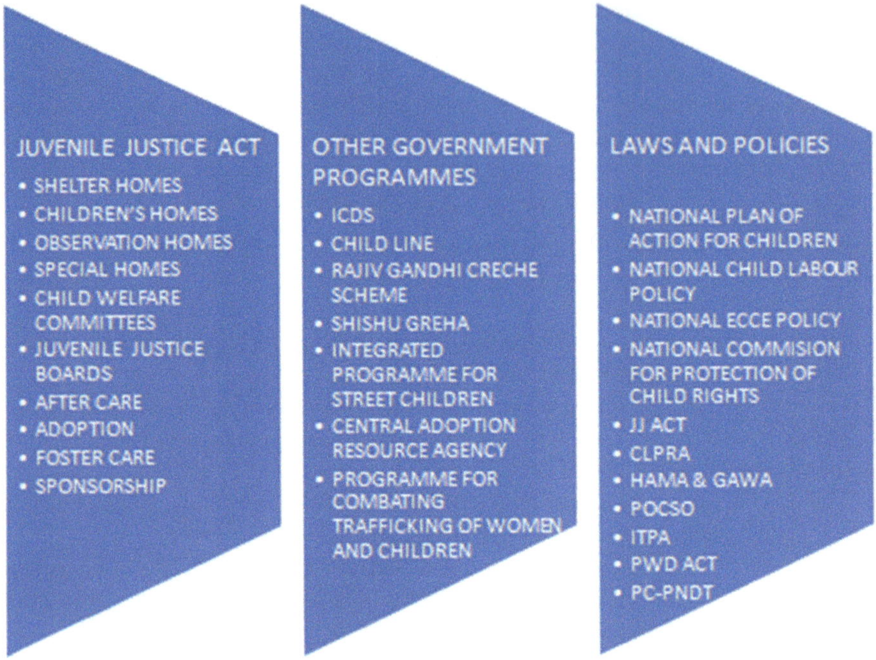

Fig. 4.1 Existing child protection mechanisms

Juvenile Justice act, The POCSO, Child Labour act, PC-PNDT act, ITPA, Persons with Disability act and so on. Yet, the plight of children has not improved. As a nation, we are struggling to give children a safe and secure environment to grow and develop.

In spite of having many legislations, policies and institutions in place (Fig. 4.1), yet the children of our country are suffering from blatant child rights violations. There are many reasons for this.

- There is hardly any effort towards raising awareness amongst people on child protection and child rights. Prevention is not happening at all.
- The implementation of laws is very weak.
- The structures in place are inadequate, dilapidated and tired. There is lack of standard of care in accommodation, leisure, food etc. in all institutions due to low funding allocated for them. The staff manning these is ill trained.
- There is inadequate sensitisation of police, judiciary and health care functionaries.
- There is inadequate number of CWCs and JJBs. The existing CWCs and JJBs are not provided with facilities for their efficient functioning.
- There is weak supervision and evaluation of children's institutions.

- Large-scale migration from villages to cities results in extreme load on city infrastructure as well as rampant poverty in the cities, severe lack of services like shelter, sanitation and water for the migrants.
- Lack of support to vulnerable families, hence making children also vulnerable.
- Serious service and infrastructure gaps leading to few adoptions. Cumbersome and time-consuming adoption services (Ministry of Women and Child Development n.d.(c)).
- Mapping of children in need of care and protection or of services available for them has not been done.

4.2.2 Integrated Child Protection Scheme (ICPS)

In order to meet the growing challenges that children face in the country, the Government of India has launched a comprehensive centrally sponsored 'Integrated Child Protection Scheme' (ICPS) aimed at providing safe and secure environment for the children of the country. ICPS brings under its umbrella several existing child protection programmes and also initiates new interventions. The scheme aims to improve the well-being of children in difficult circumstances, as well as to the reduction of vulnerability to situations and actions that lead to abuse, neglect, exploitation, abandonment and separation of children. The proposed ICPS brings together multiple vertical schemes under one comprehensive child protection programme and integrates interventions for protecting children and preventing harm.

The Integrated Child Protection Scheme is based on the cardinal principle of "protection of child rights" and "best interests of the child". The ICPS aims to promote the best interests of the child and prevent violations of child rights through appropriate punitive measure against perpetrators of abuse and crimes against children and to ensure rehabilitation for all children in need of care and protection. It aims to create a protective environment by improving regulatory frameworks, strengthening structures and professional capacities at national, state and district levels so as to cover all child protection issues and provide child-friendly services at all levels.

The guiding principles of ICPS as elucidated in the scheme (Ministry of Women and Child Development n.d.(c)) are:

- Child protection, a primary responsibility of family, supported by community, government and civil society. It is important that respective roles are articulated clearly and understood by all parties in the effort to protect children. Government, both Central and State, has an obligation to ensure a range and a continuum of services at all levels.
- Loving and caring family, the best place for the child: Children are best cared for in their own families and have a right to family care and parenting by both parents.

- Privacy and confidentiality: Children's right to privacy and confidentiality should be protected through all the stages of service delivery.
- Non-stigmatisation and non-discrimination: Each child irrespective of circumstances, as well as socio-economic, cultural, religious and ethnic background should be treated equally and in a dignified manner.
- Prevention and reduction of vulnerabilities, central to child protection outcomes: A major thrust of the ICPS will be to strengthen the family capabilities to care for and protect the child.
- Institutionalisation of children, the last resort: There is a need to shift the focus of interventions from an over reliance on institutionalisation of children and move towards more family and community-based alternatives for care. Institutionalisation should be used as a measure of last resort after all other options have been explored.
- Child-centred planning and implementation: Planning and implementation of child protection policies and service delivery should be child centred at all levels, so as to ensure that the best interest of the child is protected.
- Technical excellence, code of conduct: Services for children at all levels and by all providers should be provided by skilled and professional staff, including a cadre of social workers, psychologists, care givers, members of statutory bodies and lawyers, adhering to an ethical and professional code of conduct.
- Flexible programming, responding to local individualised needs: Customised service delivery approach is required to respond to local needs.
- Good governance, accountability and responsibility: An efficient and effective child protection system requires transparent management and decision making, accountable and responsible individuals and institutions, performance reports at all service levels and all service providers made public, including for children themselves, through child-friendly reports.

To sum up the basic principles of ICPS:

- That child protection is not a responsibility of any one institution or the family. Child protection is a shared responsibility of family, community and civil society.
- There a need to strengthen the family as the child has a right to family care. So, strengthen the capability of the family, as family is the best place for the child.
- Reduce vulnerability of children by making the families stronger through livelihood support (NREGS, Self help groups, Public distribution system, child care, health care, education).
- Institutionalisation of children should be the last resort.
- Establish standards of care and protection which all service providers and implementation agencies should adhere to.
- Train staff and equip them with skills as well as sensitivity.

ICPS considers three categories of children which are its target group:

- Child in need of care and protection (destitute, child workers, bonded labour, trafficked children, children with disabilities, street children, beggars, sexually

abused, victims of armed conflict, whose parents are unfit to take care of the child etc.).
- Child in conflict with law.
- Child in contact with law is one who has come in contact with law either as victim or as a witness or due to any other circumstances.

ICPS will function as a government—civil society partnership scheme under the overarching direction and responsibility of the central and state governments. The Government is aware that improving situation of millions of India's children in difficult circumstances requires an integrated effort and strong partnership of many stakeholders. Government cannot achieve this task alone. Therefore, the ICPS will work closely with all stakeholders including government departments, the voluntary sector, community groups, academia and, most importantly, families and children to create protective environment for children in the country. Its holistic approach to child protection services and mechanisms is reflected in strong lateral linkages and complementary systems for vigilance, detection and response (Ministry of Women and Child Development n.d.(c)).

ICPS will focus on mapping needs and services for children and families 'at risk'. It would also help provide safety to children of potentially vulnerable families and families at risk, children of socially excluded groups like migrant families, families living in extreme poverty, lower caste families, families subjected to or affected by discrimination, minorities, children infected and affected by HIV/AIDS, orphans, child drug abusers, children of substance abusers, child beggars, trafficked or sexually exploited children, children of prisoners and street and working children.

The ICPS would use the existing machinery in place for the neglected children like CHILDLINE services, the institutions set up under the JJ act like the Child Welfare committees, Juvenile justice boards, observation homes, children's homes and special homes. Depending on the need of the child, these mechanisms would be used. Adoption agencies, Shishu Grehas, after care organisations would be promoted and strengthened. Sponsorship for vulnerable families, in-country adoption, foster care, inter-country adoption would be promoted. Other programmes recommended for protection of children under the ICPS are counselling and family support, training and capacity building, research and advocacy.

As mentioned, Childline is now under the umbrella of ICPS. One of the important initiatives taken for the welfare of the children is the *Childline service*, which is a 24-h toll-free telephone service (1098) that can be accessed by children in distress or by adults on behalf of these children to seek emergency assistance and for referring the child to an appropriate organisation for long-term follow-up care. The Childline service aims to attend to children in difficulties and facilitating their rehabilitation. Childline also produces children before the CWC for ensuring care nad protection. Where required, it supports CWC in the long-term rehabilitation of children. It helps and supports the national network for tracking missing children. Through the childline, a platform is provided for networking among government and non-government agencies in the area of child welfare and sensitising those working in the police, judiciary, hospitals, etc. on child protection issues. As per the report of sub group on child protection (Ministry of Women and Child Development n.d.(b)), Childline is functional in 74 cities/towns in India offering and comprehensive child protection services. Since its inception in June 1996, a referral network has been established with over 3000 civil society organisations, academic institutes, state governments. Childline has registered to more than 96.30 lakh calls between its inception in 1996 and March 2006.

Children with or without families living in urban slums are at great risk of facing all the vulnerabilities of street life. They face exposure to abuse, drugs, AIDS and other STDs, violence, criminal activities, poverty and hunger. ICPS would provide open shelter to such children without a home particularly in urban and semi-urban areas. If not protected, these children can become a huge waste for the society. Mainstreaming of these children is a big challenge.

The ICPS would facilitate setting up open shelters particularly in urban areas. Such centres shall provide a space for children where they can play, use their time productively and engage themselves in creative activities through music, dance, drama, yoga and meditation, computers, indoor and outdoor games, etc. These activities would encourage meaningful peer group participation and interaction. This will ensure their overall growth and development, and keep them away from socially deviant behaviours in addition to fulfilling their basic requirements for food, nutrition and health. These shelters shall also have provisions for health care, quality and flexi-time education and vocational training, including provisions where children can safely keep their belongings and earnings. Counselling guidance and life skill education shall also be provided for channelling these children's energy into productive endeavours (Ministry of Women and Child Development n.d.(c)).

Central Adoption Resource Agency (CARA), which is instrumental for providing a home to orphaned and abandoned children, is now under ICPS. So, adoptions are also coordinated under the ambit of ICPS. ICPS incorporates a series of steps aimed at streamlining the adoption process; addressing identified bottlenecks and regional disparities; and promoting national adoptions.

ICPS also proposes to set up *Cradle baby reception centres*. Recognising the fact that over 80 % of districts in the country do not have facilities to receive or offer temporary shelter for infants in crisis situation, especially those who are abandoned and vulnerable to be trafficked, the ICPS envisages setting up Cradle Baby Reception Centres in each district. These Cradle Baby Reception Centres will be linked to Cradle Points at Primary Health Care Centres (PHCs), Hospitals/Nursing Homes, Swadhar Units, Short-Stay Homes and in the office of the District Child Protection Scheme (DCPS) to receive abandoned babies. For every child received by the cradle baby reception centre, the process of creating an individual care plan shall be initiated by the reception centre, to be further developed and prepared by the Special Adoption Agency in whose care the child is to be transferred after the authorisation of the CWC (Ministry of Women and Child Development n.d.(c)).

4.3 Legislative Support for Children in India

1890	The Guardian and Wards Act
1929	The Child Marriage Restraint Act (Amended in 1979)
1948	The Factories Act (Amended in 1949, 1950 and 1954)
1956	Hindu Adoption and Maintenance Act
1960	The Orphanage and Other Charitable Homes (Supervision and Control) Act
1986	Juvenile Justice Act
1986	Immoral Traffic Prevention Act
1986	The Child Labour (Prohibition and Regulation) Act
1992	The Infant Milk Substitutes, Feeding Bottles and Infant Foods (Regulation of Production, Supply and Distribution) Act
1993	The Prenatal Diagnostic Technique (Regulation, Prevention and Misuse)
1994	The Persons with Disabilities (Equal Opportunities, Protection of Rights and Full Participation) Act
2000 and 2006	Revised Juvenile Justice Act
2009	Right to Education Act
2012	Protection of Children from Sexual Offences Act (POCSO).

Major Legislations and Policies for Children: A Brief Overview

Guardians and Wards Act (GAWA) 1890 confers only a guardianship status on the parent, which ceases once the child completes 18 years of age. The Act provides for appointment and declaration of guardians, duties, rights and liabilities of guardians among others. In absence of a law governing adoption by Muslims, Christians, Jews and Parsis and India not having a common civil code, persons from these religions can take children into their families under GAWA. However, it provides them only guardianship status. The child does not enjoy the rights as those of a biological child. They cannot inherit parental property, though the guardians can will their property. As in case of Muslims, they can gift their property during their life time as Muslim personal law does not allow a person to will away his property.

However, under the JJ Act 2000 (as amended in 2006) persons of all religious groups can adopt children and these adopted children would have the same status as that of a biological child.

Hindu Adoption and Maintenance Act (HAMA) 1956 is an act to amend and modify the law relating to adoption and maintenance among Hindus. It is the only codified law available for adoption and its applicability is restricted to Hindus alone that includes Buddhists, Jains and Sikhs. Muslims and Christians cannot adopt under HAMA. The act provides for norms and standards for adoption and maintenance. The condition laid down by the act provides that only persons below 15 years are capable of being taken in adoption, unless there is some custom or usage otherwise. The act enables a person to adopt a child of either sex but you should not have a biological child or grandchild of the sex of the child that you are adopting. Child of unknown parentage and child with physical disabilities are also adopted under this act. When parents adopt, the combined age of the parents should be less than 90. A married man can adopt but he would need the consent of his wife. Though a single Hindu woman can adopt, a married Hindu woman can adopt only if her husband is of unsound mind, is divorced or has renounced the world.

As per the opinion of the Union Law Ministry (Department of Legal Affairs), nonresident Hindus (NRIs/PIOs) are not eligible to adopt a child under HAMA, but the Indian courts are passing legally binding orders in favour of adoption by NRIs and Persons of Indian Origin (PIO). These adoptions are considered as final adoptions. The JJ act allows both domestic as well as inter-country adoption. However, there is need for an independent legislation on inter-country adoption.

The Immoral Traffic (Prevention) Act, 1956: In 1986, the Government of India amended the erstwhile Suppression of Immoral Traffic in Women and Girls Act, renamed as the Immoral Traffic (Prevention) Act. The Immoral Traffic (Prevention) Act, 1956 prescribes stringent action against those inducting children (below 16 years) and minors (16–18 years) in the offence of procuring, inducing or taking a person for the sake of prostitution. As per the act, if an adult is found with a child in a brothel or a hotel with a child, it shall be presumed that the adult has committed an offence, and the onus will rest on the adult to prove that the child is not being detained for the purpose of prostitution. If the child on medical examination is found to be sexually abused, it shall be presumed that the child has been detained for prostitution and for commercial purposes. The punishment consists of imprisonment for a term which shall not be less than 7 years, but which may be for life and shall also be liable to fine, with a provision for less than 7 years under special circumstances. The act covers both the sexes exploited sexually for commercial purposes and provides enhanced penalties for offences involving children and minors.

The Child Labour (Prohibition and Regulation) Act, 1986 was enacted to reduce child labour and to have an act which is one single act and overarches the other acts for children working in various industries and processes. The act as the name suggests does not ban child labour in-toto. It just prohibits it in certain specified processes and employments which are considered 'hazardous' and regulates it with rules and regulations related to work hours, health and safety measures in certain others in the 'non-hazardous' occupations. The act provides power to state governments to make rules with reference to health and safety wherever the employment of children is permitted. The act was for children till 14 years of age, but its latest revisions also have taken into ambit adolescent children in age of 14–18 who are working. Employment of children in homes and dhabbas has also been banned. It is amply clear that the act is permitting work of children in 'non-hazardous' occupations, albeit with some regulatory provisions (Details of the act in Chap. 5).

The act is in contradiction of Constitutional guarantee of right to education for all children in the 6–14 years age group. Children can simultaneously not work and study. Therefore, an amendment to this act is urgently needed which bans child labour altogether and also puts forth a plan for rehabilitation of children who have been working due to their personal life circumstances.

Other Legislations Concerning Child Labour Include

- The Factories Act, 1948, The Mines Act, 1952
- The Plantation Labour Act, 1951
- The Merchant Shipping Act, 1958
- The Motor Transport Workers Act, 1961
- The Beedi and Cigar Workers (Conditions of Employment) Act, 1966
- The Bonded Labour System (Abolition) Act, 1976.

The Prenatal Diagnostic Technique (Regulation and Prevention of Misuse) Act 1994 (PNDT Act 1994) Parliament approved the PNDT Bill 2002 on 20 December 2002, and is now called the *Pre-Conception and Pre-Natal Diagnostic Techniques (Prohibition and Sex Selection)* act 2002. As mentioned earlier, the 2011 Census data revealed an alarming decline in the child sex ratio in India. The child sex ratio for India is a shocking 1000:914, reflecting clearly that parents do not want to have daughters. There is sex selection happening preconception as well as postconception. The PC-PNDT act prohibits just this. It prohibits the use of prenatal diagnostic techniques to detect the sex of the foetus and then to terminate a pregnancy if it is a girl. It allows the use of prenatal tests only in cases when it is medically needed (ex. There is a history of miscarriages or there is history of genetic anomalies, chromosomal anomalies, birth defects in the family etc.).

According to the statement of objects and reasons of the PNDT Bill 2002, the prenatal diagnostic techniques are being misused on a large scale to detect the sex of the foetus and to terminate the pregnancy if the unborn child is a female. It further states that the proliferation of these technologies may, in future, precipitate a catastrophe in the form of severe imbalance in the male–female ratio. It was therefore necessary to enact and implement, in letter and spirit, a law to ban preconception sex selection techniques and the misuse of prenatal diagnostic techniques for sex-selective abortions, to provide for the regulation of the techniques only for appropriate scientific use for which they are intended, and to include technologies such as preconception sex selection (Bajpai 2006).

The Persons With Disabilities (Equal Opportunities, Protection of Rights and Full Participation) Act, 1995 is an act for children and persons with disabilities. The act has 14 chapters in all. The chapters address concerns like preventing disabilities, early detection of disabilities, education of children with disabilities and employment of persons with disabilities. As per the act, all children with disabilities up to the age of 18 years are entitled to free education. No educational institution can deny them admission in their institution due to their disability. Also, there is a reservation in institutes of higher education for admission of persons with disabilities. The PWD act also addressing the concern for manpower development and research in the field of disabilities. A person with disabilities who feels aggrieved can file an appeal under the PWD act with the State Commissioners and Chief Commissioner Disabilities (Details of this act in Chap. 9).

Child Marriage Restraint Act 1929, as amended *The Prohibition of Child Marriage Act, 2006* is an Act to restrain the solemnisation of child marriages. The act prescribes a minimum age of 21 years for males and 18 years for females for marriage. This law is applicable to all whole of India except the state of Jammu and Kashmir The child marriage can be declared null if the partner who was a minor at the time of marriage approaches for its annulment. Also, all children born out of child marriage are legitimate. The act provides for punishment for solemnising a child marriage. It also provides for punishment to parent or guardian, if they marry off their children/wards before the permissible age. Under the act, any man who marries a minor girl is liable to the punishment as prescribed. Punishments for promoting or permitting solemnisation of child marriage would extend to rigorous imprisonment up to 2 years and fine up to two lakh rupees.

Juvenile Justice (Care and Protection of Children) Act, 2000 (now Amendment Act 2006) is an act to consolidate and amend the law relating to juveniles in conflict with law and children in need of care and protection. The act provides for proper care, protection and treatment of children by catering to their development needs, and by adopting a child-friendly approach in the adjudication and disposition of matters in the best interest of children and for their ultimate rehabilitation. The act defines a juvenile/child as a person who has not completed the age of 18 years. It has two separate sections for juveniles in conflict with law and for children in need of care and protection. The act defines Juvenile in conflict with law as a child who is alleged to have committed an offence and children in need of care and protection broadly as children who are neglected, abused, abandoned, victim of any armed conflict or natural calamity amongst others. It also contains an exclusive chapter concerning rehabilitation and social reintegration of children. Offences committed against a child as listed in the act, are cognizable and punishable under the provisions of this act (Ministry of Women and Child Development n.d.(a)).

The act has institutional provisions like children's homes, short-stay homes and non-institutional provisions for children like adoption. As part of reformative measure, the act prescribes community service as a 'punishment' to the offending juvenile (Details of this act in Chap. 6).

Protection of Children from Sexual Offences (POCSO) Act, 2012 To deal with child sexual abuse cases, the Government has brought in a special law, namely, The Protection of Children from Sexual Offences (POCSO) Act, 2012. The POCSO Act, 2012 is a comprehensive law to provide for the protection of children from the offences of sexual assault, sexual harassment and pornography, while safeguarding the interests of the child at every stage of the judicial process by incorporating child-friendly mechanisms for reporting, recording of evidence, investigation and speedy trial of offences through designated Special Courts. The said act recognises almost every known form of sexual abuse against children as punishable offences, and makes the different agencies of the State, such as the police, judiciary and child protection machinery, collaborators in securing justice for a sexually abused child (Details of this act in Chap. 7).

People who traffic children for sexual purposes are also punishable under the provisions relating to abetment in the act. The act prescribes stringent punishment graded as per the gravity of the offence, with a maximum term of rigorous imprisonment for life, and fine.

References

Bajpai, A. (2006). *Child rights in India Law policy and practice* (2nd ed.). New Delhi: Oxford University Press.

Laha, S. S. (2009). Work Participation Rate among Disabled Population of India. In A. Bhuimali (Ed.), *Rights of disabled women and children in India*. New Delhi: Serial Publications.

Ministry of Women and Child Development, Government of India. (n.d.(a)). *A report of the working group on development of children for the eleventh five year plan (2007–2012)*. Retrieved from http://wcd.nic.in/WG_Report.pdf.

Ministry of Women and Child Development, Government of India. (n.d.(b)). *Sub group report child protection in the eleventh five year plan (2007–2012)*. New Delhi. Retrieved from http://wcd.nic.in/wgchilprotection.pdf.

Ministry of Women and Child Development, Government of India. (n.d.(c)). *The integrated child protection scheme (ICPS)*. New Delhi. Retrieved from http://wcd.nic.in/schemes/icps.pdf.

National AIDS Control Programme. Retrieved from, http://www.archive.india.gov.in/sectors/health_family/index.php?id=5.

National Plan of Action for Children. (2005). Department of Women and Child Development, Government of India. Retrieved from http://www.wcd.nic.in/NAPAug16A.pdf.

World Bank. (2007). *People with Disabilities in India: From Commitments to Outcomes. South Asian Region*. Retrieved from, http://siteresources.worldbank.org/INDIAEXTN/Resources/295583-1171456325808/DISABILITYREPORTFINALNOV2007.pdf.

(Source: Personal collection of author)

UNITED NATIONS CONVENTION ON THE RIGHTS OF THE CHILD

Article 32 (Child labour): The government should protect children from work that is dangerous or might harm their health or their education………………………… Children's work should not jeopardize any of their other rights, including the right to education, or the right to relaxation and play.

Chapter 5
The Working and the Street Children: Where Is the Child?

Abstract This chapter is on the working and street children. It presents the magnitude of the problem. It explores the causes why children need to work and why they become part of the streets. It also defines and categorises the street and working children. The chapter analyses how this category of children are especially oppressed and the challenges that they face are unique. The laws, along with Child Labour (Prohibition and Regulation) act, related to the working and the street children are discussed and a critique is also given. The National Policy for Child Labour is also presented. The chapter proposes ways of combating child labour and suggests ideas on how to plan rehabilitation programmes for the street children and what should be the approach when working with these children. The chapter ends with a profile of leading NGOs like Butterflies, Deepalaya, M.V. Foundation and HAQ which are doing exemplary work for the prevention, protection and rehabilitation of the working and street children.

Keywords Working children · Street children

5.1 The Extent of the Problem

Children have worked in the past in most societies, but it was taken for granted and was not considered unusual or inappropriate. In the previous centuries, the concept of childhood was not given any importance because preparation of an individual child belonging to disadvantaged groups, for future responsibilities, in term of education was not as complex as it is today. Also, societies were so sharply divided on the basis of socio-economic criteria that child labour was not viewed in askance and was virtually compartmentalised and sanctified. Only children of upper castes were to be protected, while children from lower castes as well as the girl child were considered to be 'born to work'. The concept of child labour and that this should not happen, is relatively new. The concern for child labour and the social realisation of unfairness towards these children is a sign of a more aware and empathetic

G. Chopra, *Child Rights in India*, DOI 10.1007/978-81-322-2446-4_5

society. Against the backdrop of modern scientific knowledge, especially in relation to providing conducive contexts for child development, child labour appears totally dysfunctional in any society.

When we look into a child's eyes, we expect to see hope, trust and innocence but when these signs of childhood are replaced by betrayal, hunger, fear and suspicion, we need to take stock of ourselves and the society we have created (Biswas 2007). The phenomenal presence of child labour makes one wonder where has the childhood of these children gone. Truly, this is childhood lost. It is believed that India is a home to the highest number of child labourers in the world. The Census (2001) report clearly points to the increase in the number of child labourers in the country from 11.28 million in 1991 to 12.59 million in 2001. The total number of working children in the country has declined from 12.6 million as per the Census 2001 to 4.35 million as per Census 2011 which shows 65 % reduction.

According to Census 2011, the number of child labourers is 43.5 lakh in the age group 5–14 years of which 32.7 lakh are in rural areas and 10.8 lakh are in urban areas. As per UNICEF State of World's Children (2013), 12 % of India's children aged 5–14 years are child workers.

Nobody knows the exact figures. But it is known to all, they are in millions. They work everywhere—in sweatshops, in factories, in dhabas, in mines, on construction sites, in affluent households, in agricultural fields, in brothels and so on. They are estimated to be more than 100 million. A UN report claimed they are 145 million. Statistics on child labour are elusive not only because of the practical difficulties involved in the design and implementation of child survey but also because of differences in perception about what constitutes a child, or child work, or child labour (Rehman et al. 2002). The variations in estimates are due to differing notions and conceptions about working children. The conceptual and definitional differences have led to the application of different methods of estimations and surveys (Dingwaney 1988). Another serious problem which is encountered in identifying the child workers is that almost all the child workers work in unorganised non-formal sector on which there is hardly any reliable source of data. The pattern of employment also differs considerably in terms of wage, duration of work and methods of operations.

The existence of child labour, in whatever magnitude, should be a matter of concern for the working children themselves, the parents, society and the state. Whether part-time or full time, in any occupation, engagement of a child in the labour force simply means a complete or partial denial of childhood to him. He is not merely deprived of the joys and carefree life of a child but also of desirable physical and mental development. This is not only injustice to him as a child but also as an adult throughout his life. For the foundation of adulthood is built on extremely weak structure of underdevelopment (Dingwaney 1988).

The census 2011 is putting the extent of child labour to 4.35 million which shows 65 % reduction compared to census 2001 where the number was pegged at 12.6 million. According to Census (2011), the number of child labour in UP was 89630, Maharashtra 496916, AP 404851, Bihar 451590 and Rajasthan 252338.

If government claims are to be believed, then what could be the reasons for declining numbers of working children? It is not easy to reduce child labour. The government claims that its multipronged approach to alleviate poverty, universalise education along with social protection, employment generation and rescue and rehabilitation has done the work. While the government seemed content with the role, civil society activists have come down heavily on the government for not doing enough to eliminate child labour. Organisations like Bachpan Bachao Andolan (BBA) has pointed out that the samples taken for survey are very small for a country like India. Also, the assumption of the government is that children who are enrolled in school would not be part of the work force. BBA has rescued around 1,100 children from bonded labour in the past year. The rescue comes from raids conducted with help from the police and the judiciary. Of these 1,100, as per BBA, more than 800 were enrolled in schools in their respective villages. On paper they are already in schools whereas the reality is that they are bonded labour.

The Child Labour (Prohibition and Regulation) Amendment bill 2012 is in the parliament for approval. As per this bill, child labour will be completely prohibited for all children till the age of 14 years. This will link up to the Right to Compulsory and free primary education for children till 14 years. The act will also prohibit adolescence (14–18 years) from work in mines, inflammable substances and in hazardous occupations (http://www.livemint.com/Politics/FDhOcEsEiKHX572Bn7kuZJ/Number-of-child-labourers-in-country-has-declined-Govt.html?utm_source=copy).

Latest information, calculated on the basis of the worker–population ratio (WPR) based on the NSSO's revelation in its latest report, "Employment and Unemployment Situation in India, 2011–12", released in January 2014 reveals that the states which have highest number of child workers (both in urban and rural areas) are—Uttar Pradesh (28.83 lakh), Bihar (11.22 lakh), West Bengal (10.47 lakh), Jharkhand (4.75 lakh) and Andhra Pradesh (4.5 lakh). It is significant to note that the states which are good performers in overall social indicators have very few child workers. Thus, if calculations based on NSSO figures are to be taken into account, Himachal Pradesh has the lowest number of child workers, just about 4,500, followed by Kerala, about 16,000. A high proportion of child labourers implies failure of the state government's efforts to ensure universal primary education, on one hand, and the inability to implement government policies to overcome poverty and underemployment.

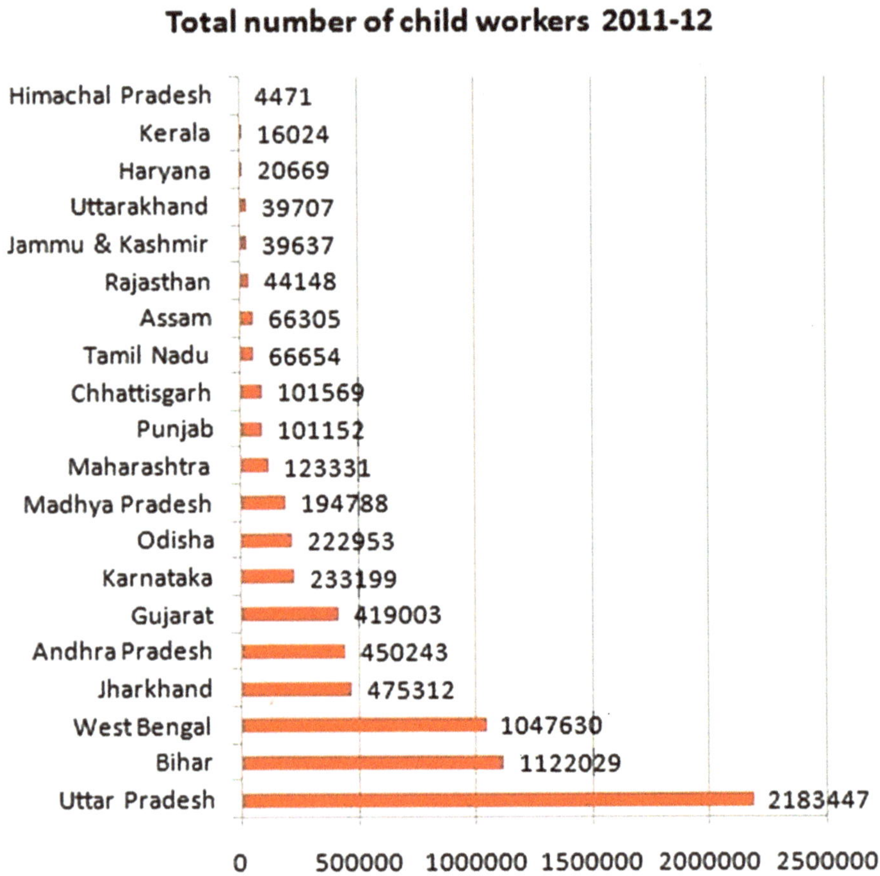

(http://www.counterview.net/2014/02/gujarat-has-nearly-42-lakh-child.html retrieved on 16th August 2014).

5.2 Defining Child Labour

There is no universally accepted definition of child labour. Various agencies have defined child labour in terms of work type and age criterion. According to ILO (1983), "Child Labour includes children permanently leading adult lives, working long hours for low wages under conditions damaging to their health and to their mental and physical development, sometimes separated from their families, frequently deprived of meaningful educational and training opportunities that could open for them a better future". The Encyclopedia of Social Sciences defines child labour as "When the business of wage earning or of participation in self or family support conflicts directly or indirectly with the business of growth and education, the result is child labour". While according to the Child Labour (Prohibition and Regulation) act (1986), a 'child' is a person who has not completed the age of 14 years.

Child labour can be defined as those children who participate in work either paid or not paid. Child labour could mean employment of children in occupations which is detrimental to their health and also deprive them from getting chances to grow, bereft of developmental opportunities and denied opportunities to acquire skills. A recent report on child labour used the term child labour to cover all economic activities carried out by persons less than 15 years of age, regardless of their occupational status (wage earners, own account worker, unpaid family worker), but not household work performed by them in their parents house, except where such work can be assimilated to an economic activity, e.g. Staying at home while parents go to work, therefore deprived them from going to school.

In the context of exploitation, UNICEF has given a very comprehensive formulation in its attempt at defining child labour:

1. *Starting Full-Time Work at too Early an Age*: This happened historically in the earlier stage of industrialisation in Europe where children begin to work in factories from 9, 8 or even 5 years. This is still the case today in many developing countries.
2. *Working too Long*: Within or outside of the family so that children are unable to attend school, where it is available, or to make the most of school due to fatigue or lack of time. In some cases, children still work 12–16 h a day.
3. Work resulting in *excessive physical, social and psychological strains* upon the child as in the cases of sexual exploitation in prostitution and pornography, work in sweatshops, as well as such dangerous work as military service and mining.
4. *Work and life on the streets* in unhealthy and dangerous conditions.
5. *Inadequate remuneration* for working outside of the family.
6. *Too much responsibilities too early* as in the domestic situations where children under 10 may have to look after young brother and sisters for a whole day thereby preventing school attendance.
7. *Work that does not facilitate the psychological and social development* of the child as in dull and repetitive tasks associated with industries like handicrafts.
8. *Work that inhibits the child's self-esteem* as in bonded labour and prostitution, and in a less extreme case the negative perception of 'street children'.

On one side of the development debate are those who believe that child labour must be defined broadly to include all children who are out of the school system as they are potential child labourers. This view is not widely shared (Burra 2002).

5.3 Classification of Child Labour

UNICEF has classified child labour into three categories:

- *Within the family*—children are engaged without pay in domestic house hold tasks, agricultural/pastoral work, handicraft/cottage industries etc.
- *Within the family but outside the home*—children do agricultural/pastoral work, which consists of migrant labour, local agriculture work, domestic service, construction work and informal occupations like recycling of waste—employed by others and self employed. Chiefly, these children are engaged with their families in some occupations.
- *Outside the family*—children are employed by others in bonded work, apprenticeship, skilled trades (carpet, embroidery, brass/copper work), industrial unskilled occupation/mines, domestic work, commercial work in shop and restaurants, begging, prostitution and pornography.

In India, the workforce is divided into:

Organised Sector
Those who are organised into trade unions—registered or unregistered; and

Unorganised Sector
Those who have not been able to organise in pursuit of a common objective because of constraints, such as casual nature of employment, ignorance and illiteracy, small size of establishment with low capital investment per person employed, scattered nature of establishments and superior strength of the employer operating singly or in combination (this definition also covers agricultural labourers).

The unorganised sector accounts for a whole army of child labour working as domestic servants, helpers or assistants in hotels, restaurants, wayside shops, canteens and similar establishments, hawkers, paper vendors, porters, shoeshine boys, sweepers and scavengers; children working in small workshops and repair shops and helpers at construction sites engaged in breaking stones, loading and unloading goods, etc. This unorganised sector is definitely the greatest employer of child labour in the country. It could be said that more the 'organised' sector is brought under protective and prohibitive regulations as far as work of the child is concerned, the greater is the extent to which child workers are pushed into the unorganised sector (Dingwaney 1988). Employers engaging children in the unorganised sector are not answerable to anyone, hence free to act in their own self interest.

In almost all societies, children work, though the forms of their involvement vary. Many children work in hazardous, abusive and exploitative conditions. They are found working among others in the following conditions:

- Agriculture labour
- Plantation workers
- Cultivators
- Dangerous industries like lock making, fire works, bangle making, glass factories
- Carpet weaving

- Handloom industry
- Construction workers
- Tea stalls, road side dhabhas
- As domestic workers carrying out arduous work sometimes all alone at home, sometimes facing physical and sexual abuse
- Bonded labour
- Shops and establishments
- Mines and quarrying
- As family labour in traditional occupations like embroidery, zari work
- On the streets as rag pickers, beggars, vendors, shoeshine boys, newspaper and magazine sellers, hawkers, puppeteers and acrobats

The following health hazards have been identified with work in these sectors (Table 5.1):

Report of the International Labour Conference, 1983, asserts that child labour in urban activities, though sometimes found in the organised sectors, can be considered to be a problem mainly of the unorganised sector. The report points out the economic activities in which children participate:

1. Domestic Work such as cleaning, cooking, childcare and other chores in the child's own household undertaken by children in almost all societies.
2. Non-domestic but non-monetary work: this covers such activities as farm work, fuel and water collection and hunting. Even in the urban sector many urban household production units engaged in trade and services as well as in artisanal manufacturing production rely on children for activities such as running errands, guarding goods, marketing etc.
3. Bonded labour: illegal, it arises as one of the obligations to landlords whereby the provision of child to the landlord is part of the family's rent or in a situation where children are given in exchange of settlement of debts.
4. Wage employment: children working as a part of the family group or an individual in agriculture sites, in domestic services, in manufacturing and services activities, etc. They may work on piece-rate or time-rate basis, as regular or casual workers, in jobs that may or may not involve some training.
5. Marginal work: the types of activities in this category vary in nature and intensity. They may be irregular or of a short-term nature such as selling

Table 5.1 Health hazards (Dingwaney 1988)

S. No.	Occupation	Type of health hazard
1	Bidi Industry	Chronic bronchitis and tuberculosis
2	Glass Industry	Asthma, bronchitis, tuberculosis, eye defects
3	Handloom Industry	Asthma, tuberculosis
4	Zari and embroidery	Eye defects
5	Gem cutting and diamond cutting	Eye defects
6	Construction	Stunts the growth of the child
7	Rag pickers	Tetanus, skin disease
8	Pottery	Asthma, bronchitis, tuberculosis
9	Stone quarries/slate quarries	Silicosis

Table 5.2 Number of child workers (5–14 years) engaged in hazardous occupations as per 2001 Census

1	Pan, bidi and cigarettes	252,574
2	Construction	208,833
3	Domestic workers[a]	185,505
4	Spinning/weaving	128,984
5	Brick kilns, titles	84,972
6	Dhabas/restaurants/hotels/motels[a]	70,934
7	Auto-workshop, vehicle repairs	49,893
8	Gem cutting, jewellery	37,489
9	Carpet-making	32,647
10	Ceramic	18,894
11	Agarbati, dhoop and detergent making	13,583
12	Others	135,162
Total		1,219,470

[a]Ministry has recently issued notification to include children working as domestic workers and in dhabas/restaurants, hotels, etc. in the list of hazardous occupations w.e.f. 10th October 2006
Source Planning Commission (n.d.)

newspapers, shoe-shining, 'looking after' cars, garbage collection and sorting out objects from garbage.
Table 5.2 shows the number of child workers engaged in hazardous occupations as per census 2001.

5.4 Causes of Child Labour

Child labour is one of the pernicious and evil manifestations of the growing volume of all engulfing poverty and exploitation. Today, the third world is a basketful of cheap labour force: the adult labour is cheap and child labour is the cheapest for the capitalists, and for any owner of means of production to reap profits. Child workers are the most vulnerable human factor in the production process. Today, the existence of 250 million working children in the world is not a coincidence. It is a systematic outcome engendered by the process of capitalist exploitation (Rehman et al. 2002).

The Indian position rests on deeply held beliefs that there is division between people who work with their minds and rule, and people who work with their hands and are ruled, and that education should reinforce rather than break down this division. These beliefs are closely tied to religious notions and to the premises that underline India's hierarchical caste system (Weiner 1991). No doubt, children who work do come from highly impoverished homes mostly from the lower castes.

The causes of why children work when they should be enjoying childhood and learning skills which would make them functional and productive adults are many. Poverty has been accused to be the biggest reason for swarming child labour in India. Poor parents perceive many advantages in children taking up jobs. They feel that job disciplines them, protects them against delinquency and also provides opportunity for learning financially viable work.

ON DOMESTIC CHILD LABOUR—Point to Ponder

I recruited a young 16–17 year old girl to do my house hold jobs. She was to stay with me for all 24 h. I housed her in my servant quarters with my other two maids who had been with me for past 2 years or so. Her mother lived in a close by slum. This girl had been with me for about 3 weeks when she developed a strange pain in her chest. I had her mother's mobile number, and I called her. Once she came, I decided to send her home. I gave her mother some money for her treatment and told her to get her back when she was better.

After a few days, I checked her condition, her mother said she was better but not fit enough to join back. I called after a few days again, she said she will come and meet me soon. Her mother came in the next day with her little son, who looked 8–9 year old to me. She said 'munni' was still unwell, so she was planning to take her to Kolkata where her father lived, so I should pay her whatever was her due. I did so. Then came a strange request. She said, keep my son in your house. He will do dusting, washing, running errands, small jobs. Pay him whatever you wish to. She added, "he is full day loitering in the slums with his vagrant friends. I am not home to keep an eye on him. If this continues for some more time, he will be totally spoilt". She pleaded to me, "please keep him at your house. He will serve you and also learn some work in the process and also stay away from bad company".

Here was the dilemma!! We say no child labour. Was this little boy better-off working in my home or staying unsupervised at his own house in the thick of urban slums of Delhi, in company of anti-social influences? We can succeed in abolishing child labour from our country only if we simultaneously have a rehabilitation plan in hand for children freed from the labour force.

For the curious readers, I did not hire the boy for my household work. I also learnt that the girl working for me, 'munni', had been married away within just a few days of leaving from my home. She was certainly a sick girl. And now a child bride. But these are the compulsions of poverty!

The root cause of child labour lies in abject poverty. Instances where social and economic condition of family have improved, children go to school and child labour has virtually disappeared. So any society, which wants its children to be free to learn and play, must first free its entire population from fear of want, thus ensuring fulfilment of basic needs of all people. This includes such essentials as food, shelter, clothing, water and education for children, and training and provision of gainful employment for parents. But, can poverty alone or even public apathy explain the fact that thousands of children spend their childhood rummaging through dustbins and heaps of filth to pick rags, waste paper, used polythene bags and bits of broken glass or scraps of metal to enable them to earn a few rupees a day, which is not enough to buy them even dry rotis and dal? They often look through the same dustbins to pick up food thrown away by the affluent (Dingwaney 1988).

Mostly children work as the parents are not able to financially support their families. Parents are forced to send their children to work for reasons of survival, at times even in hazardous occupations, ignoring the fact that this is wrong. Monetary constraints, need for food, shelter, clothing forces the children to premature labour. Overpopulation has been also cited as another reason for child labour. When there are limited means and many mouths to feed, there are few options but each feeds self as well as supports the remaining family. Children loose out on childhood and now are performing adult role of being economically productive. Parents themselves are uneducated, ignorant and unexposed and do not realise the salience of education and developmental opportunities in early childhood, which would prepare children much better for their impending future adult roles. Children miss on prospects of wholesome physical, social, emotional and cognitive development. The family practice to inculcate traditional skills in children also pulls little ones inexorably in the trap of child labour, as they never get the opportunity to learn anything else.

The more generally held is the view that in a society where basic needs have not been satisfied, the income of the chid is critical to the family's survival. It is often argued that poverty is a 'harsh reality' and children have to work in order to survive. How will poor families survive without the additional income of the children? It is seldom taken into account that children's earnings are pathetically meagre, and that it is precisely because of the vast numbers of children in the workforce in all the sectors of the economy that adult wages are depressed (Burra 2002).

"People are poor so they need the income from their child's labour. Therefore to eliminate child labour you must eliminate poverty, else people will starve"-this argument may sound convincing, but is erroneous. The situation persists because neither the policy makers nor the influential voices in the society believe that we can eliminate child labour. That is a problem to be solved on another day, in another realm (Sinha 2011).

Given the need to meet subsistence requirements on the one hand and growing pauperisation resulting from land alienation on the other, the pressure on rural households to find alternative sources of survival by all means, including the labour of the children, whether under family control or under contract to prospective employers and labour recruiters, becomes almost insurmountable.

Ineffective child labour laws and the tacit acceptance these provide to child labour in non-listed processes and occupation becomes a hindrance in combating child labour. As per Child Labour Prohibition and Regulation Act (CLPRA), child labour is NOT banned in toto in India. It is prohibited in certain 'hazardous' occupations and processes, while child work conditions are regulated in certain other occupations and processes. Children working as part of family are exempted from the penal provisions of the law, the act is also silent about children working in the agriculture sector and other unorganised informal sectors.

Adult unemployment and urbanisation also causes child labour. Adults often find it difficult to find jobs because factory owners find it more beneficial to employ children at cheap rates. A 1997 AusAid report has it that in Bangladesh 'one in ten in the labour force is under 14, displacing two to ten million adults from employment'. The report further says that in the absence of an effective compulsory education system, increasing number of children are coming to the labour market, to compete with adults in both the formal and informal sectors (AusAid 1997).

Also, children are easy to exploit as they are not part of trade unions, protest little, are easy to mould and work enthusiastically. This attitude also makes it difficult for adults to find jobs in factories, forcing them to drive their little ones to work to keep the fire burning in their homes.

It is documented in the literature as to how alcoholism and entertainment needs of the fathers contributes substantially to the poverty of the family and propels children into work in order to sustain wasteful expenditure (Burra 2002). In India, children are considered a property of parents and in many poor households, children are considered an economic asset. It is difficult to find remorse among parents who not only make children work, but also sell them to rich landlords to pay off their debts etc. Adult exploitation of children is also evident on many occasions. Elders relax at home and live on the labour of poor helpless children.

Broadly, the reasons for child labour can be classified as under:

1. Social Reasons

As we have noted above, India's social structure is highly differentiated in terms of caste, religion, race, etc. In the social hierarchy those who are placed at the lower rung are generally the labouring masses without any means of production except their own labour power. As a result, as observed by Voll (1999), we find that "By far the majority of child labourers in India belonged to the so-called 'lower castes' (Dalits/Harijans), the so-called 'tribals' (Adivasis) and to the Muslim religious minority. Most child labourers do not belong to the 'upper castes', which constitute about 17–18 % of Indian society" (Voll 1999). It has been a common practice in the society for children from lower castes to work, while children from upper castes went to school.

2. Economic Reasons

Lack of family's ability to take care of the needs of children due to monetary constraints is a major reason for child labour. The adult members may be unemployed, or be working on low wages which are insufficient to manage the needs of the family. The basic survival of these children at times depends on the wages that they earn.

3. Legal Reasons

The Child Labour (Prohibition and Regulation) act does not summarily ban child labour. With a weak legislation, we have little hope to fight against child labour. The penal provisions are not deterrent enough. Also, there are too many loopholes in the act which can provide an escape route to the offenders.

4. Political Reasons

In a democratic political system where there is universal franchise and all citizens can vote, one cannot but wonder if people are deliberately kept vulnerable and dependent. It is very easy to buy the loyalty of people in extreme poverty. So, would it be fair to say that it suits our political system to have poverty and child labours?

5. Education System

India has just made 'Right to Education' as a fundamental right for all its children. With this new development, only time will tell if children will start compulsorily attending school. The school system is not inspiring for the child. In many cases, child workers are school dropouts who felt that they were wasting time in school. So, the ability of schools to retain children and provide meaningful education would be a very significant factor which can retain children in school rather than joining the work force.

Prevailing education infrastructure is highly unsuitable to many economically deprived families. Many a time the unfeeling attitude of the teachers, depressing school environment, outdated curricula, lack of teaching material, etc., deter children from socio-economically deprived families from going to educational institutes (Anker and Melkas 1996). Our education system does not draw the child towards the school but drives the child away.

6. Employers Preference for Child Labour

Many employers prefer child labour because children could be easily coerced and used for anything without opposition. Anker and Melkas (1996) have given reasons for employers preference:

- More docile and less troublesome. Can be beaten up to submission
- Greater willingness to do repetitive work
- More trustworthy and innocent, so less likely to steal
- Less absenteeism (no absenteeism if bonded labour)
- Do not form trade unions
- Tradition of hiring child labour by employers
- Traditional occupations have children working alongside parents
- Employers need labourers. Children come asking for jobs. So why not hire them?
- Children have better health

7. Adult Unemployment

A major reason cited for child labour is that children need to work because their parents are not employed. But the fact is otherwise. It is because children work, the opportunities available to adult workers become less, rendering them unemployed. If child labour stops, fewer adults would be unemployed. With more adults working, fewer child will need to take up jobs to survive. The contention of the author is that child labour perpetuates adult unemployment than otherwise.

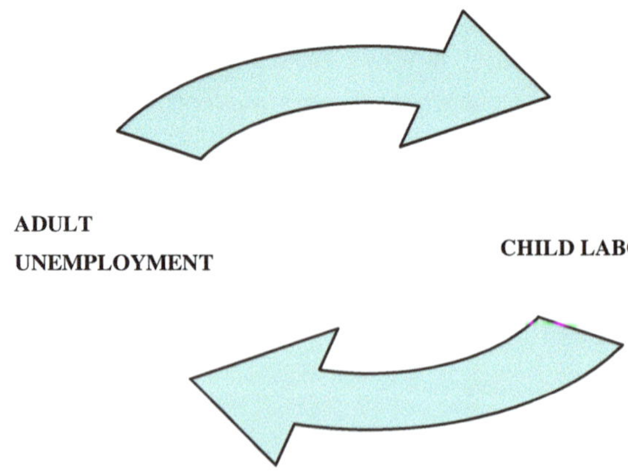

8. Demographic Reasons
Factors like size of the family also compel children to work. Larger the sizes of the families which are poor, greater the chance of employment of children for their own maintenance, as well as for adding financially to the family's kitty add to child labour.

9. Migration to Cities
Migration to cities by rural population is another major cause for child labour in cities.

10. Family Conditions
Child abuse, poverty, unequitable distribution of family resources, illness, debts and incapacitation and death of adults can all lead to child labour.

5.5 Combating Child Labour

Childhood is period in life when the child should be provided with chance to develop a healthy body, a sound personality and cognitive abilities. But when these early years are lost in trying to survive, childhood is a missed prime time for these children. Weiner argues that other countries, developed as well as developing, have sought to deal with child labour by introduction of universal education through legal enforcement of school attendance. Child labour and compulsory education cannot co-exist. Education by itself will not eradicate child labour but will reduce and discourage it. Employers will find child labour uneconomic as children will now be available only for half a day (Jaiswal 2000). Also, children will be less available, leaving more employment opportunities for adults. Education will improve the capability of children, have a positive impact on the health, mortality and family life.

The M.V. foundation's experience of removing over 100,000 children from work has shown that there is a deep and extricable link between universalisation of elementary education and elimination of child labourer and does not choose to distinguish between children engaged in different forms of work. The foundation's work, therefore is based on the premise that the only way to eliminate child labour is to universalise education (Sinha 2002). With the notification of RTE act, there is fresh hope of eradication of child labour in our country via the implementation of compulsory education of all children between 6 and 14 years.

A CHILD WORKING IN A SHOP…
I often visited a grocery shop in my local market where I always found this young boy (maybe 10–11 years old), efficiently handing over whatever items customers asked for, be it soaps, soups or shampoos. On one of the days, my 15 years old son, studying in a leading school of Delhi, very aware, who read his newspaper daily and had also read that Child Labour now is prohibited in shops and homes, came with me to this shop. He bought his stuff from the shop and as soon as he stepped out, he told me "Ma, Child Labour". I responded,

"hu". He realised that I had I was not considering it important enough. He again repeated, "Ma, Child Labour". I looked at him and said, "Yes". He said, "Call the police. She can not make such a small child work". I said, the child looked happy, efficient, well engaged and neatly turned out. But my son was very firm and persuasive. He picked up my cell phone and called 100 number.

The police reached the shop and did whatever they were to do. But I still wonder, if that was the right/wise thing to do. Without work, I really wonder in what condition that child must be in!

MY CONCERN IS, DO WE HAVE A CONTINGENCY PLAN TO REHABILITATE THESE CHILDREN BEFORE WE DISPLACE THEM FROM WORK!!

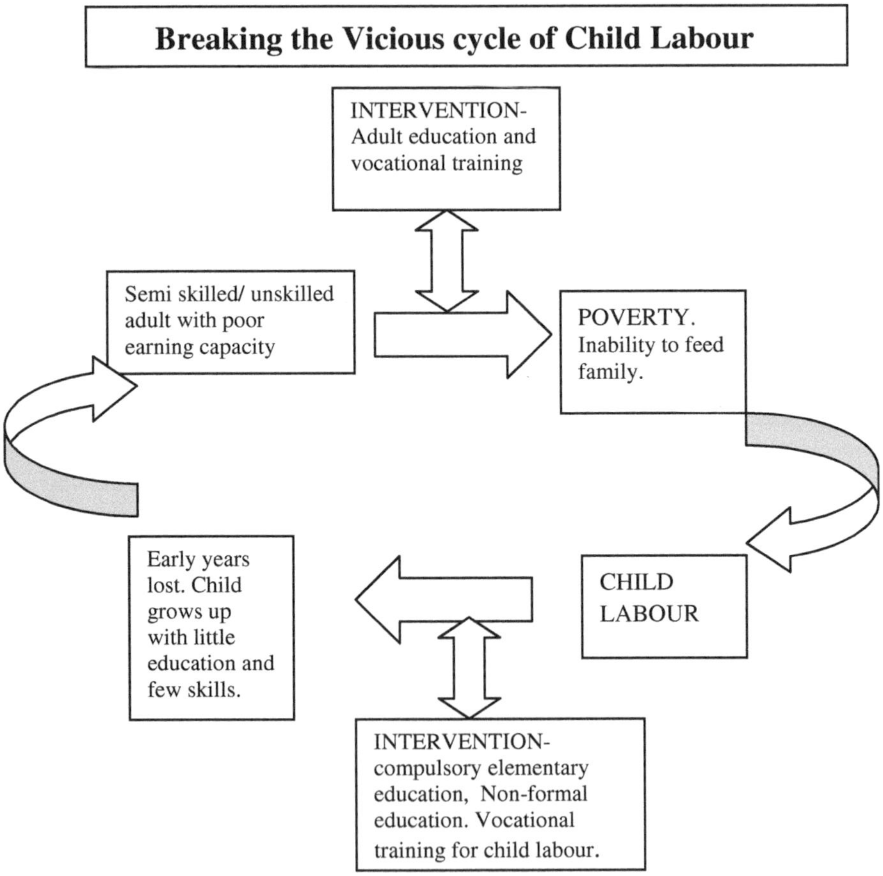

When childhood is burdened with the adult role of earning for a living, the crucial years when normally children study and acquire skills which would equip them to lucrative jobs in future, are lost in the drudgery of child labour. When this child grows up to be an adult, he is unskilled, unequipped to earn well, as well as weak since his physical development and health status has also got affected due to prolonged years of labour and related physical abuse. When he produces his own children, he does not have enough earning to support his family and provide for decent meals. His own children then become child labour and the vicious cycle continues.

Single most important intervention is strict enforcement of compulsory education for all children till 14 years of age is a single most important step to combat child labour. But other interventions like upgrading the skills of parents so as to improve their capacity to earn and having provision for night schools and other non-formal education options for working children should also be simultaneously implemented.

If children are working then to combat child labour, interventions can come at two points. We start night schools and other non-formal schools for the working child and while they are working, they also acquire functional literacy and other vocational skills. The second intervention can be for the parents who can also receive adult education and vocational training to learn semi-skilled and skilled jobs, hence improving their ability to earn better, so that they no longer need to send their children to work.

As also referred by Dingwaney (1988), there exists a vicious cycle—most of the occupations in which children are employed neither offer them any skills nor education, long hours of work affects their overall development, their present economic situation and work environment retards their future—leaving them no option but to rope in their little ones, thus condemning generations to a bleak and bereft future.

In most countries, and particularly in India, legislation concerning minimum age for admission to employment or regulations about the employment of children exists and at least covers industry. But it is the ineffectiveness of enforcement of legislation which allows child labour to persist. An effective inspection system is not adequately developed. Also, legislation often excludes traditional work, ignores quasi family undertakings, petty commerce, street trades and agriculture where majority of the children work and the enforcement of legislation, if any, is extremely difficult (Dingwaney 1988).

The Ranga Reddy district in Andhra Pradesh has shown the results of continuous engagement in over 1000 villages, where children of the poor have begun to go to school. Ranga Reddy effort happened because of clarity of overall framework and trust in people. Experience over the years has shown that in every village there are a number of poor parents sending their children to school even as some of the relatively better-off families are sending theirs to work. How does one explain this? There is no 'poverty line' or a level of poverty below which parents are compelled to send their children to work. There are thousands of parents, among the poorest in the country, who are in debt and bondage, from different family sizes and background but still send their children to school because they believe that their children must not work. Any new and sincere effort by the state to provide a complete measure of schooling has seen a surge in the number of those attending school, reaffirming the latent desire to learn. We are dealing therefore with not an issue of bare economic need as the motivator for child labour, but a complex compact of attitudinal, social and policy neglect that reinforces a current practice rather than question it (Sinha 2011).

What are the ways to prevent child labour? The existing law does not ban child labour This is the first amendment that is required in the law. The law divides children into children and adolescents. But adolescents are also vulnerable to exploitation and of being denied of development opportunities. The law should be extended to children up to 18 years. It is also recommended that RTE should cover children till they complete 18 years of age. Another road block in the prevention of child labour is that for children who are taken out of work force, there is no rehabilitation plan in place to make sure that after some time they do not regress to becoming a part of the work force again. Rehabilitation of the working child has to be an integral part of the child labour laws. In addition, social protection schemes, entitlements and increased livelihood opportunities for poor and vulnerable families need to be seriously brought into effect.

Make it mandatory that children under 14 years of age have to attend school, then we would have no children working as labourers. This is the contention of many social activists across the world who feel that the only way to combat child labour is to make elementary education compulsory for all children. India has recently amended the constitutional provision and as per The Constitution (Eighty-Sixth Amendment) Act, 2002, Article 21A of India's Constitution now establishes free and compulsory education for all children aged 6–14 years as a fundamental RIGHT. Right To Education, notified in February 2010, is a fundamental right of every child in India who is between the age 6–14 years. The result of this change are still to be seen for the millions of child workers in the country who are found toiling in the fields, factories, mines and even affluent urban homes, rather than attending school. It is worth mentioning here that Article 51 fixes the responsibility on parents to ensure that their children are attending school.

NEWS PAPER EXCERPTS ON CHILD LABOUR

As said by Sh Kailash Satyarthi, Nobel Laureate, to Pandey and Haider (2014) 'It is an absolute myth that poverty causes and perpetuates Child Labour. The reality is that Child Labour causes poverty and child labour perpetuates illiteracy'.

Singh (2014) in 'Government may bring total ban on Child Labour' reports that the government is likely to introduce a key legislation that proposes a complete ban on child labour in all sectors in the coming winter session of Parliament.

The legislation aims to amend the Child Labour (Prohibition and Regulation) Act to bring it in tune with the Right To Education (RTE) Act, which makes education compulsory for all children up to the age of 14. Though the proposal for complete ban on child labour up to 14 years of age was once cleared by the Cabinet, it could not get parliamentary approval. Under existing laws, child labour is not a punishable offence in some "non-hazardous" sectors such as farming. It was argued that there should not be any discrimination on working in hazardous or non-hazardous industry in terms of the ban. The proposal aims to ban all work for children under the age of 14 and restrict non-hazardous work to adolescents between the age of 14 and 18. Employing a child under 14 for any work—hazardous or non-hazardous—will be a cognizable offence punishable with imprisonment up to 2 years or a fine up to Rs. 50,000 or both, an increase from the current 1-year jail or Rs. 20,000 punishment. Repeat offenders can be imprisoned for up to 3 years.

Varma (2014) in 'Census shows India Frittering away demographic dividend' reports that the traditional gender differences in education and work are diminishing. The much anticipated advantage of having an enormous population of young people seems within India's grasp. And yet the system is pressing them down. An unconscionable number of adolescents are already working although they should be studying. In rural areas, staggeringly high numbers of youth are working as agricultural labourers. And over 20 % are jobless. These are some of the findings of the latest Census 2011 data. Although the census does not give detailed educational qualifications, literacy rates among this young population are indicative. Over 90 % of adolescents and 86 % of youth are literate compared to an overall literacy rate of 63 %. This particular slice of census data provides a picture of employment trends among the young, but only in broad strokes. The most startling figure in this is that nearly four crore adolescents, making up nearly 15 % of the 10–19 age group, are working. About 80 % of these are in the 15–19 age group. This is a testimony to the fact that entry into higher education—the natural objective of this age group—is still not in their grasp. Economic compulsions force them to take up jobs, killing any dream of higher skills or education.

5.6 Street Children

Children, especially children of the deprived, marginalised and disadvantaged, occupy no space in the public debate and discourse in contemporary Indian society and polity. In spite of their omnipresence, and our daily lives being connected, these children are still invisible—the 'missing children'. We see them every day, all around us, vending flowers, newspapers or cleaning car windshields at traffic signals, and homes working as domestic help. They are in *dhabas,* herding cattle and sheep, in farms, brick kilns, railway bogies and platforms. We depend on their sweat and labour in every grain of rice and wheat, all the vegetables and meat we consume, the clothes we wear and the buildings we live in. Yet, we pretend they do not exist and accept the fact that nothing much can be done for them (Sinha 2011).

The operational research group estimated that there are 44 million working children in India, of which, 11 million are street children (UNICEF 1988). The 'Street Child' is any child for whom the street is the habitual abode and who is without adequate protection. The two major elements in this categorisation are attachment to the street and lack of protection. The term 'Street Children' along with defining a place of congregation, also includes certain set of working and living conditions. A vast majority are on the streets to make a living for themselves and their families. The returns may be paltry and may be in cash or kind. They live on the street, wasteland and public places most of the time. They work on the streets on jobs of low status and low income. Most make their way in the informal sector as petty hawkers, shoeshine boys, scavengers, thieves and even street prostitutes. There is no adult guiding them, nurturing them or protecting them.

By the nature of their jobs, they live exposed on the streets, largely on their own, unprotected. They have either continuous, intermittent or no parental contact at all. They could be earning on the streets and going back to their families at night, or they could even be children who are orphans or have been abandoned or have run away from home and have just no contact with their families. This makes them vulnerable to many dangers and abuses. They receive few services essential for their protection.

According to UNICEF, three types of children belong to the category of street children. The first is *street-living children* who ran away from their families and live alone on the streets. The second is *street-working children* who spend most of their time on the streets fending for themselves, but return home on a regular basis. The last category is *children from street families* who live on the streets with their families (Bhaskaran and Mehta 2011).

Street children are a specially vulnerable group because of the way they are forced to live, homeless, out on the street. Their mobility is high, they are without parental guidance and with little family love and affection; hence, they are subjected to the grimness of an existence not suitable for their physical and psycho-social development. They have to work to make a living and are constantly exposed to the dangers and the unhealthy life of the city and the streets. They face physical abuse, the callousness of policemen, are vulnerable to drugs and sexual abuse and other health insecurities. Due to their distrust and hatred for any form of authority, it is hard to reach this group of children.

Street children work as ragpickers, in tea stalls and dhabha, as shoeshine boys or vendors. While engaged in various trades which directly and indirectly serve the city dwellers, they do not have sufficient access even to basic services required for their healthy growth and development.

The young boys and girls struggle for their daily existence, with little or nil parental support or guidance. Life on the streets is doubly hard with cruel reality of physical and sexual trauma always lurking in the background. They do not have role models, live as social outcastes, end up disillusioned, violent and at risk of being juvenile offenders.

There are problems that are peculiar only to street children. Years of neglect and hard work leave physical as well as emotional scars. These children do not even have the basic amenities like food, clothing and shelter, things they can never take for granted. Diseases among street children range from nutrition deficiency disorders like PEM (Protein Energy Malnutrition), anaemia, night blindness, rickets and scurvy, infectious diseases, viral hepatitis, gastroenteritis, worm infestation, typhoid, upper and lower respiratory tract infections. Also featured in this milieu, are skin irregularities and diseases like scabies, boils, cuts and injuries and physical and mental disability conditions. And if this was not enough, they are vulnerable to innumerable health insecurities and risks like T.B., HIV and AIDS, drug abuse and peddling, hepatitis, skin infections, child trafficking etc. They receive very few services essential for their protection and development.

ILO-IPEC (2007) revealed that more than 60 % of the street children are ragpickers and more than 50 % of these boys were some way or other attached to different 'Rag shops' (Places to exchange recyclable materials for small amounts of cash). In many a case, the children pledge themselves to the rag shop owners by borrowing money from them. Later, with the meagre amounts of money, which the children make, they are not in a position to pay back the borrowed money. In fact, they borrow even more which make them "Bonded Child Labourers". The henchmen are there to hunt them out bringing them back, if they try to run away from the respective shop owners. An investigation by the street educators reveals a fact that apart from girl children, the cases of sexual abuse of male children are also on the rise in the city. Most of the street children live in dirt and filth. Some of them are severely malnourished, and are the victims of diseases such as tuberculosis, typhoid, malaria, jaundice, hepatitis B, kidney disorders, etc., which often go untreated and result in death. Many of them are victims of drug abuse and liquor addiction. Sexually transmitted diseases, especially HIV/AIDS, are becoming rampant. Needles to say, the vast majority of these innocent children, unless rescued and rehabilitated at an early age, are prone to become anti-social elements. The reality of the street child is the naked and vicious face of broken home, poverty and exploitation. Apart from these, street children who have no contact with their families, there are a huge number of children on the streets, flowing onto the city's streets from its slums to be engaged in various works to them an income to their families.

Using a multi-method approach, this study identifies the stresses and coping strategies of street children in Bombay, particularly of the 'children of the street'. Semi-structured in-depth interviews, focus group discussions, informal interviews and a case study were used to collect data from 73 street children, five agency social workers and three street workers. The results suggest that children face several challenges in their search for food, safety, employment, shelter and medical care. They commonly depend on their peers, non-governmental agencies and their own resourcefulness to survive on the streets. While the majority use positive mechanisms to cope with their daily stresses, some children also employ maladaptive strategies such as using alcohol, drugs and visiting prostitutes. The study also reveals that these 'children of the street' are not entirely on their own but depend on various connections with substitute family members and/or their peers to cope with life. The stresses and coping strategies of the 'children of the street' are similar to those of other street children who live with their families and work on the streets. Agencies that work with street children may need to recognise these challenges and strengths to provide needed services to improve their condition (Kombarakaran 2004).

There are no reliable statistics available on street children and street child labour, as this group is highly mobile and are likely to drift in and out of different places and occupations. India reportedly has the highest number of street children in the world. At least 18 million children live and/or work on the streets of urban India, labouring as porters at bus stops or railway stations, mechanics at auto repair shops, as street vendors, or as rag pickers picking through garbage (United Nations Development Programme 1996).

Findings of the Census of Street Children in Delhi conducted by Save the Children and Institute of Human Development (Bhaskaran and Mehta 2011) are being shared

- 50,923 children below 18 years of age were identified as street children in Delhi during 12 July to 28 August 2010. Street children in Delhi constitute nearly 0.4 % of the total population. Street children below 18 years constitute nearly 1 % of the total number of children in Delhi.
- A majority of the street children (36.03 %) belonged to the category of children from street families. Children who work on the streets constituted 29.05 % and street-living children constituted 27.91 % of the total street children population in the city.
- Only 20.5 % of the street children in Delhi were girls.
- One out of every five (20.3 %) of the street children was involved in rag picking. This was followed by street vending (15.18 %), begging (15 %), working in roadside stalls or repair shops (12.19 %), *dhabas*/hotels (6.24 %), and manufacturing units (1.22 %). Reasons why street children worked varied from survival, to funding healthcare for parents, sending remittances home (usually somewhere far-off), and earning something extra for personal and family use.
- Social class is a key determinant in leaving a child on the streets to work or live because one out of three street children was a dalit (36 %), 17 % were adivasis, and 38 % belonged to Other Backward Castes (OBCs).
- One out of every three children (34 %) was on the street due to poverty and hunger. Around 30 % were on the street in search of jobs; they had either come by themselves (17.7 %) or were sent by their parents (12.6 %), 9 % were on the street after running away from home (the reasons for running away included out

of curiosity, escape from abuse, and family issues), or they had been kidnapped, orphaned, or because of incidents such as riots, accidents and natural calamities or because they had inadvertently lost contact with their parents while travelling.

Study on Child Abuse in India (Ministry of Women and Child Development 2007) reported, that most street children, 51.8 % slept on the footpath, 17.5 % slept in night shelters and 30.7 % in other places including under flyovers and bridges, railway platforms, bus stops, parks, market places, cinema theatres etc. They did not seem to have much access to sanitary places for defecation as a result of which majority of children (70.6 %) were defecating on railway lines or road side ditches. Bathing is not a priority for most street children, they do not bathe at all.

Approaching the Problem
Street children are the most vulnerable group requiring innovative, empathetic and positive developmental approach to their rehabilitation. Any rehabilitation programme should be rooted in a strong belief:

- Each child has a potential, waiting to be harnessed
- A multi-disciplinary team and 'Whole child' approach
- Collaboration and cooperation with other NGOs working with this group
- Focusing on the strengths, resilience and adaptability among street children
- Building competencies rather than just attempting to cure
- Taking context into consideration and understanding the needs of the child.

5.7 Causes Which Render Children on the Street

1. *Socio-structural causes*: new industries not only provide new opportunities for employment but also displace traditional workers from their place of work. Dwindling opportunities in the rural areas induce migration to cities. This population along with their families, live in city slums. Rarely, migrant population manages a roof over their head in the cities, and children are found wandering on the streets. In India, an estimated one-third of the population resides in the urban areas, compared to a one-fourth a decade ago.
2. *Economic Compulsions*: In many instances, the income of the parents is insufficient to provide for the family's minimum needs. Children have to be sent to work to supplement the family's income.
3. *Poor quality of school education*: absence of school teachers from schools, poor infrastructure, unimaginative curriculum and understaffed schools are some of the several reasons resulting in a high school drop-out rate. School dropouts often end up as street children.
4. *Natural calamities* and wars result in disintegration of families; as a result, children of affected families are often compelled to be on the streets and sometimes are begging for survival.

5. *Poor parenting*: parents have been divested with the responsibility of nurturing their off springs. In families where violence is common or parents are alcoholic children suffer from trauma. In the absence of parents caring touch, the child may find home a hostile and threatening place. They may run away from their home, hence adding to the population of street children.
6. *Peer influence*: truancy, lack of parental control may find the child drifting on the street in the influence of a peer, hence providing the child with a sense of independence. It is easy in such situations to commit petty crimes while in the company of truant friends.

It is admitted today that the phenomenon of street children is not simply a consequence of poverty; rather it is the sum of different phenomena that explains it. The following causes are currently being put forward:

- rapid and uncontrolled urbanisation and migration to cities;
- lack of family support and a sense of anonymity;
- population explosion;
- family disintegration;
- unemployment and insufficient income;
- inadequacy of educational and social systems;
- maladjustment of formal education systems leading to school failure, drop-out and insufficiency or lack of care of children who have dropped out of school, etc.

5.8 Approaches to Rehabilitate the Street and Working Children

Some suitable approaches tried by the NGOs as well as the government which are quite in sync with the nature of the problem are included here:

a. Mobile schools may be opened for children who are not organised.
b. Organising training programs in slums on better parenting methods using appropriate audio-visual aids.
c. Provide training to slum dwellers for starting self help groups.
d. Opportunities for skill development of children to enhance their employability in short time.
e. Multi-purpose centres may be opened where there is concentration of street children. These centres can be equipped with toys, indoor games and other options for entertainment and development of hobbies.
f. Content of education as well as transaction of the content in the classrooms needs urgent reforms. School environment needs to be child friendly, and both the teacher needs to be motivated to teach and learner interested to learn.
g. Need more night schools for the child who cannot give up working during the day. These night schools to provide functional literacy, which not just includes 3

R's, but also vocational training, counselling, information on health and hygiene, medical checkups, legal literacy and options for small savings.

h. It is high time that India has a legislation which primarily focuses on protecting the street and working children's rights and needs.

With 'Right to Education' as a fundamental right of every child, all children between 6 and 14 years of age in India should be attending school. If all children are in school, then there would be no children wondering on the streets or working at a young and vulnerable age.

A more comprehensive and targeted approach is required to deal with the specific situations of all street children. These children must be provided necessary care and protection under the juvenile justice legislation. Instead of conducting raids and treating them as criminals, the victimisation of these children needs to be addressed and they need to be provided a protective environment. A cadre of counsellors need to be built in the years to come to prevent children from running away from homes or taking to drugs etc. and also to help children post-victimisation. Dearth of counsellors and social workers has led to a catastrophe, as there is nobody to reach out to children when they require emotional and psychological support. Necessary institutions and courses may be initiated to develop such trained personnel and place them in every school, panchayat, childline centre, police station or any other point of contact for children in distress.

A PROFILE OF 'CHILDREN ON THE STREETS' IN DELHI

Street Children are so much a part of the urban roads that they are impossible to ignore. They are a part of our day-to-day consciousness, knocking at the window panes of our cars at red lights of the crossings or selling news papers or flowers at road interjections. A small group of street children, in all 24 in number were studied to understand their living and work conditions (Chopra 2005). These children were mostly stationed at the traffic signals of busy roads of South Delhi. Some were even working at prominent temples of Delhi, begging alms. Of these 24 children, 18 were males and 6 females. 8 of them were less than 10 years of age while 16 fell in the 10–14 age group. The occupations that they were engaged in were ragpicking (n = 5), beggars (n = 3), boot-polish (n = 2), hawkers (n = 8) and others (n = 6). 9 of them had never been to school and 9 had attended school until grade V. As far as their parents education is concerned, fathers of 14 of them and mothers of 17 of them were illiterate. 9 of them had migrated from Bihar, 3 from U.P., 2 each from M.P. and Rajasthan and 2 were non-migrants. The reason for work given by children were monetary, for survival, own will, family pressure and poverty.

The children expressed harassment by police, insecurity, problems of food, clothing and shelter and people thinking of them as thieves, as some of the day-to-day challenges faced by them. They worked for more than 10 h every day. They reported that they had no time for pursuing their hobbies. Most of them disliked their jobs. Most of them were unsure about their future. They wanted to do something so that they could earn more money. Some even said they wanted to be doctor or police.

5.9 Constitutional Provisions for Child Labour

The concern of policy makers for the child labour is reflected in the following articles:

Article 24—No child below the age of 14 years shall be employed to work in any factory or mine or engaged in any other hazardous employment.
Article 39-E—The state shall direct its policy towards securing that the health and strength of workers, men and women and the tender age of children are not abused and that they are not forced by economic necessity to enter vocations unsuited to their strength.
Article 39-f—Children shall be given opportunities and facilities to develop in a healthy manner and in conditions of freedom and dignity and that childhood and youth shall be protected against moral and material abandonment.

As per The Constitution (Eighty-Sixth Amendment) Act, 2002, *Article 21A* of India's Constitution establishes free and compulsory education for all children aged 6–14 years as a fundamental right.

Article 45 of the Constitution provides for early childhood care and education for all children until they reach age six. As an amendment of *Article 51A*, the following clause shall be added, namely: "… who is a parent or guardian to provide opportunities for education to his child or, as the case may be, ward between the age of 6 and 14 years"; Article 51A fixes the responsibility on parents as well to ensure that their children are attending school.

5.10 UN Convention on the Rights of the Child

The UN adopted the Convention on the Rights of the Child (CRC) in 1989. The preamble of the CRC recognises that "every child, for the full and harmonious development of his or her personality, should grow up in a family environment, … the child should be brought up in the spirit of peace, dignity, tolerance, freedom, equality and solidarity." …. "in countries where children are living in exceptionally difficult conditions, such children need special considerations." The CRC is a wide spectrum international treaty to ensure the rights of the child. India ratified the CRC in 1992. Although the CRC does not refer to the street children but several articles therein indirectly deal with the problems of street and working children since their survival violates the protection and normal development rights of the child, the Convention includes such and many more rights of the child.

The UN CRC, article 32, deals with child labour by recognising the right of a child to be protected from economic exploitation and from doing hazardous or harmful work. This deals not only with physical harm, but also to the mental, social, spiritual and moral development of the child.

5.11 Legislative Support

Based on recommendations made by various committees on child labour, there was national consensus in favour of a uniform comprehensive legislation to prohibit the employment of children in various employments. To achieve this goal, the parliament in 1986 enacted *The Child Labour (Prohibition and Regulation) Act* (CLPRA) to prohibit the engagement of children in certain employments and to regulate the conditions of work of children in certain other employments. The Act provides for power to state governments to make rules with reference to health and safety wherever the employment of children is permitted. The salient features of the Act include:

- Defines child as a person who has not completed 14 years of age
- Prohibition of employment of children in certain occupations and process
- Regulation of conditions of work of children including fixing hours and period of work, weekly holidays, provision for resolving disputes as to age, maintenance of registers and for health and safety, etc.
- Lays down penalties for employing any child or permitting any child to work, procedures relating to offences, appointment of inspectors
- Has appointed Child Labour Technical Advisory Committee

Objectives of CLPRA include:

- Banning the employment of children, i.e. those who have not completed their fourteenth year, in specified occupations and processes
- Laying down procedures to decide modifications to the schedule of banned occupations or processes
- Regulating the conditions of work of children in employment where they are not prohibited from working

PART A of CLPRA lists out occupations in which child labour is prohibited. Some of the prohibited occupations include working transport of passengers, goods or mails by railways; cinder picking, clearing of an ash pit or building operation in the railway premises; work in a catering establishment at a railway station, involving the movement of a vendor or any other employee of the establishment from the one platform to another or into or out of a moving train; work relating to the construction of a railway station; Work relating to selling of crackers and fireworks in shops with temporary licenses; in mines, automobile workshops, foundries, slaughter houses, explosives, handloom and power loom industry; plastic units and fibreglass workshops; domestic workers or servants and dhabas (roadside eateries), restaurants, hotels, motels, tea shops, resorts, spas or other recreational centres.

PART B of the act enlists processes in which child labour is prohibited. These include beedi-making, carpet weaving, cement manufacture, including bagging of cement, cloth printing, dyeing and weaving, manufacture of matches, explosives and fireworks, mica cutting and splitting, shellac manufacture, tanning, building and construction industry, manufacturing processes using toxic metals and substances such as lead, mercury, manganese, chromium, cadmium, benzene, pesticides and asbestos. Brick kilns and roof tiles units, gem cutting and polishing, manufacture of glass, glassware including bangles, fluorescent tubes, bulbs and other similar glass products, manufacturing or handling of pesticides and insecticides, oil expelling and refinery etc. There are 65 such processes listed out in the act in which children are prohibited from working.

The act clearly spells out health and safety guidelines and directs appropriate government to make rules for the health and safety of children employed or permitted to work in any establishments. The rules may provide for cleanliness in the place of work and freedom from nuisance; disposal of wastes and affluents; ventilation and temperature; lighting; drinking water; latrine and urinals; employment of children on dangerous machines; protection of eyes; precautions in case of fire among others.

Hours and Period of Work Prescribed in the Act Include

- A child shall be permitted to work only for 2 shifts a day, each shift spread over 3 h.
- A minimum rest period of 1 h must follow the 3 h shift.
- The maximum work period must not extend beyond 6 h a day including a 1 h break.
- The section prohibits night work between 7 pm and 8 am.
- It does not allow double employment or working over time.

Penalties Under Act

Severe penalties with imprisonment extending up to 3 months or fine up to Rs. 20,000 but not less than Rs. 10,000 or both. In case a person is convicted for a second time, then he will be punished with imprisonment for 6 months extending up to 2 years.

Critique of the Act

- Almost 75 % of the child labour works as agriculture labour. CLPRA does not cover agriculture labour. Infact, it covers only 10 % of working children.
- It is not easy to impose CLPRA in unorganised sector as the units are small, dispersed and unregistered. At times, these units crop up for a very brief duration and they disappear also as fast. Since these are not registered, keeping a track of these is very difficulty.
- At times the units are small and family based. Implementing CLPRA gets difficult here. Also, the act keeps occupations and work carried out as part of family out of purview of CLPRA. So when caught in work, the child can readily be presented as part of family, or helping in household work.
- The word 'hazardous' is not clarified in the act.
- The act does not ban child labour in any sector, rather it just regulates at some places while prohibits at other instances. It would be most legitimate to assume that for the occupations not listed in the act, child labour is tacitly allowed. Do we assume that in occupations other than listed, children of any age can work?
- Elimination of child labour should be statutory in all government organisations.
- The present definitions of establishments has considerable scope for extension and enlargement.
- Determining the age of children can be a big issue as most children in India do not have birth certificates. It becomes very easy to produce fake age certificates.
- No lower age limit of children employed in non-hazardous occupations has been spelt out.

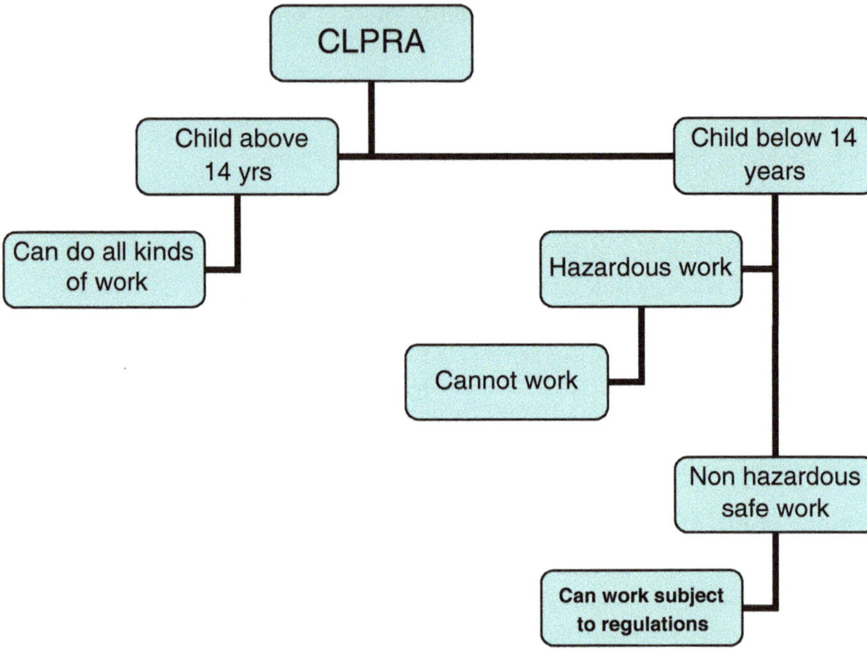

The Child Labour (Prohibition and Regulation) Act 1986 is inadequate to address the real problem. The law makes a fallacious distinction between 'hazardous' and 'non-hazardous' sectors, negating the fact that any employment of children violates a child's basic rights to survival, development, protection and participation. Prohibition of employment in the so-called 'hazardous' sectors and regulation in the 'non-hazardous' allows for employment of children and weakens law enforcement. Moreover, this is in contradiction with the Constitutional guarantee of right to education for all children in the 6–14 years age group. Therefore, an amendment to this Act is urgently needed (Ministry of Women and Child Development n.d.).

THE CHILD LABOUR (PROHIBITION AND REGULATION) AMENDMENT BILL, 2012

Presented to Lok Sabha on 13th December, 2013

Laid in Rajya Sabha on 13th December, 2013

Salient Features of the Bill are being presented:

1. The title of the act "the Child Labour (Prohibition and Regulation) Act, 1986", the "the Child and Adolescent Labour (Prohibition and Regulation) Act, 1986" shall be substituted.
2. Definition of "Adolescent" is a person who has completed the age of 14 years but not 18 years.

3. The definition of "child" to provide that child means a person who has not completed his fourteenth year of age or such age as may be specified in the Right of Children to Free and Compulsory Education Act, 2009, whichever is more.
4. The bill prohibits the employment of children below 14 years in all occupations and processes except those where the child is helping his family after school hours, in fields, home-based work, forest gatherings and apprenticeship.
5. The insertion of a new section to prohibit employment of adolescents in any hazardous occupations and processes specified in the proposed Schedule.
6. The punishment has been increased to imprisonment from at least 6 months which may be extended to 2 years (which was 3 months earlier extendable to 1 year) and a fine of Rs. 20,000–50,000 (which was Rs. 10,000–20,000 earlier) or both.

Other legislations concerning Child Labour include The Factories Act, 1948, The Mines Act, 1952, The Plantation Labour Act, 1951, The Merchant Shipping

Table 5.3 Major features of Acts relating to Child Workers[a]

Sl.No	Act	Minimum age	Hours of work	Prohibition of night work
1	The children (pledging of labour) act	15 years	No specification	–
2	The plantation labour act	12 years	Not more than 40 h per week	6 p.m–7 a.m
3	The employment of children act	15 years	–	10 p.m–7 a.m
4	The apprentices act	14 years	Up to 48 h per week	10 p.m–6 a.m
5	The beedi and cigar workers (conditions of employment) act	14 years	Not specified	7 p.m–6 a.m
6	The factories act	14 years	6 h maximum	10 p.m–7 a.m
7	The mines act	16 year	4½ h	6 p.m–6 a.m
8	The motor transport workers act	18 year	6 h	10 p.m–6 a.m
9	The shops and commercial establishment act	Varying state-wise between 12 and 15 years	30–42 h per week	Hours that constitute night work have been specified differently in different states

[a]Adapted from Dingwaney (1988)

Act, 1958, The Motor Transport Workers Act, 1961, The Beedi and Cigar Workers (Conditions of Employment) Act, 1966, The Bonded Labour System (Abolition) Act, 1976. All these acts prohibit employment of children under 14 years only, which is not in accordance with the UNCRC and the Juvenile Justice legislation in India. Therefore an amendment to these acts is required for ensuring that children are protected from economic exploitation and their rights are not violated. A brief overview of the acts is presented here (Table 5.3).

5.12 National Policy on Child Labour

National Policy on Child Labour was formulated in 1987. The Policy seeks to adopt a gradual and sequential approach with a focus on rehabilitation of children working in hazardous occupations and processes. Under the National Child Labour Project (NCLP) Scheme, special projects are set up at sites which have large concentration of working children. The project aims at withdrawing and rehabilitating children working in identified hazardous occupations and processes through special schools and finally mainstreaming them to the formal education system.

Education, vocational training, health checkups, nutrition and monthly stipends for children are essential components of the scheme.

The action plan outlined in the policy for tackling this problem is three fold. The policy identifies three main strategies to handle child labour. It recognises the need for a strict enforcement of Child Labour Act and other labour laws to ensure that children are not employed in hazardous employments, and that the working conditions of children working in non-hazardous areas are regulated in accordance with the provisions of the Child Labour Act. It also entails further identification of additional occupations and processes, which are detrimental to the health and safety of the children. Second, it emphasises the need to design and implement development programmes for the working children. As poverty is the root cause of child labour, the action plan emphasises the need to cover these children and their families also under various poverty alleviation and employment generation schemes of the government. Third, recognising that child labour is endemic in some areas, NPCL envisages starting of projects in areas of high concentration of child labour.

Pursuant to this, *National Child Labour Project Scheme* was launched in 1988 to rehabilitate the working children starting with 12 child labour endemic districts of the country. Under the Scheme, working children are identified through child labour survey, withdrawn from work and put into the special bridge schools, so as to provide them with enabling environment to join mainstream education system. In these special schools, besides formal education, they are provided stipend of Rs. 100/per month, nutrition, vocational training and regular health checkups. In addition, efforts are also made to target the families of these children so as to cover them under various developmental and income/employment generation programmes of the government. The scheme also envisages awareness generation campaigns against the evils of child labour and enforcement of child labour laws. The government decided to expand the coverage of the scheme from 100 districts in the 9th plan to 250 districts in the 10th Plan. The components of education, health care and vocational training were greatly reinforced under the 10th Plan. So far 3,74,255 children have been mainstreamed under the Scheme (Planning Commission n.d.).

5.13 Interventions and Strategies by Non-Government Organisations for Working and Street Children

Some exemplary and path-breaking initiatives have been taken by NGO's working for the care, development and rehabilitation of street and working children. *Butterflies*, which mainly works from the interstate bus terminals and railway stations in Delhi, also has its presence in Chennai, Andaman-Nicobar, Jammu and Kashmir, Kolkata and Bihar among others. It has been working with street and working children in Delhi since 1989. The philosophy at Butterflies is that it is the right of every child to have a full-fledged childhood where she/he has the right to protection, respect, opportunities and participation for his/her growth and development. Rights of working and street children are no exception. Butterflies adopts a participatory approach where they let their work be guided by the views and suggestions of children. They purport is to give the necessary tools to the vulnerable children which can equip them to facilitate change in their lives and which will make them useful and productive citizens. The effort is to ensure that children reach their full potential and are also capable to protect their lives. Attempt is also directed towards reinstating them in their families.

The approach of Butterflies is democratic, participatory, rights based, and non-institutional. When in contact with any child, the first effort is to build a rapport and encourage a child to return to his/her family as it is believed that family is the best and the right institution for every child to grow up in. In case this is not possible due to the child being an orphan, or belonging to a dysfunctional family or rejected by step parents, the child is encouraged to get associated with the programme of Butterflies. As the first step, every child is encouraged to go to a formal school or get enrolled in the National Institute of Open School (NIOS). The child benefits from the various programmes of Butterflies such as health, participation in media-related activities, legal aid, counselling, cultural, art, sports, vocational training and Children's Development Bank. The alternate education programme is conducted at places where street children are available, like the bus stations, rail stations, etc. the curriculum has been developed within the framework of the formal primary school syllabus in consultation with children, includes vocational training, life skill education and computer literacy. Children's theatre group is an active part of Butterflies through which children's feelings get a voice. Children also come out with a newspaper and radio programme. Children run their own thrift and saving bank where children save money and can even borrow money at some interest. Butterflies publishes a periodical journal called My Name is Today (MNT), a compilation of news items on children in Indian and Foreign Newspapers/Magazines. It has a mobile health team which regularly visits street children. Children are trained on culinary and catering skills as well.

Butterflies also has an emergency resilience centre which houses childline and is a short stay crisis centre; night shelter for homeless children and night outreach programme (http://www.butterflieschildrights.org/).

Deepalaya was established in 1979 in urban slums in Delhi and has also made inroads into rural development in the states of Haryana and Uttarakhand. Deepalaya is working on issues affecting the urban and rural poor, with a special focus on children. They provide institutional care for the vulnerable sections namely the children who are under difficult circumstances like children of the drug addicts, or children with HIV+ parents or their parents are in jail or have run away. Deepalaya also works towards the care and inclusion of the differently abled. They also work for the capacity building of functionaries of various small and young NGO's and networking, advocacy and policy intervention. The long-term strategy of Deepalaya is emancipating the whole community, through interventions at three levels, i.e. the child, the family and the community with extra emphasis on child specially girl child, street child and disabled child.

Deepalaya enrolls students with the National Open School for both academic and vocational streams. As part of institutional care, at Haryana, they run a shelter home for street children at Deepalaya Gram, in the village Gusbethi. Deepalaya Gram today is home to over 80 children (both boys and girls) in difficult circumstances, e.g. street and runaway children, victims of child abuse, children of lifetime convicts, HIV/AIDS patients, sex workers and other vulnerable categories. At the centre, children are provided with formal and informal education, life skill training, counselling and medical care. Moreover, they support the severely mentally challenged with institutional care and provide the elderly a family-like atmosphere—so that they can lead a mutually supportive and emotionally satisfying life in a community. The vocational centres of Deepalaya are providing training in computer hardware/software, air conditioning and refrigeration, beauty culture, tailoring and fashion designing, photography and videography, electricals and electronics. An additional class on spoken English is also imparted every week. The courses are structured to compliment the needs of an individual as well as the market demands. The trained students then are helped to find a job. Caring for children with special abilities became a part of Deepalaya 15 years ago, when disability was included as a programme. The programme aims to be that platform from where the special children could jumpstart their journey and be mainstreamed into regular education. Deepalaya is working for gender equity in which they want women to have enhanced socio-cultural, economic and political opportunities, enabling them to take crucial decisions which affect them and their families.

The *Mamidipudi Venkatarangaiya Foundation* (MVF), a registered trust, was established in 1981 in memory of educationist and historian Prof. Mamidipudi Venkatarangaiya. It began as a research institution on issues relating to social transformation. Today, the Foundation is building the capacities of the community in rural and urban areas for abolition of child labour by universalising school education. It also works towards empowering women.

MV foundation adopts ‘area based approach’ in which it takes in its universe all children in the age 5–14 years. This approach deems all children out of school as child labour and understands that being out of school is intrinsically hazardous to their growth and well-being. It keeps track of all school going children and ensures that all of them reach class 10 without disruption. It feels that any child dropping out of school could get pushed to join child labour force. MVF does not set up parallel institutions to the schools, social welfare hostels, gram panchayats and other state institutions. The MVF program has blended with the existing government programs enriching rather than supplanting them.

The major campaign of the MVF is total abolition of child labour. The panacea offered for the malaise is that if all children in the age group 5–14 years are school, then they would not be at work. The MVF has the firm conviction that abolition of child labour and the realisation of the right to education are closely interrelated. The MVF mobilised mass support to establish a norm that all children should attend full-time school. As a spin off of this effort, collectives of villagers formed Child

Rights Protection Forums (CRPF) from different parts of the State of Andhra Pradesh, Maharashtra, Orissa and Assam. The members of the CRPF include gram panchayat members, school committee members, youth, school teachers, erstwhile employers, women group members and political leaders. Cutting across caste and class barriers, the members of the CRPF are the conscience keepers in the village playing the role of spokespersons for child rights in the community. The CRPF members monitor all child-related institutions at the village level, resolve problems relating to children's needs, ensure no child rights violations occur and share such experiences at various forums. The MVF provides intervention in health for children up to 3 years of age, pregnant women and adolescent girls.

HAQ which means 'right' in Urdu is a national-level organisation working for the rights of children. HAQ strives to propel child rights into all mainstream development efforts, governmental and non-governmental, and place it on the centre stage of national debate. Performance of any state related to realisation of rights is linked to governance. It has been recognised across the world that improved or good governance is a precondition for sustained poverty reduction and a peaceful and stable society. HAQ believes that it is primarily the duty of the state that all children realise their rights. HAQ has engaged itself in monitoring the performance the performance of states on child rights. It also analyses gaps and documents them and brings it to the notice of the government. It believes that child rights can be realised through law, policy and subsequent action. HAQ works with children in the age group of birth–18 years. It works within the constitutional framework of India as well as the UNCRC. The chief concerns redressed by HAQ are child labour, education, children in conflict with law, abandoned and orphaned children, girl child, child trafficking and victims of child abuse and violence. It targets its goals through advocacy, research and training and capacity building and providing legal aid.

References

Anker, R., & Melkas, H. (1996). *Economic incentives for children and families to eliminate or reduce child labour*. Geneva: International Labour Organisation.

AusAid (1997). Child labour in Asia: Some perspectives on selected countries. *International Development Issues, 49*.

Bhaskaran, R., & Mehta, B. (2011). *Surviving the streets a census of street children in Delhi*. New Delhi: The Institute for Human Development and Save the Children.

Biswas, S. A. (2007). Child worker-poverty and hunger: A study among the stone crushers of Balasan river bed. In S. C. Singh (Ed.), *Rights of child*. New Delhi: Serial Publication.

Burra, N. (2002). Rights versus needs: Is it in the 'best' interest of the child? In N. Kabeer, G. B. Nambissan, & R. Subrahmanian (Eds.), *Child labour and right to education in South Asia-Needs versus rights?*. New Delhi: Sage Publication.

Census India (2001). Retrieved January 12, 2009, from www.censusindia.net.

Census India (2011). Retrieved from http://censusindia.gov.in/.

Chopra, G. (2005). *A profile of the street child on the streets of Delhi*. Paper presented at a symposium organised by Katha. New Delhi.

Dingwaney, M. (1988). *Children of darkness: A manual on child labour in India*. New Delhi: Rural Labour cell.

ILO-IPEC (2007). *International programme on the elimination of child labour and street children*. Evaluation Report IPEC in India.

Jaiswal, P. (2000). *Child labour-a sociological study*. New Delhi: Shipra Publications.

Kombarakaran, F. A. (2004). Street children of Bombay: Their stresses and strategies of coping. *Children and Youth Services Review Volume 26*(9), 853–871.

Ministry of Women and Child Development, Government of India (2007). *A study on child abuse: India 2007*. Retrieved from http://wcd.nic.in/childabuse.pdf.

Ministry of Women and Child Development, Government of India. (n.d.). *A report of the working group on development of children for the eleventh five year plan (2007–2012)*. Retrieved from http://wcd.nic.in/WG_Report.pdf.

National Sample Survey Office (2014). *Employment and unemployment situation in India (NSS 68th round July 2011–June 2012)*. Ministry of statistics and programme implementation. Retrieved from http://mospi.nic.in/Mospi_New/upload/nss_report_554_31jan14.pdf.

Pandey, N., & Haider, F. (2014, October 10). The award will benefit the movement, says Kailash Satyarthi. *Hindustan Times*.

Planning Commission (n.d.). *Report of the working group on child labour for the 11th five year plan*. Government of India. New Delhi. Retrieved from http://planningcommission.nic.in/aboutus/committee/wrkgrp11/wg11_rpchlab.pdf.

Rehman, M. M., Rehman, K., & Begum, S. M. (2002). *Child labour and child rights. A compendium*. New Delhi: Manak Publications Pvt. Ltd.

Singh, M. K. (2014, November 12). Government may bring total ban on Child Labour. *The Times of India*.

Sinha, S. (2002). Schools as institutions for the elimination of child labour: The experience of the M.V. foundation in the Ranga Ready District. In N. Kabeer, G. B. Nambissan, & R. Subrahmanian (Eds.), *Child labour and right to education in South Asia-Needs versus rights?* New Delhi: Sage Publication.

Sinha, S. (2011). Getting children out of work and into schools. In E. G. Thukral (Ed.), *Every right for every child*. New Delhi: Routledge.

UNICEF (1988). Annual report. In R. Agarwal (Ed.), *Street children: A socio-psychological study*, 1st edn (1999). Delhi SHIPRA Publication.

United Nations Development Programme. (1996). *Human Development Report 1996*. New York: Oxford University Press.

Varma, S. (2014, November 2). Census shows India Frittering away demographic dividend. *Times of India*.

Voll, K. (1999). *Against child labour: India and international dimensions and strategies*. New Delhi: Mosiac Books.

Weiner, M. (1991). *The child and the state in India*. New Delhi: Oxford University Press.

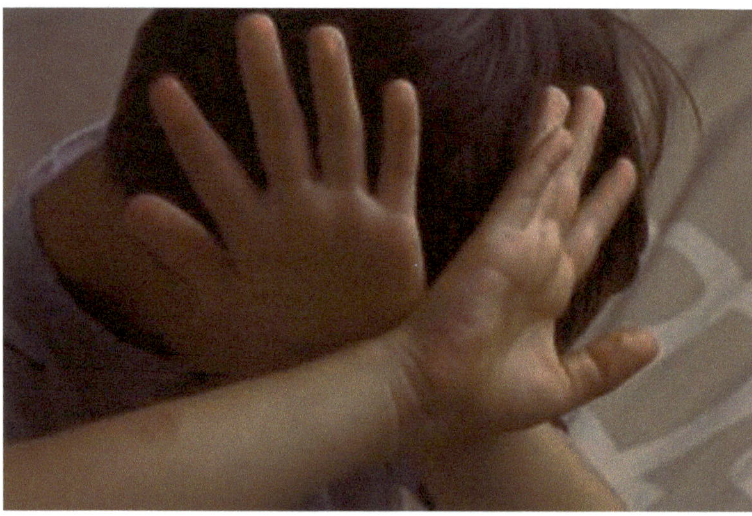

UNITED NATIONS CONVENTION ON THE RIGHTS OF THE CHILD

Article 40 (Juvenile justice): Children who are accused of breaking the law have the right to legal help and fair treatment in a justice system that respects their rights. Governments are required to set a minimum age below which children cannot be held criminally responsible and to provide minimum guarantees for the fairness and quick resolution of judicial or alternative proceedings

Chapter 6
Children in Conflict with Law: The Child Offender

Abstract This chapter is on the sensitive area about children taking to crime and coming in conflict with law. The magnitude of the problem is put up front. The factors responsible for children coming in conflict with law are discussed. The concept and principles on which juvenile justice rests are presented, describing the difference between restorative justice and retributive justice. Children in conflict with law and children in need of care and protection are differentiated. The salient features of the Juvenile Justice act (1986 and 2000) are discussed in detail and the loopholes also are critiqued. The proposed Juvenile Justice 2014 bill which is pending with the parliament is also presented. The contentious issue of whether the age of juvenility must be brought down is dispassionately presented, along with the findings of adolescent brain research. The chapter outlines the institutional provisions like shelter homes, children's homes and observation homes for children in conflict with law and children in need of care and protection. The chapter also briefly sketches non-institutional care options like adoption, foster care and sponsorship for children. NGOs working for adolescents and youth like Prayas, ICCW and Manzil are profiled at the end of the chapter.

Keywords Children in conflict with law · Juvenile justice

From Jesus to Gandhi, before and after, every sublime soul has beheld divinity in juvenility. Yet, we have young offenders!! What went wrong? There are many questions that come to ones mind. Is it poverty? But children of rich parents also take to crime. Is it poor upbringing? Is it peer pressure? Is it urbanisation and marginalisation? Young children are committing crime and this is a testimony of state of social and moral fabric of the society.

Vagrancy, delinquency and crime are emerging as serious social problems in India. Children who are run away, abandoned or come from broken homes form a vulnerable group.

Children in conflict with law or the child offenders are most commonly referred to as juvenile delinquents. As per the Juvenile Justice (Care and Protection of Children) Act, 1986, males below 16 years and females below 18 years were considered as a

G. Chopra, *Child Rights in India*, DOI 10.1007/978-81-322-2446-4_6

child. Covered under the Juvenile Justice (Care and Protection of Children) Act, 2000, the age has been increased for boys also to 18 years hence the number of such children in conflict with law has increased over the years, from 17,203 in 1994 to 30,943 in 2004. Not only has the number of offenders gone up, even the percentage of juvenile crimes to total crimes has virtually doubled from 0.5 to 1.0 %. While part of this increase in juvenile crimes may be attributed to the inclusion of boys aged 16–18 years in the definition of child in the revised juvenile justice law of 2000, the fact remains that the rate of juvenile crimes is fairly high and more and more children in the 16–18 years category are coming in conflict with law (Table 6.1).

Juveniles Apprehended Under IPC and SLL Crimes by Sex (1994–2004)
As per National Crime Records Bureau (2013), a total of 41,639 juveniles were apprehended in 2013 under IPC and Special laws (SLL) of which only 4.3 % were girls. Of these, bulk of juvenile (28,830 which is 66.3 %) were in the age group 16–18 years. Juvenile crime under IPC has risen from 27,936 in 2012 to 31,725 in 2013.

6.1 Factors Responsible for Children Coming in Conflict with Law

To be born in happy and comfortable homes and a caring society is not a destiny that all children enjoy. There are several social and economic factors that push children to committing crimes. Inadequate care and protection systems create multiple levels of

Table 6.1 Incidence and rate of Juvenile Delinquency under IPC (1994–2004)

S. No.	Year	Incidence of		Percentage of juvenile crimes to total crimes
		Juvenile crimes	Total cognizable crimes	
1	1994	8,561	16,35,251	0.5
2	1995	9,766	16,95,296	0.6
3	1996	10,024	17,09,576	0.6
4	1997	7,909	17,19,820	0.5
5	1998	9,532	17,78,815	0.5
6	1999	8,888	17,64,629	0.5
7	2000	9,267	17,71,084	0.5
8	2001	16,509	17,69,308	0.9
9	2002	18,560	17,80,330	1.0
10	2003	17,819	17,16,120	1.0
11	2004	19,229	18,32,015	1.0

Source Crime in India 2004
Note As per revised definition of juveniles in the Juvenile Justice (Care and Protection of Children) Act, 2000, boys in the age group of 16–18 years have been included

violence against children and bring girls and boys into conflict with the law. Broken homes, poverty, illiteracy, living with criminal parents, harsh disciplining, physical abuse and neglect, migration from villages to urban slum squatters, loss of identity in cities and hence a search for a sense of belongingness albeit a negative one, peer influence, exposure to anti-social activities, gang membership and lack of parental guidance could be some of the many reasons which result in inadequate care and protection mechanisms bringing children in conflict with law.

In India, a vast majority of children are impoverished, which puts them in especially difficult circumstances where they are in crying need for care and protection. Children are destitute, neglected and marginalised, often living away from their parents, deprived of family care, shelter, clothing, food, health and education. All these factors put them at a greater risk of taking to criminal activities.

The impact of media on children is an important factor. Violence in today's cinema, acceptable aberrations shown in TV serials, advertisements, fashion shows and crime-related TV programmes. Many times crime is glorified rather than abhorred. All of these give ideas to the young mind.

In India, at times the policing system treats a child who is a victim of crime in the same manner as a child who has committed a crime. Children who are used, trafficked and forced into begging, drug peddling, prostitution etc. are actually victims of crime. These children cannot be treated in the same manner as those who are caught committing a crime and are juvenile offenders. At times, some children also become victims of legal apathy when they could be detained for crimes which they have not committed. The overwhelming majority of children in the criminal justice system do not belong there. The vast majority of youngsters are deprived of their liberty, who have not been convicted of a crime and are yet to be brought to trial. Misuse and overuse of detention and lack of alternatives put large numbers of boys and girls at risk of violence. At times child beggars and vagrant children are put in the same category as children who have committed serious offences. Such children face the discriminatory component of law and could then take on to become regular offenders. Also, booking children for minor crimes decreases their chances to become productive, contributing adults, and is a disservice to communities. At times, children could be falsely implicated so that police can claim that they have taken some action on cases pending with them. Inadequacy of law and the behaviour of police add to the woes of children.

In the year 2004, out of the total juveniles involved in various crimes, 9,273 were illiterate and 10,771 had education up to primary level. These two categories have accounted for 64.8 % of the total juveniles arrested during the year 2004. Children living with parents/guardians (23,701) have accounted for 76.6 % of the total juveniles arrested. The share of homeless children who were involved in various crimes was just 7.5 %. A large chunk of juveniles (72.3 %) belonged to the poor family whose annual income was up to Rs. 25,000/. The share of juveniles hailing from middle-income group (Rs. 50,000–2,00,000) was 8.7 %. The share of juveniles from upper middle income (Rs. 2,00,000–3,00,000) and upper income (above Rs. 3,00,000) was considerably low at 0.3 and 0.02 %, respectively (National Crime Records Bureau 2004). These figures indicate that a vast majority of children coming in conflict with law are either illiterate or have low levels of literacy and majority belong to poor families.

As per National Crime Records Bureau (2013), out of the total juveniles involved in various crimes, 8,392 were illiterate and 13,984 had education up to primary level. These two categories together accounted for 51.9 % of the total juveniles arrested during the year 2013. Children living with parents (35,244) have accounted for 81.0 % of the total juveniles apprehended. The share of homeless children (2,462) who were involved in various crimes was just 5.7 %. A large number of juveniles (50.2 %) belonged to the poor families whose annual income was up to Rs. 25,000. The share of juveniles from families with income between Rs. 25,000 and 50,000 was 27.3 %. The share of juveniles hailing from income group Rs. 50,000 to 2,00,000 was 20.2 %. The share of juveniles from families in income group Rs. 2,00,000–3,00,000 was 1.4 % and income group above Rs. 3,00,000 was 0.6 %.

6.2 What Do We Mean by 'Juvenile Justice'?

The term juvenile justice emanates from the word 'juvenis', which is a Latin word for young, and hence, it is a justice system for the young. Juvenile justice is a framework and a system that protects, reforms and rehabilitates the young. The concept of juvenile justice is derived from the belief that both problems of delinquency as well as children and youth in abnormal circumstances cannot be resolved by the traditional processes of criminal law. The system is not designed to deal with young offenders alone. Its role is to provide specialised and preventive treatment services for children and young persons as a means of 'secondary prevention, rehabilitation and socialization' (HAQ: Centre for Child Rights and Leher, n.d.).

According to the United Nations Convention on the Rights of the Child, "State Parties recognize the right of every child alleged as, accused of, or recognized as having infringed the penal law to be treated in a manner consistent with the promotion of the child's sense of dignity and worth, which reinforces the child's respect for the human rights and fundamental freedoms of others and which takes into account the child's age and the desirability of promoting the child's reintegration and the child's assuming a constructive role in society".

The term "juvenile justice" would refer to all measures taken by the state and society specially for the juvenile offenders. It would include legislations, norms and standards, procedures, mechanisms and provision, institutions and bodies which the state machinery has developed for the juvenile offenders. It is important to note that juvenile justice includes the measures to prevent children from coming in conflict with law. Hence, it also includes efforts to address the root causes of offending behaviour and implement measures to prevent such behaviour.

Government responses to children in conflict with the law almost always involve dealing with the child through a formal justice system. Due to their specific needs and circumstances, children and adolescents should always be treated outside the regular adult criminal system.

Fundamental Principles of a Juvenile Justice System

- The juvenile justice system shall be child-centred that all actions pertaining to the child have to be in his/her best interest.
- Children need to be treated with humanity. They are not hardened criminals and have a life time ahead to them to put their lives together.
- Children to be kept away in confinement with liberty taken away only as the last resort and for the shortest period possible. Detention only as a last resort, for the shortest time possible.
- The child should have access to legal assistance.
- No capital punishment. Currently there are only 6 countries in the world that still have juvenile death penalty.
- No life imprisonment. About 12 countries in the world allow for minors to be given a life sentence with no provision for release.
- There should be reduced pre-trial detention. Children should not be kept away from their families due to delay in trial as this moves them away from protective societal networks, reinforces stigmatisation and discrimination.
- Attempt should be to reach the root cause of offending behaviour, explore circumstances which led to the offence, the familial conditions, the motivations for offending and what corrections can be made hence forth.
- There should be diversion and alternative to detention in the form of social work, and involving children in socially meaningful activities. This would also help mainstream the child and reduce alienation.
- Specialisation and multidisciplinary approach: when the 'criminal' is a child, then a multidisciplinary team of people is recommended which should try to help this child. The team should not only just include the police and the judiciary but also a social worker, a psychiatrist, a child psychologist, persons belonging to the civil society like the teachers, panchayat members, head masters, lawyers, probation officers to name some. What this refers to is not a single juvenile justice system, but multiple, inter-connected systems.
- After care and reintegration to prevent re-offending.

'Restorative Justice' Approach to Juvenile Justice Versus 'Retributive Justice'
Criminal justice systems in many countries are 'retributive'—i.e. they are concerned with punishing the offender, concentrating more on the crime itself than on the people involved. However, this is often not in the best interests of the victim, the

offender, or society in general. This would be most counter productive specially in the context of the child offender.

In the 'restorative justice' approach, the focus is on 'restoring' damaged relationships and make things right as much as possible. This approach looks for solutions to restore harmony and to rehabilitate the offender as well as the victim. The ultimate aim of restorative justice is healing. It emphasises the active participation of the offender, victim and community in listening to the facts and feelings of those involved, and identifying and implementing solutions which balance the best interests of all sides involved. The offender takes responsibility for their crime and makes amends to the victim and to the community. It allows for repentance, forgiveness and reintegration. Restorative justice is much more likely to reduce re-offending.

Restorative justice applies to people of all ages but it is especially important in relation to young offenders as it provides the option of having a lasting impact on their emotional and moral development which is positive, rather than negative: it can stop the process of a young offender turning into an adult offender.

Restorative justice involves these strands (www.juvenilejusticepanel.org, retrieved on 4 January 2014):

- *Prevention*—In order to ensure that boys and girls do not come into conflict with the law in the first place and therefore do not come into contact with the formal criminal justice system;
- *Diversion*—To ensure that at all possible stages girls and boys are diverted away from the formal justice system and into community-based and restorative processes that address effectively the causes of their behaviours and identify strategies at the community level to effectively prevent re-offending e.g. victim-offender mediation, family group conferencing, referral to an NGO or other community or social programme, including substance abuse programmes, family reunification, community service, police warnings, behaviour contracts, conditional or unconditional release; and
- *Protection*—Of children who are already in conflict with the law from human rights violations, focusing on their development in order to deter them from re-offending and to promote their rehabilitation and smooth their reintegration back into society e.g. care, guidance and supervision orders; probation; community service orders; financial penalties, compensations and restitution; intermediate treatment and other treatment orders; orders to participate in group counselling and other similar activities; orders concerning foster care, living communities or other educational settings.

Restorative justice is about balancing the rights of offenders, rights of victims and concern for public safety and crime prevention. Police officers have a key role to play in this important process. Their actions can make the difference between a good outcome and a bad outcome for all those involved.

The UN Guidelines on the Prevention of Juvenile Delinquency (Riyadh Guidelines), 1990 cover both general, 'developmental' prevention (addressing the root causes of the creation of social problems such as poverty and inequality) and 'responsive' prevention (programmes targeted at those children most at risk of coming into conflict with the law). The Riyadh Guidelines encourage a positive emphasis on socio-economic support and quality of life rather than a 'negative' crime prevention approach. They cover virtually all social areas such as family, school, community, media, social policy, legislation and juvenile justice administration.

6.3 Legal Reforms Recommended in Laws for Juvenile Offenders

Laws and legal systems fashioned according to norms of justice, and international human rights represent a universal common heritage for ensuring that state power does not emerge as authoritarian. It is vital that the standards set in the CRC are incorporated in the national legal system. Keeping in view the UNCRC and other UN guidelines on juvenile justice (including the Riyadh Guidelines and Beijing Rules), any laws relating to juvenile offenders should incorporate these principles for according justice to them:

- *Ensure the protection of all children*, regardless of gender, race, ethnicity, sexuality, disability and social, economic or any other status from discriminatory laws and practices.
- Ensure that children below the age of 18 are accorded the protection of *separate justice provisions* and are not treated as adults criminals.
- *De-criminalise* 'vagrancy', 'loitering', victims of commercial sexual exploitation and status offences such as truancy and 'running away'; and 'survival' activities like beggary.
- *Outlaw the death penalty and life imprisonment* for crimes committed by children under the age of 18 at the time of the offence and commute any existing death sentences passed on children.

The Beijing rules are not a treaty and are not binding per se. These provide that:

- A comprehensive social policy is in place to ensure the well-being of the juveniles.
- Reaction to juvenile offenders is always to be in proportion to both the circumstances of the offender and the offence.
- Police officers who deal extensively with juveniles shall be specially instructed and trained.

- Detention pending trial is to be used as a last measure of last resort and for the shortest period of time.
- The placement of juveniles in an institution is always to be a last resort and for the minimum necessary period.
- Necessary assistance such as housing, vocational training and employment is to be provided to facilitate the rehabilitative process (Mitra 1999).

6.4 The Indian Law

6.4.1 The Juvenile Justice Act, 1986

The Juvenile Justice (Care and Protection) Act, 1986 was enacted by the Parliament of India in recognition of the commitment that the country has made in respect of the care protection, treatment, development and rehabilitation of neglected children and juvenile in conflict with law. The act marked the beginning of a new era in seeking to promote the 'best interests of the juveniles'. The act brought about a uniform juvenile justice system through out the country by consolidating some of the major provisions and clauses of the Indian constitution and all related legislations on the subject.

Objective of the Juvenile Justice Act

- To lay down a uniform framework for juvenile justice in the country so as to ensure that no child under any circumstances is lodged in jail or police lock up.
- To provide for a specialised approach towards the prevention and treatment of juvenile delinquency.
- To spell out the machinery and infrastructure required for the care, protection, treatment, development and rehabilitation of various categories of children coming under the purview of the JJ system.
- To establish norms and standards for the administration of juvenile justice.
- To develop appropriate linkages and coordination between the formal system of juvenile justice and voluntary agencies.
- To constitute special offences in relation to juveniles.

Salient features of the Juvenile Justice Act 1986:

1. Envisages a comprehensive approach to justice for juveniles in situations of abuse, exploitation and social maladjustment.
2. JJA totally renounces the term 'custody' and replaces it with 'care'.

3. As per the JJA, a 'juvenile' means a boy who has not attained the age of 16 years and a girl who has not attained the age of 18 years.
4. It categorically spells out that no juvenile is to be kept in a police station for more than 24 h.
5. The JJA classifies juveniles in two categories; '*neglected juveniles*' and '*delinquent juveniles*'. 'Neglected Juvenile' is a child found begging, is a destitute, has inadequate parental support and guidance, who lives in a brothel or with a prostitute, or is likely to get exploited for criminal and immoral purposes. 'Delinquent Juvenile' is a child found to have committed an offence which is punishable as per Indian laws.
6. It stipulates two main authorities in the administration of juvenile justice; '*Juvenile Welfare Boards*' to deal with the neglected juvenile and the '*Juvenile Court*' to deal with juvenile delinquents and to decide on the cases concerning them.
7. JJA stipulates the establishment of certain institutions which are as follows: '*Juvenile homes*' for the reception of neglected juveniles so as to provide them with shelter, food, education, counselling, medical care, vocational training and rehabilitation, '*Special homes*' for the reception of delinquent juvenile so as to provide them with shelter, food, education, counselling, medical care, vocational training and rehabilitation and opportunities for reformation, '*observation homes*' are meant for the reception of juveniles during the pendency of any inquiry regarding them, '*after care organisation*' are meant to take care of the juveniles after they have been discharged from juvenile homes or special homes with a view of enabling them to have an honest, industrious and useful life.
8. It lays lot of emphasis on involvement of voluntary agencies in welfare of neglected, marginalised and socially maladjusted children. The act permits that the neglected juvenile can be brought before a competent authority not just by the police but by any person authorised to do so.
9. As per the act, no juvenile can be sentenced to death or life imprisonment, or committed to prison in default of payment or fine imposed or furnishing security.
10. No juvenile is to be tried like an adult. The following factors are considered when making an order under the act: age of the juvenile, the state of physical and mental health of the juvenile, the circumstances under which the juvenile lives, the report made by the probation officer and any other circumstances.

The act provides a protective cover for the neglected and the delinquent juveniles. Offences committed by the adults against the juveniles are now to be punished in a stringent manner. As per Chapter IV of the JJA, these offences and their corresponding punishments are as follows:

- Cruelty to juvenile (assault, abandoning etc.) would call for Imprisonment up to 6 months or fine or both.
- Employment of juveniles for begging would call for Imprisonment up to 3 years and fine.

- Giving intoxicating or narcotic drugs or psychotropic substances to juveniles would call for imprisonment up to 3 years and fine.

The history of the implementation of the Juvenile Justice Act is a history of hopes unrealised and dreams unfulfilled (Bajpai 2006). In light of the various loopholes in the act and its implementation, the Juvenile Justice Act, 2000 was passed, which is summed up briefly.

6.4.2 The Juvenile Justice Act, 2000

In this act, 'juvenile' or 'child' means a person who has not completed 18 years of age, where as the 'juvenile in conflict with law' means a person who is alleged to have committed an offence. Thus there are two categories of children:

- 'juvenile' for children in conflict with law; and
- 'child' for children in need of care and protection.

The act has now included children with disabilities, sick children, children tortured and abused and children affected by natural calamities and armed conflicts also in its list of children in need of care and protection.

JJ act 2000 has brought in many changes to make the juvenile justice system more child friendly. These include the following:

- As act defines the child as a person up to 18 years of age. The disparity vis-à-vis defining the child between boys and girls has been removed. The JJ act now conforms with the CRC on the chronological definition of the child which is 18 years.
- The 1986 act classified children in need of care and protection as 'juvenile', while the 2000 act refers to them as 'child'.
- The 1986 act classified children in conflict with law as 'delinquent', while the 2000 act refers to them as 'juvenile'.
- The JJ mechanism has also been revisited. As per 1986 act, the children in need of care and protection were taken care by the 'juvenile welfare boards'. The 2000 act has constituted the 'child welfare committees' for their care and protection.
- The children in conflict with law were produced for justice in front of 'juvenile courts' as per the 1986 act. As per the 2000 act, the 'juvenile justice boards'.
- Non-institutionalised services are an important part for the social reintegration of the child. A major change that has been brought about is that the Juvenile Justice boards can now give the orphaned, abandoned and neglected children in adoption. Parents can adopt the child of any sex irrespective of the sex of the existing biological children. Also single parents can adopt.

- The new act recognises the inherent potential of the young child and includes group counselling and community service as part of rehabilitation and social integration strategy.
- There is provision of children's homes and shelter homes for children in need of care and protection. But the prime objective of these institution care organisations is to restore the child to their family. The monitoring and evaluation of these homes are to be done by the respective state governments.

The juvenile in conflict with law is brought before the '*Juvenile Justice Boards*'. The JJBs consist of a bench of metropolitan magistrate or a judicial magistrate of the first class and two social workers of which at least one should be a woman. The judges and the social workers who are the members of the JJBs are so selected so that they are sensitive to the social realities in which children live, understand child psychology and have at least 7 years of experience of working with children. As soon as the juvenile in conflict with law is apprehended by the police, he shall be placed in charge of the special juvenile police, who shall then inform the parents of the child and also ask them to be present at the board. A probation officer then seeks information about the circumstances in which the child lives, information related to his parents and family antecedents. The orders that can be passed for juvenile in conflict with law include the following:

- Allow the juvenile in conflict with law to go home after counselling and some admonition;
- Order the juvenile to perform community service;
- Order the parent of the juvenile to pay a fine;
- Order the juvenile in conflict with law to remain under the supervision of a probation officer for up to 3 years; and
- To be placed in a fit institution/special homes.

It has been specified that no juvenile in conflict with law will be sentenced to death penalty or life imprisonment.

The JJ act also provides for setting up of *Special Juvenile Police Units* (SJPUs) in every district and city to coordinate and upgrade the police force to manage children who come in conflict/contact with law.

However, many loopholes still remain in the JJ act 2000. The act has not clearly laid down the age of innocence, i.e. the minimum age below which the act is not applicable. The act still remains dependent on adult criminal justice system, the police, lawyers, magistrate etc. there is no concept of parental responsibility in the act. CWC members are to play a very important role in the implementation of the act. Their posts remain adhoc and honorary. Training of functionaries on child development, child welfare and child rights is not a part of the act. Although adoption has been included in the act, the act remains silent on inter-country adoption. As the adoption by Muslims, Christians, Parsis and Jews is not covered by any act, it is not clear if the JJ act 2000 can give them a right to adopt which has not been conferred on them by any other law directly. Also with the special law for Hindu adoption, Hindu Adoption and Maintenance act, 1956 it is not clear that which law would take precedence. There is no linkage between JJ act 2000 and other acts related to children on child labour, health, adoption, child abuse, disabilities and education. The act should have provided for an upper limit within which preliminary enquiry is completed. Children are kept in observation homes for long periods of time.

6.4.3 Provisions for Rehabilitation of the Child—Institutional Care Options in the JJ Act

Chapter IV of the JJ act 2000 provides for social integration and rehabilitation of the child in the *shelter homes, children's homes, observation homes and special homes.*

Shelter homes: The JJ act provides financial assistance to voluntary organisations to set up shelter homes for children without parental care, run away children, migrant children. These are institutions providing residential care for temporary period. Shelter homes offer day and night shelter facilities to children in need of this kind of support.

Children's Homes: A large number of children who enter the JJ system through the CWCs are in need of residential care during the course that the enquiry is taking or for long-term treatment, education, training and development. Children's homes are established to provide shelter for children in need of care and protection. The JJ act empowers the states to set up Children's homes either by itself or in collaboration with NGOs in every district as residential care service for neglected, abandoned children. These homes are to serve as homes away from homes and are to be geared to provide comprehensive services for complete development and mainstreaming of children.

Observation Homes: are to be established under the act for the juvenile in conflict with law by the state governments in alliance with NGOs in every district. Observation homes are for housing the juvenile in conflict with law while the case is under consideration and the decision is pending. Juveniles in conflict with law are housed in an 'observation' home temporarily before being handed over to a parent or guardian. The observation home would keep the juvenile at its premise and would be especially useful if the parent of the juvenile is not available/competent to take charge on the juvenile pending enquiry. During this time, age of the juvenile is also ascertained so as to decide on what legal action needs to be taken. Due consideration is given to physical and mental health and the degree of offence committed.

Special Homes: At times, juveniles convicted of a crime are ordered to be sent to a 'special home' for a period not more than 3 years so as to reform and rehabilitate them. Children are provided with residential care, treatment, education and vocational training in these homes.

After Care: The JJ act provides institutional care for juveniles in need of care and protection up to the age of 18 years. These juveniles have no where to go to on turning 18 years. It is also observed that institutional life does not equip them to meet the challenges of the real world which they would have to face on their own. After care service is to prepare children to have a transition from institutional life to independent life. Organisations are identified for running after care homes for such individuals. The ICPS scheme provides grant Rs. 2000 per child per month to these after care organisations to meet the needs of these individuals.

6.4.4 Non-institutional Care Support and Rehabilitation Services—Adoption, Foster Care and Sponsorship in the JJ Act

Keeping in spirit with the UNCRC, it is in the best interest of the child that the child should live with her family. But when the child is orphaned, has been abandoned by the parents or has been left as a destitute due to war, terrorism or civil unrest, and in these circumstances, when the child does not have the biological family to fall back on, in such cases, non-institutional care in the form of adoption, foster care and sponsorship is the best option for the child as these are family-based care options.

Whenever a child is abandoned or orphaned, keeping in mind the best interest of the child, the following options are considered in this order of preference:

i. Preserving the biological family.
ii. Sponsorship for very poor families (though this scheme has to still pick up).
iii. Foster Care (though this scheme too has to still pick up).
iv. In-country adoption.
v. Inter-country Adoption.

The JJ Act also provides for non-institutional services like the following:

- Adoption,
- Foster care, and
- Sponsorship.

Adoption is an option which can now be legally exercised using the JJ act 2000 for the abandoned, orphaned and neglected children. Each state runs its own children's homes for the orphaned and abandoned children which are recognised as the adoption agencies under the act. The officers of these homes scrutinise families which want to adopt the child, and do the due diligence before approving them as adoptee parents. At the same time, they ensure that the children placed for adoption are legally free for such a placement when the case is of an abandoned child. If the child was surrendered by the parents, then the wait of 2 months given to parents for reconsideration should be over before a child is considered as legally free for adoption. It is important that if the child is old enough to understand, then the consent of the child is also obtained when being placed for adoption. As per the JJ act 2000, the juvenile justice board can give the child to single parent for adoption. If parents have a biological child, they can adopt another child of the same sex, which is not permitted as per the Hindu Adoption and Maintenance act. Let us discuss non-institutional options in details.

Adoption

> ...the child, for the full and harmonious development of his or her personality, should grow up in a family environment, in an atmosphere of happiness, love and understanding...
>
> Preamble to the UN Convention on the Right of the Child

Children without parental care or children separated from their parents often live in difficult circumstances or in conditions of moral danger. In such cases, the concept needs to be applied by the State so that absence of parental care does not hamper their holistic growth. This theoretical underpinning has an impact on formulation of policies in most of the modern states, where the latter takes pro-active role in addressing the issues and concerns of childhood in a holistic manner. Children without parental care need alternative family environment.

UNICEF estimates that there are 25 million orphaned children in India in 2007. Another study estimates that there are 44 million destitute children in India and over 12 million orphans and abandoned children, yet there are only 5,000 (0.04 %) adoptions every year (http://www.childlineindia.org.in/children-without-parental-care-india.htm, retrieved January 2015). This is indeed a shame!!

Adoption and informal foster care are part of India's tradition. It was common for parents to adopt boy children to perpetuate the family name. The examples of adoption are also available in Indian mythology where Lord Krishna was adopted by Yashoda and Nand Kishore while his biological parents were Devaki and Vasudeva. Adoption is not a new concept in the Indian subconscious.

Adoption is a process by which a child who is permanently separated from biological parents becomes a legitimate child of another set of parents. This way, the child gets parents and the parents get a child to nurture and take care. The adoptive parents give to the adopted child all rights privileges and responsibilities that are associated with this relationship. Adoption in the present context is the legal placement of a child with any person other than his/her biological parent.

At the time of independence, adoption was governed by personal laws of each religion as there was refusal to have a uniform civil code by the religious groups. Hence we had legislations like HAMA which catered to adoption by Hindu parents and GAWA which helped non-Hindu parents to become guardians. With the revision of Juvenile justice act, adoption and foster care came in its ambit too. JJ act is a secular act and people belonging to any religion can adopt under it.

In India at present adoption is done under three legislations:

(a) Hindu Adoption and Maintenance Act (HAMA) 1956 applicable to Hindus, Sikhs, Jains and Buddhists where in the child gets all the rights of a biological child.
(b) The Guardian and Wards Act 1890 which is applicable to all other communities other than those covered under HAMA where couples can at best become a guardian of the child and where in the child does not have the rights of a biological child.
(c) The Juvenile Justice Act 2000 provides for Adoption as a rehabilitative measure for an abandoned child, but JJ act is silent on the issue of inheritance and other rights of the adopted child.

As per a judgment given by the honourable High Court, Mumbai, the HAMA and the JJ act must be harmoniously construed. HAMA deals with conditions of adoption by Hindus while JJ act is more secular law enabling adoption and rehabilitation of abandoned and orphaned children. According to the high court orders, the Juvenile Justice Act would prevail over the Hindu Adoption and Maintenance Act as HAMA puts too many restrictions on adoption. Also, the JJ act permits parents to adopt a child of the same sex even if they have a biological child of the same sex.

Adoption is coordinated by Central Adoption Resource Agency (CARA) which was set up in 1990 and is an autonomous body that comes under The Ministry of Women and Child Development. Adoptions are done by Child Welfare organisations who are licenced by state governments for Indian adoptions and in the case of Inter-country adoptions the organisations are recommended by state governments to CARA for recognition. At state level, there are Adoption Coordination Agencies (ACA) which have been set up under the ICPS scheme. There are Specialised Adoption Agencies (SAA) where the abandoned and orphaned child is kept. The health, nutrition and emotional needs of children are taken care of at SAA. SAA also report all cases of admissions, restorations, transfers, adoptions and death of children, and any children missing from the institution to CWC, SARA/ACA and any other appropriate authority. SAA is responsible for birth registration of a child placed in its care. Some of the prominent organisations which under take adoption are Delhi Council of Child Welfare, Missionaries of Charity and SOS Children's Village.

Agencies Involved in In-Country Adoption

- Competent Court in India,
- State Adoption Resource Agency (SARA),
- Adoption Coordinating Agency (ACA),
- Child Welfare Committee (CWC),

- Recognised Indian Placement Agency(RIPA), and
- Specialised Adoption Agency (SAA).

Who Can Adopt

As per Juvenile Justice (Care and Protection of Children) Act 2000 as amended from time to time, the court may allow a child to be given in adoption

1. to a person irrespective of marital status; or
2. to parents to adopt a child of the same sex irrespective of the number of living biological sons or daughters, or
3. to a childless couple.

Additional Eligibility Criteria

1. 2 years of stable relationship in case Prospective adoptive parent (PAPs) are married.
2. To adopt children in the age group of 0–3 years, the maximum composite age of the PAPs should be 90 years wherein the individual age of the PAPs should not be less than 25 years and more than 50 years.
3. To adopt children above 3 years of age, the maximum composite age of the PAPs should be 105 years wherein the individual age of the PAPs should not be less than 25 years and more than 55 years.
4. A single PAP desiring to adopt should not be less than 30 and more than 50. The maximum age shall be 40 years to adopt children in the age group of 0–3 years and 50 years for adopting children above 3 years.
5. PAPs should have adequate financial resources to provide a good upbringing to the child.
6. PAPs should have good health and should not be suffering from any contagious or terminal disease or any such mental or physical condition which may prevent them from taking care of the child.
7. A second adoption is permissible only when the legal adoption of the first child has been finalised.
8. Single male is not permitted to adopt a girl child.

Adoption Steps

CARA has set out both the In-country and Inter-country guidelines and procedures for adoption. Procedures for in-country adoption are as follows:

(http://www.childlineindia.org.in/central-adoption-resource-agency-cara.htm retrieved August 2014)

Stage I

Prospective Adoptive Parent (PAPs) should register themselves with the local RIPA/Adoption Coordinating Agency or with the State Adoption Cell.

Stage II

- A home study report of the prospective adoptive parents will be prepared by the social worker of the Agency. To allay the fears and apprehensions of the prospective adoptive parent(s), pre-adoptive counselling sessions will be undertaken by the social worker during the preparation of the home study report. Assessing the ability of a couple to parent a child not born to them is of crucial importance in a successful adoption. Therefore, their suitability to care for an unrelated child is assessed through this home study and counselling. Documents relating to the financial and health status of the prospective parent(s) will be part of the Home Study Report.
- The Agency will make a suitable reference from amongst the admitted children legally free for adoption. If no suitable child is available, the family will be referred to the ACA.

Stage III

- After a Home Study has been accepted and approved, a child will be shown to the parent(s). The agency will take care to match a child meeting the description, if any, desired by the parent(s).
- In case of placement of older children (above the age of 6), both written and verbal consent of the child will be obtained.

Stage IV

- Once a successful matching has been done, the agency will file a petition in the Court/JJB for obtaining the necessary orders under the relevant Act. The above process will normally be completed in 6–8 weeks.

The current situation can be assessed by the woefully few children who can be adopted in the country as shown by the following statistics.

Status of Adoption in India

See (Table 6.2).

The total number of in-country adoptions is so meagre in comparison to innumerable number of destitute and orphan children in the country. There is a need to widen the adoption programme across the country. There is also a need to arrest illegal adoptions and address the gaps in the existing system, such as no centralised

Table 6.2 Status of adoption in India

Year	In-country adoption	Inter-country adoption
2010	5693	628
2011 (Jan 2011 to March 2012)	5964	629
2012–2013 (financial year)	4694	308
2013–2014	3924	430

Source Central Adoption Resource Authority. Retrieved from http://adoptionindia.nic.in/Resources/Adoption-Statistics.html

database on all such children; myths and misconceptions relating to adoption; lack of transparency, adoption programme being confined to some selected pockets/cities in the country; lack of availability of professional services (adoption counselling and preparation of home study report etc.); lack of comprehensive database on institutionalised children, specially in government institutions, who can be declared free for adoption; poor system of monitoring and inadequate child care standards etc. (Ministry of Women and Child Development, n.d.(a)).

Why are there such long waiting lists with children in institutions? The reasons stated by the agencies were that at any given time, not all children are 'free' for adoption. Children who are relinquished by their parents have to remain in institutions for a mandatory two-month period, giving the biological parents this time to reconsider their decision. A child who is abandoned or lost must be first declared 'free for adoption' by the juvenile justice system. Various agencies such as police, medical institutions and a probation department are involved and each takes its own time to file a report. Besides the legal clauses, the high incidence of morbidity in children in institutions becomes a reason for their non-adoptability. The incidence of transitory health problems like low birth weight, tuberculosis or hernia during infancy is another significant reason for children remaining in institutions for long periods (Bhargava 2005).

Another reason for not initiating early placements within the country was vested interests of agencies working in this area. Some agencies were not committed to the principle of giving priority to the child's own community or country and merely paid it lip service. Financial considerations made international adoptions attractive. Placement agencies received large donations from foreign countries, escorting children or otherwise. If a child remained in an institution for several months or was more than an year old at the time of placement, the chance of an Indian family adopting was slim. Delaying early placements, therefore, became a strategy for obtaining the required three rejections from Indian families and applying for inter-country placement (Bhargava 2005). These reasons try to explain the low adoption rates in our country.

Foster Care

Foster care facilities are for families which are in temporary distress and for some time are incapacitated in terms of taking care of their children. It could be that a parent is having a prolonged illness, or there is substance abuse, or is deserted or death of a parent. In such cases, the child is taken away from the family and put in another family for a brief period of time, i.e. till the time that the biological family can come out of distress and is ready to take care of the child again. The aim is to eventually reunite the child with the family. Foster families could be extended family of the child or some unrelated persons.

Foster care services are almost non-existent in our country. To give impetus to this, under the ICPS scheme, Sponsorship and Foster Care fund has been floated which would be made available to the District Child Protection Society to support foster care families. As per ICPS, the Child welfare committees either by itself or with the help of Special Adoption Agencies (SAA) shall identify suitable cases and order children to be placed in foster care. The quantum of support to families who take in children for foster care would be Rs. 750 per child per month. The SAA would periodically report about the progress of the child to the CWC and the DCPS.

Sponsorship

The CRC is convinced that family is the fundamental unit of the society. The natural environment for the growth and well-being of all the members of family, particularly children should be the goal. For this purpose, necessary protection and assistance should be extended to the families; so that it can assume its responsibility within the community. The CRC also recognises that the full and harmonious development of a child's personality can be made possible in a family environment in an ambience of happiness and understanding.

There are families which are very poor and unable to provide for the basic necessities of children. Children belonging to such families are 'at risk' of being abandoned by them, or in instances not unheard of in our country, sold to traffickers. In such instances it is important that the family's resources are strengthened so that they do not move children away from the family into institutions. It is an accepted fact that children should live with their family and institutionalisation should actually be the last resort.

The Government of India also realises the need to provide support and supervised financial assistance to such extreme cases as a preventive measure to keep children within families and remain protected. In order to achieve the above, the Government of India proposes a Pilot initiative under the ICPS to provide support services to families at risk. ICPS shall create a special Sponsorship and Foster Care Fund within the DCPS. Sponsorship will offer supplementary financial support to families to meet the educational, medical, nutritional and other needs of children with a view to improving the quality of their lives (Ministry of Women and Child Development, n.d.(b)).

Families with annual income less than Rs. 12,000 are selected for sponsorship. The quantum of sponsorship is Rs. 500 per child per month which is put in child's bank account, which is operated preferably by mother. There is no cash transfer of money. Duration of sponsorship is not exceeding 3 years.

Sponsorship support will be provided as a preventive measure to families so that they do not abandon their children due to sheer poverty. This support will also be extended to children who are already in institutions. Their families will be located and children will be restored to the families and their resources augmented through the sponsorship scheme. So, this scheme is preventive as well as rehabilitative. The SAA will monitor the sponsorship programme and send reports to DCPS and CWC.

6.4.5 Areas of Concern in the Implementation of the JJ Act

According to Report (Ministry of Women and Child Development, n.d.(a)) of the SUB GROUP on Child Protection in the Eleventh Five Year Plan (2007–2012) Ministry of Women and Child Development Government of India, the following problems remain in the implementation of the JJ act:

1. JJ act has identified justice delivery system for Children in Conflict with Law which includes the JJBs, probation officers, police and special juvenile police units, NGOs, various ministries like Home affairs, Railways, WCD, NHRC and State Human Rights Commissions. The co-ordination and interaction between different wings of the juvenile justice delivery system is poor. Coordination is also missing between the States, and juvenile justice mechanisms set up the different states. This is important particularly if a case of a child in conflict with law needs to be shifted or transferred to his native state.
2. A fairly significant number of children in conflict with law are released on probation. However, a good probationary service programme, where the child is supervised, monitored and provided support on being released on probation, does not exist in India. Neither are there any successful experiments available to provide a model for developing effective probationary service programmes. This is an area that needs urgent and utmost attention to ensure a reformative approach to juvenile justice rather than a punitive approach.
3. Even when education is guaranteed as a fundamental right for 6–14 year olds, for those held in institutions, this right stands violated. The facilities where they are detained fail to provide adequate medical care, mental health intervention, or rehabilitative services. Drug and substance abuse, sexual abuse, physical punishment and inhuman treatment are rampant and often reported in the media.
4. There is no age-specific segregation and treatment of children inside the observation homes and special homes. Smaller children being physically and sexually abused by the older ones is often reported and found to be true. Perhaps the spaces and facilities for children in conflict with law need to be separated to cater to different age groups and their needs.
5. The whole atmosphere in the JJBs is unfriendly to the child. While JJBs were created under the juvenile justice system to be a child-friendly mechanism, they continue to function like any other adult court. Although training is mandated for the JJB members, it does not happen in most cases. There is limited use of non-institutional options for rehabilitation and social integration. Due to heavy pressure on the JJBs with regard to the number of cases handled in a day, children have to wait long hours till they are called in. In fact they have to be there the whole day, often without food, water and proper toilet facilities as they are all brought together from the institution in the morning and taken back together at the end of the day.

6. Violence and abuse faced by children in conflict with law, from the time they are apprehended till they are released, tells a lot on the existing system and its inadequacies. Children in conflict with law face abuse and other human rights violations during arrest, interrogation and detention, including arbitrary arrest, physical abuse during interrogation, and routine harassment and physical abuse by police and by private security guards. They are held in overcrowded and unsafe conditions, denied basic sanitary facilities, and sometimes commingled with adults. They are also denied family visits, religious services, and other important contacts with their communities and even adequate food at times.

Hindustan Times (Nov. 18 2014) 'Dramatic escape bid at juvenile home' In what could be the plot of a prison break movie, five juveniles allegedly attempted to escape from their observation home in North Delhi's Mukherjee Nagar by digging a hole on a wall on Sunday afternoon. For around 4 h, the boys dug a hole in the wall and drowned the noise of digging by singing loudly and allegedly banging the dormitory door. While they thought they had acted smart and managed to dodge the guards, it was this act that got the security personnel suspicious. To conceal their tracks, the boys, all aged between 16 and 18 years, hid the hole with a carom board. "They hid the cement in the garbage bin and dumped leftover food on top of it", the official added. Around 2 pm on Sunday, a guard noticed the prolonged singing session. "The boys were singing and banging the door, as if it were a drum, for almost four straight hours. They managed to dig a one square foot hole in the room wall", said a staff member. On investigating, the guards heard digging sounds. The authorities rushed to the room and found the hole at the knee level on a side wall. They found an iron rod. "They had broken the rod from the window and used that to dig a hole in the wall", said an official. While officials of the observation home maintained that the boys could not have escaped from the premises, sources in the department claimed that they could have been successful in their plan had their singing had gone unnoticed. "The boys could've easily made out of the premises had they managed to escape from the room," said a staff member. The five boys, observation home officials said, were repeat offenders and had been admitted before. These boys were kept separately because they would often bully other children of the house. Officials said while the police was alerted after the incident, a case was not registered.

In the past decade, the number of crimes committed by juveniles has doubled. This is primarily due to increasing the age of the child to 18 years even for boys. But the infrastructural and administrative support has not increased proportionately to address the issues related to children in conflict with law. Children are deprived of their right to be properly defended, denied bail even when they have committed petty offences or are first time offenders, and hoarded in institutions, in conditions detrimental to their growth, development and protection. Child beggars continue to be governed by the Bombay Prevention of Begging Act. As a result, their cases are dealt with in the Beggars Courts and they are also held in the beggar's homes, which is for both adult and child beggars. Children are not given bail as most have to depend on sub-standard lawyers to present their cases. As a result, not only does the number of cases pending disposal goes up and the institutions receiving such children remain overcrowded, but the child's right to be heard and have a say in his own disposition also stands jeopardised.

The JJB decides on grant or denial of bail on the basis of the Special Investigation Report prepared by the Probationary Officers for every child. This report is supposed to provide an indepth view of the circumstances in which the juvenile lives and also the circumstances of the crime. With the number of cases of juvenile crime going up, it is quite expected that the Special Investigation Report are not as indepth as they should have been. As a result, there is no real assessment of the child's situation and circumstances and his/her family environment. Even a good case of bail gets rejected in the absence of a fair social investigation report.

In *Sheela Barse versus Secretary, Children's aid society* (*air 1989 sc 1278*) case, the grievances of the petitioner were delay in restoration of children to their parents; non-application of mind in the matter of taking children into custody and directing production in front of the juvenile court; absence of proper follow up action after admission of children in the homes; detention being illegal, it amounts to harassment. The Supreme Court ruled that children should not be made to stay in the observation homes for too long. While they are there, they should be suitably occupied, intending to bring about adaptability in life, self confidence, and development of human values. The juvenile courts should be run by a judicial officer with some special training (Bajpai 2006).

In *Krist Pereira v The State of Maharashtra and others* (Criminal writ petition no. 1107 of 1996, Mumbai High court) filed after the death of a child in a remand home in Bhiwandi under mysterious circumstances. A committee of experts was constituted to examine the condition in different remand homes, children's homes and special homes in the state of Maharashtra. The report of the committee brought to light the extremely distressing and pathetic conditions prevailing in the various homes of the state (Bajpai 2006).

6.5 Proposed Juvenile Justice Bill 2014

The gang rape and heinous murder of a young physiotherapist in Delhi on 16th December 2012 woke up the entire nation to the safety of women. Half of us are women, yet we cannot walk alone in our own country. The youth came out in large numbers to protest on the streets, asking for strict laws to protect women against sexual abuse and changes in the patriarchal mind sets which commodified women.

The nation also woke up to the fact that one of the rapists was a juvenile. Although he had participated in the act with the remaining four men, he was likely to get away with much lighter punishment for the same crime. This stroked the debate on whether a young person who commits an adult crime which is heinous, should he be tried as an adult offender? Hence, should the age for juvenile offences for heinous crimes be reduced to 16 years? There has been heated discussion on this issue.

The ones who feel that the age should not be brought down are mostly the activists and social workers. They argue that universally, age of child is 18 years. India is a signatory to UNCRC as well as well as Riyadh guidelines, so India should abide by that.

The second powerful argument is that neuroscience research on the development of brain shows that adolescent brain is still a work in progress.

A long-range study by Jay Giedd and his colleagues at the National Institutes of Mental Health (NIMH.) has involved using functional Magnetic Resonance Imaging (fMRI) to scan the brains of nearly 1000 healthy children and adolescents aged 3–18. Giedd discovered that just prior to puberty, between ages 9 and 10, the frontal lobes undergo a second wave of reorganisation and growth. This growth appears to represents millions of new synapses. Then around age eleven a massive pruning of these connections takes place which is not complete until early adulthood. The brain is getting rid of the least-used pathways, a method for ensuring that the most useful synapses are maintained which in turn allows the brain to operate more efficiently. One of the final steps in developing an adult brain is myelination. Myelin increases the speed of the axon potential travelling down the axon, up to 100 fold compared to neurons that have no myelin. So, during the teen years not only does the number of connection change, the speed of the connections becomes faster. Myelination occurs in the frontal lobes last. This is the last part of the brain to mature: full myelination is probably not reached until around age 30 or perhaps later (Wolfe 2011).

Why are these changes in the frontal lobes significant? The frontal lobes—specifically the area right behind the forehead called the prefrontal or orbitofrontal cortex—is often referred to as the CEO of the brain. It is in this part of the brain that executive decisions are made and where ethical/moral behaviour is mediated. In fact, this part of the brain has been dubbed "the area of sober second thought". Persons with damage to this part of the brain often know what they are supposed to do but are unable to do it. In these persons, the damage also appears to impair their ability to imagine the future consequence of their actions. They tend to be more uninhibited and impulsive. Many researchers suspect that an unfinished prefrontal cortex, with its excess of synapses and unfinished myelination, contributes to the adolescent's deficits in these areas (Wolfe 2011). Scientists have discovered that in the teen brain, the emotional center matures before the frontal lobes. Emotion therefore often holds sway over rational processing. Giedd comments that adolescents can be thought of as trucks with no brakes! (Wolfe 2011).

So the argument is that the adolescent is more prone to risk taking behaviour and mistakes because his brain is not like that of an adult and is unable to assess and make sound judgements. Hence adolescent coming in conflict with law is still neurologically immature.

The next rationale is summed up in jail committee report which states, 'the ordinary healthy child criminal is mainly the product of unfavourable environment and that he is entitled to a fresh chance under better surroundings. There is a general consensus of opinion that as youth is the time when habits are not fixed, the prospects of reformation are then most hopeful' (HAQ: Centre for Child Rights and Leher, n.d.).

As per 'We must stop Juvenile Injustice' (HAQ: Centre for Child Rights and Leher, n.d.), National Crime Records Bureau data tell us that juvenile offenders commit less than 2 % of all crimes. They are less than 4 % of those offended for rape. It is not that if juveniles are locked up, women will become safe. The number of young offenders committing a heinous crime like rape is so small that changing the law without looking at the real figures is being called a knee jerk reaction.

The general population as well as the political system is very firm in its belief that a 16–18 year old youngster is old enough to understand the grievous nature of the crime. If a crime has been committed which has put to risk or taken away somebody's right to live, it is a crime which should be met with an equal punishment. Further to this, if two people have committed the same crime, one is 17-year old and other one has crossed the 18 year of age, is it justified to let one get away with 3 years in a reform home and the other with say life imprisonment? The general feeling is that the reform homes do not reform them. In fact they walk away committing big crimes getting small punishments. At times, young children are misused by organised crimes to commit offences for which, if caught, these children would get very small punishments, compared to an adult who would have to spend many years behind bars. Hence, the discussion and the proposed JJ 2014 bill to reduce the age from 18 to 16 years for heinous offences.

The other proposals in the new law are setting the age of consensus sex to 18 years. So, if young people less than 18 years have consensual sex, it would be considered rape as per the Protection of Children against Sexual Offences act (POCSO), and the punishment would be as per POCSO. Also, it is not just rape and murder which are being considered as heinous crimes. Even possession of narcotic drugs can put children behind bars for a life term.

6.6 Interventions and Strategies by Non-Government Organisations in Need of Care and Protection

Prayas was born in the year 1988. Prayas started its activities by providing non-formal education to 25 children, today it serves around 50,000 neglected street and working children in Delhi. The thrust areas of Prayas are Child Protection, Juvenile Justice, Education and Child Labour. Mission of Prayas is to protect the children's rights, to help them meet their basic needs and to expand opportunities to achieve their full potential. Prayas believes that every child has needs and has the right to adequate food, clothing, shelter, education, recreation, medical facilities, love and care. Prayas today has expanded its outreach with programmes in Haryana, Rajasthan, Gujarat, Bihar, Arunachal Pradesh, Andaman and Nicobar Islands.

Children served by Prayas include rag pickers, shoeshine boys, street vendors and trafficked children. Aims and objectives of Prayas are to undertake welfare programmes for care, protection and development of disabled children, youth and women, fulfilling basic needs of destitute street and neglected children, running vocational training programme, sensitising government, community and civil society about needs of children.

Prayas runs many activities and programmes of children. The alternative education program is run for children who are nout of regular school system. This program is contributing to India's target for making elementary education reach all. Prayas is catering to the educational needs of approximately 10,000 children through more than 110 alternative Education Centres, which adopts a multidimensional approach for the rehabilitation of needy children. The vocational training centre trains children in 23 trades mechanics, tailoring, beauty culture etc. The highlight is that children trained here are provided with job placements and the more enterprising ones are even helped to arrange for funds for starting their own enterprise. Prayas runs six shelter homes for children in the age group of 6–18 years. A working girls hostel and night shelter for homeless are also being run by Prayas. The combined capacity of these homes is 1000 children at any given point of time. Institutional care is one of the chief activities of Prayas. Childline is India's first 24 h free emergency telephonic helpline and outreach service for children in need of emergency assistance. Prayas runs a free telephone helpline for children in North Delhi. Any child in distress can get immediate medical aid, shelter, protection, counselling etc. on dialling the Childline number 1098. The other activities of Prayas include research and documentation, training, information education and communication (IEC), media resource unit and education resource training centre.

Indian Council for Child Welfare was established in 1952. It is the single largest agency in the voluntary sector engaged in promoting development services for the child. The objectives of ICCW are to initiate and undertake services for child welfare and development in India, promote enactment of legislation and reforms for benefit of children, cooperate and collaborate with government, non-government, national and international organisations to meet the needs of children.

ICCW is spread all over India. ICCW runs balwadis, crèches and ECE centres all over the country. Council has also set up centres to train grass root level child care workers. Anganwadi workers and helpers are trained through short-term courses to equip them to deliver the package of integrated services effectively. ICCW also acts as a scrutiny agency for cases of in-country and inter-country adoption and guardianship. Underprivileged and socially handicapped children between 6 and 18 years of age are provided with financial assistance to help them grow as educated, efficient and useful members of society.

ICCW also brings out a quarterly journal. In addition, State Councils for Child Welfare run Juvenile Guidance centre, family consoling services, drug consoling/de addiction centre, vocational training programmes, programmes for destitute children, bal bhawan and implement other programmes which address identified target groups.

Manzil is a non-profit organisation registered under the Societies Registration Act 1860, since March 1998. Activities are carried out from centres at Kotla, Pandara Park and Khan Market. Kotla centre reaches out to children between age group of 2 and 5 years and to young girls and women. Khan market and Pandara Park centres reach out to children and youth of nearby areas. All classes are held free of cost.

At Manzil, Pandara Park and Khan Market, New Delhi, local youth from low-income backgrounds come to learn, teach, be creative, and see the world in new ways. Manzil serves those living in the servant quarters and one-room tenements that cohabitate this affluent area of New Delhi. They are children of housemaids and cooks and electricians and barbers and drivers and servants. Manzil encourages all students to discover their own interests, talents and guides them towards actualizing their dreams and aspirations with or without school. Most children being first generation learners, they receive input in Maths, English and Computers. Creative talents are nurtured through music, dance and painting. Theatre is another engaging passion for many students. Theatre, not in terms of a product to be put up on stage, nor to usher students towards acting as a profession, but more as a constant process of observing, exploring, revisiting and representing our feeling emotions and realities of life. Through various workshops, students have acquired a more confident outlook, a reflective openness and sensitivity to various issues, ideas and relationships around them.

Regular visits to places within Delhi like museums, trade fair, book fair, zoo are also arranged. Outstation visits are a constant source of learning for the Manzil youth, who in the past visited Kutch-Gujrat after 2001 earth quake, to Ladakh where they were hosted by a local NGO which with a complete solar campus organised educational activities for students and teachers from all over Ladakh, to a tribal area in Madhya Pradesh where they stayed in a novel local school and also with a farmers facing displacement due to the upcoming Narmada dam. Manzil has got involved in setting up a small hydro-power station in the remote un-electrified village of Newalgaon in Tehri-Garhwal district of Uttaranchal to generate livelihoods for rural youth.

By providing a safe space for students with diverse talents, strengths, needs, abilities, backgrounds, perspectives, funds of knowledge, cultural and social capitals, intelligences and learning preferences, Manzil attempts to put in action the often repeated slogan "equal education for all students".

References

Bajpai, A. (2006). *Child rights in India Law policy and practice* (2nd ed.). New Delhi: Oxford University Press.

Bhargava, V. (2005). *Adoption in India*. New Delhi: Sage Publications India Pvt Ltd.

Central Adoption Resource Authority, Government of India, Ministry of Women and Child Development. *Adoption Statistics*. Retrieved from http://adoptionindia.nic.in/Resources/Adoption-Statistics.html.

Dramatic escape bid at juvenile home (2014, November 18). *Hindustan Times*.

HAQ: Centre for Child Rights and Leher (n.d.). *We must stop Juvenile Injustice*. A Brochure.

Ministry of Women and Child Development, Government of India. (n.d(a)) *Sub group report Child protection in the eleventh five year plan (2007–2012)*. New Delhi. Retrieved from http://wcd.nic.in/wgchilprotection.pdf.

Ministry of Women and Child Development, Government of India. (n.d.(b)). *The integrated child protection scheme(ICPS)*. New Delhi. Retrieved from http://wcd.nic.in/schemes/icps.pdf.

Mitra, N. L. (1999). *Policy and Law in Juvenile Justice*. Bangalore: National Law School of India University.

National Crime Records Bureau (2004) *Crime in India 2004*. New Delhi: Ministry of Home Affairs. Retrieved from http://ncrb.gov.in/.

National Crime Records Bureau (2013) *Crime in India 2013*. New Delhi: Ministry of Home Affairs. Retrieved from http://ncrb.gov.in/.

Wolfe, P., (2011). *The Adolescent brain a work in progress*. Retrieved from http://patwolfe.com/2011/09/the-adolescent-brain-a-work-in-progress/.

UNITED NATIONS CONVENTION ON THE RIGHTS OF THE CHILD

Article 34 (Sexual exploitation): Governments should protect children from all forms of sexual exploitation and abuse.

Chapter 7
Child Abuse in India: The Battered Child

Abstract The chapter begins with identifying abusive acts like hitting, punching, emotionally depriving, and touching the child inappropriately, which would help the reader to understand the meaning of child abuse. The act of child neglect, whether inadvertently or out of want, is also put under child abuse. Child abuse is defined and categorised. Features of child sexual abuse (CSA) are delineated and how to prevent CSA is covered in one of the sections. Information on the extent of child abuse, both physical and sexual, in India is put together from different sources. Statistics on Crimes committed against children are taken from National Crime Record Bureau, form a part of the chapter. The laws Prevention of Children against Sexual Offences act 2012, Prohibition of Child Marriage act and Prenatal Diagnostic Technique act 1994, which address some aspect of abuse of children are discussed. National level NGOs working against CSA and Child Abuse, TULIR and RAHI are profiled.

Keywords Child abuse · Child sexual abuse

Traditionally, in India, children were valued and pampered. But today the truth is different. Children face all kind of abuses within the family space as well as in public life. Violence against children includes, physical abuse, sexual abuse, pornography, pedophilia, child marriage, child trafficking, child labour, child bonded labour and infanticide to name some. Children get worse affected by communal violence, civil conflicts and natural calamities.

Child abuse includes all forms of physical or emotional ill treatment, sexual abuse and exploitation which results in actual or potential harm to child's health, survival and development. Abusive acts include a wide range of acts including grave sexual offences to corporal punishment to scolding a child which lowers the self-esteem of the child. Some abusive acts could be

- Verbally abusing a child
- Teasing a child
- Hitting and punching a child
- Corporal punishment in school

G. Chopra, *Child Rights in India*, DOI 10.1007/978-81-322-2446-4_7

- Twisting arms
- Ignoring the child and not listening to him
- Ridiculing and putting the child down
- Emotionally depriving the child
- Touching the child's private parts
- Engaging the child in sexual activities
- Showing sexually explicit material to the child

Child neglect can also fall in the category of child abuse as it would deprive the child, the opportunities for health, education, recreation and safe living. It includes failure to properly supervise and protect children from harm, provide them with education, health care and nutritious food. Neglect can be willful and intentional. But in the context of our country, it could even be an outcome of ignorance or inability of the parents to meet the health, education, recreation and nutrition needs of their children, hence unintentional and situational.

Harmful traditional practices like child marriage, caste system, discrimination against the girl child, child labour and Devadasi tradition impact negatively on children and increase their vulnerability to abuse and neglect. Lack of adequate nutrition, poor access to medical and educational facilities, migration from rural to urban areas leading to rise in urban poverty, children on the streets and child beggars result in break down of families. This increases the vulnerability of children and exposes them to situations of abuse and exploitation (Ministry of Women and Child Development, n.d.).

Over 44,000 children go missing every year of which 11,000 remain untraced. Traditional forms of violence against children like child marriage, economic exploitation, and Devadasi tradition continue in many parts of the country (Ministry of Women and Child Development, n.d.).

Mowli (1992) observed that religious prostitution is practised in various parts of India and Nepal. Devdasi cults are found in Southern India and also practised in other parts of the country such as Uttar Pradesh and Orissa. They derive customary sanction from oppressive upper-caste temple traditions. Pre-pubertal girls, aged between 5 and 9 years, from poor, low-caste homes, are dedicated by an initiation rite to the deity in the local temple during full moon. After a girl is married to the deity by the tali rite, she is branded with a hot iron on both shoulders and her breast. She is then employed by the temple priest. Sometimes, even before menarche, she is auctioned for her virginity; the deflowering ceremony known as udilumbuvadu becomes the privilege of the highest bidder. Religious prostitution is known by different names such as venkatasani, jogini, nails, muralis and theradiyan. Tiwari (2011) points out that the Devdasi practice is illegal, after the Prohibition of Dedication Act was passed in 1982. However, no one pays heed to this law, as many believe that it is part of their culture to continue this act.

According to Thukral et al. (2008), children get recruited to perpetuate violence in almost all conflict regions of India, and are exploited on daily basis. They are trained to use fire-arms and brainwashed to believe in fighting for a 'cause'. The state of Chattisgarh has been in news for using children as combatants and in other war activities. In Manipur, Chattisgarh, Kashmir and other states affected by armed conflicts, it is the youth that is pulled in. This would also fall in the category of child abuse.

7.1 Definition of Child Abuse

The term 'Child Abuse' may have different connotations in different cultural milieu and socio-economic situations. A universal definition of child abuse in the Indian context does not exist. According to World Health Organization (1999):

1. Physical Abuse: Physical abuse is the inflicting of physical injury upon a child. This may include burning, hitting, punching, shaking, kicking, beating or otherwise harming a child. The parent or caretaker may not have intended to hurt the child. It may, however, be the result of over-discipline or physical punishment that is inappropriate to the child's age.
2. Emotional Abuse: Emotional abuse is also known as verbal abuse, mental abuse, and psychological maltreatment. It includes acts or the failures to act by parents or caretakers that have caused or could cause serious behavioural, cognitive, emotional, or mental trauma. This can include parents/caretakers using extreme and/or bizarre forms of punishment, such as confinement in a closet or dark room or being tied to a chair for long periods of time or threatening or terrorising a child. Less severe acts, but no less damaging, are belittling or rejecting treatment, using derogatory terms to describe the child, habitual tendency to blame the child or make him/her a scapegoat.
3. Neglect: It is the failure to provide for the child's basic needs. Neglect can be physical, educational, or emotional. Physical neglect can include not providing adequate food or clothing, appropriate medical care, supervision, or proper weather protection (heat or cold). It may include abandonment. Educational neglect includes failure to provide appropriate schooling or special educational needs, allowing excessive truancies. Psychological neglect includes the lack of any emotional support and love, never attending to the child, substance abuse including allowing the child to participate in drug and alcohol use.

Child abuse is a violation of the basic human rights of a child and is an outcome of a set of inter-related familial, social, psychological and economic factors. The problem of child abuse and human rights violations is one of the most critical matters on the international human rights agenda (Shweta 2012).

Sexual abuse, cyber abuse, constant and persistent bullying, abduction, emotional abuse, physical abuse, bonded labour, child labour and negligence of the girl child are major problems faced by children. India is found to be the sixth most dangerous place for children. The well-known example is that the country and the world watched in horror and disgust as the remains of 34 children were pulled out of the gutters of a suburb close to Delhi. These were children from the village of

Nithari, who were lured by sweets and other platitudes, abused, sexually assaulted and killed with impunity (Suseela 2007).

Sexual Abuse: Sexual abuse is inappropriate sexual behaviour with a child. It includes fondling a child's genitals, making the child fondle the adult's genitals, intercourse, incest, rape, sodomy, exhibitionism and sexual exploitation. To be considered 'child abuse', these acts have to be committed by a person responsible for the care of a child (for example a baby-sitter, a parent, or a daycare provider), or is related to the child. If a stranger commits these acts, it would be considered sexual assault and handled solely by the police and criminal courts.

Child Sexual Abuse (CSA) has been defined as any kind of physical or mental violation of a child with sexual intent usually by a person who is in a position of trust or power vis-à-vis the child. CSA is also defined as any sexual behaviour directed at a person under sixteen, without informed consent (Bajpai 2003).

The Children's Act 1989 of Great Britain defines sexual abuse as the involvement of dependent, developmentally immature children and adolescents in sexual activity they do not normally comprehend, to which they are unable to give informed consent, or that which violate the social taboos of family roles. This definition introduces the concept of 'informed consent' and 'dependent'. It is the dependent nature of child and young people that make child sexual abuse a particular problem (Bajpai 2003).

INCEST—Any physical sexual activity between family members; it can include step-parents, upper siblings, grandparents, father, aunts and uncles and brother–sister. MOLESTATION—A vague term that includes "indecent liberties", such as touching, foundling, kissing, single or mutual masturbations, or oral–genital contact. EXHIBITIONISM—Indecent exposure, usually exposure of the genitals by an adult to children or other adults. CHILD PORNOGRAPHY—Arranging and photographing in any media sexual acts involving children, either alone or with adults or animals, regardless of consent by the child's legal guardian; also may denote distribution of such material in any form with or without profit. CHILD PROSTITUTION—Involving children in sex acts for profit and usually with changing partners. PEDOPHILIA—Literally means "Love of child" and does not denote a type of sexual activity but the preference for pre-pubertal children as the means of achieving sexual excitement.

Effects of child sexual abuse on the victim(s) include guilt and self-blame, nightmares, insomnia, fear of the abuser or things associated with the abuse (including objects, smells, places etc.), lower self-esteem, sexually transmitted diseases, chronic pain, self-injurious or suicidal tendencies, depression, stress disorders, personality disorders or other psychiatric problems.

Unfortunately, in most of the child sexual abuse cases, offenders are acquainted with the victims, being family members, relatives, neighbours etc. Strangers are the offenders in very less child sexual abuse cases. Hence, it is very essential for parents and school to give sex education to children so that they are able to differentiate between 'good touch' and 'bad touch' and feel free to discuss about it with their parents.

Sexual abusers incite children with gifts of privileges to begin with. They will confuse the child by wrongly presenting the moral standards by saying that 'it is ok' to engage in a sexual act. They also tell the victim that the act is a secret between them and the child and that the child should not tell it to anyone. If the child expresses fear, they could play on the fear of the child, threaten her/him or coerce her/him. It is also worth noting that children who are emotionally weak are more at risk of being sexually abused.

Adults should be alert to any sudden changes in the child's behaviour. There could be sudden emergence of sexually related problems, including excessive or public masturbation, age in appropriate sexual play, promiscuity or overtly seductive behaviour. It is also possible that the child becomes suddenly very quite or withdrawn or refuses to participate with the peer group. The child could look lost in her own world and be excessively inattentive. There could be a dip in school performance or participation in class. The child might look depressed or may even try to run away from home. There could be suicidal attempts or ideation. She may display unusual fears or phobias, may want to be close to mother or even display fear of strangers or of men.

7.2 Factors Contributing to Child Abuse

Child abuse and violence against children has emerged as one of the most crucial and alarming problems in this country. Factors such as growing industrialisation, liberalisation, urban bias, inter-state and rural–urban migration, economic poverty, breakdown of family and community values and support systems have resulted in children being the most marginalised and vulnerable victims (Thukral et al. 2008).

Instead of discussing the issue or guiding children, physical abuse in the form of corporal punishments in the pretext of disciplining the child continues in our schools unabated. As a society, we are quite insensitive to violence against children. Protectors have turned abusers. It is common to find the worst form of violence against children being reported from children's institutions, where orphans, destitute, children with disabilities and girls have been kept for their care and protection.

Callous attitude of adults towards children is the major factor for Child Abuse. As a society, we turn a blind eye towards children on the streets who might get rebuked or physically abused in front of us. Do we really care if a child domestic help is over worked? Child beggars on the street elicit no reaction from us. It is as if we have become desensitised to the misery of children. A parent who thrashes his child draws no reaction at all and is more of a norm in our society rather than a one-off event. We have to take the onus ON-US.

The chief underlying causes of Child Abuse and Neglect are poverty, lack of education, migration to big cities and large family size. It is obvious that being born in poor families denies in many instances the provision of basic health and nutrition care and educational opportunities. This is a major cause of neglect which could also be called abuse to some extent. Poverty leads to children taking to work which exposes them to all kinds of abuses. Migration to cities in search for work leads to further destitution of children as city life exposes to them to dangers of day to day existence. Migrants live in overcrowded dwellings which are impoverished. Children get exposed here to many inhuman conditions. Substance abuse and STD's are common in these children.

Theoretical understanding: Parents could be violent or alcoholic which leads to abuse. It is also possible that family culture permits abusing children. Theoretical perspectives point out that parents who abuse their children are mentally ill. The parents need help. In the Environment Model, two factors that interact to precipitate abuse are a violent environment and stress. The violent environment can be found either in society or the family. Abusive parents ideologically belong to that segment of society that approves of physical violence against children in certain circumstances. According to this theory, the violence has to be a result of child behaviour. This model is used to explain intergenerational abuse and those instances of abuse where children are exposed to an environment that tolerates and even sanctions child abuse as a method of problem solving. Social Psychological Model states that for abuse to occur, three variables must be present: A special parent, a special child and stress. The parent can be "special" in a number of ways, including being immature having unrealistic expectations of the child, having poor impulse control and failing to recognise and respect the child as a unique individual. The child can also be special in several ways; "wrong" sex, physically or mentally disabled, "different" from the other children in the family.

Reasons for Child sexual abuse can be very complex. This can happen to any child irrespective of the family's economic condition. For CSA to happen, the perpetrator must first overcome his own internal conscience which would initially stop him from engaging in this act. Subsequent to this, he has to be confident that he will not be caught/discovered, so he has to overcome the fear of the external environment. It is likely that the child also resists his overtures. He will have to surmount the resistance of the child as well. Children play a vital role in whether they can be sexually abused or not.

7.3 Preventing Child Sexual Abuse

It is of utmost importance to take all possible measures to prevent Child Sexual Abuse (CSA). Information about CSA should be provided to school teachers, panchayat officers, health workers, parents and children themselves. Children should not keep quiet about CSA but tell their parents or teachers about it. Schools should teach children such skills that help them identify dangerous situations, refuse an abusers approach, break off an interaction and summon help. Although it is controversial and not openly talked about subject, it is important that some brochures and material are developed for advocacy and education of children. Children should be allowed to speak. Encourage disclosure and reduce self-blame. A repository of habitual sexual offenders should be maintained at the district level. Register sex offenders, notify communities about their presence and impose long prison sentences for offenders.

Parents are surrounded by messages about child sexual abuse. Talk shows and TV news warn parents about dangers at school, in the home and on the internet. Despite all the media coverage, parents do not get much advice about how to talk to their children about sexual abuse and how to prevent it. Parents should teach children the names of their body parts including the genitalia so that if they want to tell about someone touching them, they have a vocabulary to express the same. Parents should tell the child that no one is allowed to touch their private parts, and if anyone does so, there is no 'secret' about it and the child should inform the parents. Children sometimes feel that they cannot talk to their parents. Know the other trusted adults in your child's life. Spend time with the child. Develop a relationship of trust. Talk in a matter-of-fact way about our body so that the child does not shroud this fact in mystery. If your child comes to you reporting about any sexual abuse, it is important to follow it up. When you empower your child to say "no" to unwanted touch and teach them that they can come to you with questions and concerns, you take critical steps to preventing child sexual abuse.

7.4 Extent of Child Abuse in India

There are no macro-level statistics available on the number of abused children, especially those who are sexually abused, given the sensitive nature of the issue, the criminal and covert nature of these violations and the limited research conducted to date. However, whatever little is available is being shared.

A study was undertaken by Ministry of Women and Child Development (2007), 'A study of Child Abuse in India' in 13 states of India. Respondents included children (5–18 years), young adults (18–24 years) and stakeholders. Child respondents included the following five categories of children:

(a) Children in family environment, not attending school,
(b) Children in schools,
(c) Children in institutional care,
(d) Working children, and
(e) Street children.

Data were collected from more than 12,447 children. It has very clearly emerged that across different kinds of abuses, it is young children, in the 5–12 year group, who are most at risk of abuse and exploitation. Here is the summary of the key findings:

Physical Abuse

1. Two out of every three children were physically abused.
2. Out of 69 % children physically abused in 13 sample states, 54.68 % were boys.
3. Out of those children physically abused in family situations, 88.6 % were physically abused by parents.

4. 65 % of school going children reported facing corporal punishment i.e. two out of three children were victims of corporal punishment.
5. 62 % of the corporal punishment was in government and municipal school.
6. The State of Andhra Pradesh, Assam, Bihar and Delhi have almost consistently reported higher rates of abuse in all forms as compared to other states.
7. Most children did not report the matter to anyone.

Sexual Abuse

1. 53.22 % children reported having faced one or more forms of sexual abuse.
2. Andhra Pradesh, Assam, Bihar and Delhi reported the highest percentage of sexual abuse among both boys and girls.
3. 21.90 % child respondents reported facing severe forms of sexual abuse and 50.76 % other forms of sexual abuse.
4. Out of the child respondents, 5.69 % reported being sexually assaulted.
5. Children in Assam, Andhra Pradesh, Bihar and Delhi reported the highest incidence of sexual assault.
6. Children on street, children at work and children in institutional care reported the highest incidence of sexual assault.
7. 50 % abusers are persons known to the child or in a position of trust and responsibility.
8. Most children did not report the matter to anyone.

Emotional Abuse

1. Every second child reported facing emotional abuse.
2. Equal percentage of both girls and boys reported facing emotional abuse.
3. In 83 % of the cases parents were the abusers.

A study on Child Sexual Abuse carried out by Ray and Iyer (2006) looked at the prevalence and dynamics of child sexual abuse among school going children in Chennai. The study was conducted with a view to add to the scarce indigenous body of knowledge on child sexual abuse and with the aim of breaking the silence around the issue, dispelling certain myths and providing research-based information on child sexual abuse. The team followed major ethical standards of confidentiality, freedom to participate, informed consent and a multi-disciplinary team. The major findings of this study include as follows:

1. Out of the total of 2211 respondents, 42 % children faced at least one form of sexual abuse or the other.
2. Among respondents, 48 % of boys and 39 % of the girls faced sexual abuse.
3. The prevalence of sexual abuse in upper and middle class was found to be proportionately higher than in lower or in lower middle class.
4. Sexual abuse was found to be prevalent in both joint and nuclear families.

5. Majority of the abusers were people known to the child and strangers were a minority.
6. Sexual harassment in public places and exhibitionism was higher by strangers.

The WHO estimates that 150 million girls and 73 million boys under 18 have experienced forced sexual intercourse or other forms of sexual violence involving physical contact, though this is certainly an underestimate. Much of this sexual violence is inflicted by family members or other people residing in or visiting a child's family home-people normally trusted by children and often responsible for their care. A review of epidemiological surveys from 21 countries, mainly high- and middle-income countries, found that at least 7 % of females (ranging up to 36 %) and 3 % of males (ranging up to 29 %) reported sexual victimisation during their childhood. According to these studies, between 14 and 56 % of the sexual abuse of girls, and up to 25 % of the sexual abuse of boys, was perpetrated by relatives or step-parents. In many places, adults were outspoken about the risk of sexual violence their children faced at school or at play in the community, but rarely did adults speak of children's risk of sexual abuse within the home and family context. The shame, secrecy and denial associated with familial sexual violence against children foster a pervasive culture of silence, where children cannot speak about sexual violence in the home, and where adults do not know what to do or say if they suspect someone they know is sexually abusing a child (Ministry of Women and Child Development 2007).

Data on offences against children reported by the National Crime Records Bureau (NCRB) is an authentic source to estimate the number of children in abusive situations. The cases in which the children are victimised and abused can be categorised under two broad sections:

(1) Crimes committed against children which are punishable under Indian Penal Code (IPC).
(2) Crimes committed against children which are punishable under Special and Local Laws (SLL).

Specific sections/Acts under above two categories are as follows:

(1) Crime against children punishable under the Indian penal code (IPC) are as follows:
    (a) Murder,
    (b) Foeticides,
    (c) Infanticides,
    (d) Abetment to suicide (abetment by other persons for commitment of suicide by children),
    (e) Exposure and abandonment, and
    (f) Kidnapping and abduction for ransom, murder, marriage, begging, slavery, selling of girls, prostitution and rape.
(2) Crime against children punishable under 'Special and local laws' get covered under these laws:

(a) Immoral Traffic Prevention Act, 1956 (where minors are abused in prostitution).
(b) Child Labour (Prevention and Regulation) Act, 1986.
(c) Prohibition of Child Marriage Act 2006.
(d) Protection of Children from Sexual Offences Act 2012.

As per Crime in India 2013 (National Crime Records Bureau, National Crime Records Bureau 2013), a total of 58,224 cases of crimes against children were reported in the country during 2013 as compared to 38,172 cases during 2012, showing an increase of 52.5 %. Some IPC crimes have shown a substantial increase during 2013 as compared to 2012. These crimes were kidnapping and abduction (54.2 %), procuration of minor girls (51.3 %), abetment to suicide (49.3 %) and rape (44.7 %). The crime rate i.e. incidence of crimes committed against children per one lakh population of children was observed as 13.2 at all India level during 2013. The crime rate was highest in Delhi (132.3) followed by Chandigarh (55.6), Goa (53.3), A&N islands (40.6), Chhattisgarh (37.7) and Madhya Pradesh (27.8) as compared to the national average of 13.2. A total of 1,739 cases of murder of children (including infanticides) were reported in the country against 1,678 cases in 2012 resulting in an increase of 3.6 % in 2013 over 2012. A total of 82 Infanticide cases were reported in the country during the 2013. The incidents increased by 1.2 % in the year 2013 over 2012. A total of 12,363 cases of child rape were reported in the country during 2013 as compared to 8,541 in 2012 accounting for an increase of 44.7 % during the year 2013. A total of 28,167 cases of kidnapping and abduction of children were reported during the year 2013 as compared to 18,266 cases in the previous year accounting for an increase of 54.2 %.

A look at the data maintained by NCRB shows the following:

1. There is a record of only those crimes which can be registered under the IPC or other criminal Acts. Corporal punishment, use of children for creation of pornography, exposure etc. are not reflected in NCRB data as they are not offences under the IPC.
2. There is a gross under-reporting of crimes against children, which in itself is indicative of the low priority accorded to children by parents, caregivers and the police and the state.

The data available with NCRB constitutes a miniscule of crimes/violence committed against children (Ministry of Women and Child Development 2007). The reason being that crimes against children are either not reported or cognisance is not taken. Also, many crimes are reported in state records; example, crime under Devadasi tradition is reported in the Karnataka/Andhra Pradesh data. Some crimes against children are not covered under existing legislations.

Child sexual abuse is not restricted only to girls. It cuts across gender, class, caste and regions. Yet NCRB does not report on child sexual abuse against boys. A study carried out in Chennai revealed that, contrary to popular belief, boys (48 %) were more often sexually abused than girls (39 %). Not only is the number of boys more, but they also are victims for severe form of sexual abuse compared to girls (Thukral et al. 2008). A trial court judgment in December 2006 branded sodomy and rape equal under the law, with the chief metropolitan magistrate stating, "there is no reason why sexual assault on a male child should be treated differently from a similar act committed on a female child" (Mahapatra 2006).

For sexual abuse of boys, India only has Section 377 of IPC under which cases get registered. This legal provision relates to unnatural sexual offences and sex with boys seen as a part of it. Being seen as a 'unnatural offence' is in itself a reflection of the taboos attached to the sexual abuse of boys and the archaic mind sets that are not willing to accept this stark reality (Thukral et al. 2008).

7.5 Legal Frame Work for Protection of Children Who Are Abused

The various laws for protecting children from abuse that will be discussed in this section are as follows:

1. Protection of Children from Sexual Offences Act (POCSO), 2012.
2. Prohibition of Child Marriage Act, 2006.
3. The Pre-natal Diagnostic Techniques (Regulation and Prevention of Misuse) Act, 1994

Highlights of the Acts

Protection of Children from Sexual Offences Act, 2012
The data collected by NCRB and put in the previous sections clearly shows that crimes against children are on a rise. The Ministry of WCD "Study on Child Abuse: India 2007" also shows an increase in sexual offences against children. Sexual offences against children where addressed in the IPC and most of the crimes were either not penalised or were inadequately penalised under the IPC. POCSO is a landmark legislation to protect children of India against crimes of sexual nature. It addresses sexual offences against children explicitly and also specifies commensurate penalties for the offences. It is a self-contained comprehensive legislation to protect children less than 18 years of age against sexual abuse. Unlike the rape provisions of IPC which are woman centric, POCSO is gender neutral legislation both for the victim as well as the perpetrator. Broadly, children are protected against the offences of sexual assault, sexual harassment and pornography. The act safeguards the interest and well being of the child at every stage of reporting, inquiry, investigation and trial.

POCSO has two categories of offences:

1. Sexual Assault: In this category, the victim comes in physical contact with the perpetrator. The assault is further classified as penetrative and non-penetrative. *Penetrative sexual assault* does not necessarily mean penile entry, but it could

be entry of any object or any part of the body into the vagina, urethra or anus or the child. He may penetrate the penis into the vagina, mouth or urethra or anus of the child or make the child do so with him or another person. The punishment for penetrative sexual assault is 7 years which may extend to life imprisonment. When the assault is not penetrative, i.e. it is *sexual assault*, then the person committing the act on the child may be touching the private parts of the child, or making the child touch his private parts or do any other act with sexual intent without penetrating. The punishment for sexual assault is not less than 3 years which may extend to 5 years. When a person in position of authority like a policeman, teacher, persons of armed forces, or those who are supposed to protect the child like management or staff of jail or children's home or a hospital, or a blood relative of the child commits a sexual offence, the offence is taken even more seriously and is termed as an 'aggravated' offence. *Aggravated Penetrative Sexual Assault* is penetrative sexual assault committed by a person of authority. When the penetrative assault is done by a group of persons or the assault injures the child grievously or makes the child pregnant or passes the HIV infection, who commits the crime on child younger than 12 years of age, all these come in the category of aggravated penetrative sexual assault. The quantum of punishment goes up in these instances to rigorous imprisonment of at least 10 years which may go up to life term. *Aggravated Sexual Assault* is also crime committed by persons of authority as just mentioned. The punishment for this is an imprisonment term of at least 5 years which may extend to 7 years.
2. Sexual Harassment: the child's body is not touched in sexual harassment but many actions with sexual intent get covered like uttering words, making sounds and gestures, exhibiting body parts or objects, making the child exhibit body parts. These offences have been defined for the first time clearly in law. The punishment is up to 3 years. The child may be used for pornographic purposes in any form of media—T.V., films, internet, in real or simulated sexual acts or as indecent representation, is liable to imprisonment of up to 5 years.

It is observed that there are further provisions of the Act which draw reference to the Child Welfare Committees and entrust them with certain functions. There is, therefore, a relationship between POCSO and the JJ Act. The Act entrusts the Special Juvenile Police Units or local police with an obligation to report the matter to the Child Welfare Committee and the Special Court or with in the absence of Special Courts to the Court of Sessions, within 24 h. Specifically, in case the abuse of the child is by a family member, the power is given to CWC to adjudicate within 3 days whether the child should stay with the family or not.

The act incorporates child friendly procedures for reporting, recording of evidence, investigation and trial of offences. For a speedy trial, the act provides that the evidence of the child be recorded within 30 days. Also, the special court is to complete the trial within 1 year. The Act also criminalises disclosing the identity of the child victim in the media and the entire publisher or owner of the media are jointly or severally liable for the acts and omissions of his employees.

Prohibition of Child Marriage ACT, 2006

(1) As per this act, a 'child' is a male who has not completed 21 years of age and a female who has not completed 18 years of age.
(2) 'Child marriage' means when any of the contracting parties is a child.
(3) Every child marriage solemnised before or after commencement of the act shall be voidable at the option of the contracting party which was a child at the time of marriage.
(4) The petition can be filed at any time but before the child filing the petition completes 2 years of attaining majority.
(5) The court would pass a decree on annulment of marriage directing both the parties to return to the other party all money, ornaments, gifts and valuables exchanged during the marriage.
(6) The male contracting party can be asked to pay maintenance to the female, and if the male is a minor, his parents to pay maintenance to the female till her remarriage.
(7) Legitimisation of children born of a child marriage even if the marriage has been annulled, including providing for the custody and maintenance of the children born of child marriages.
(8) The court shall make appropriate order for the custody of the child which is in his best interest.
(9) If a male adult above 18 years contracts child marriage, he shall be liable to a fine of up to one lakh rupees and rigorous imprisonment up to 2 years.
(10) Other adults who are responsible for the solemnisation of such a marriage shall be punishable to a fine of up to one lakh rupees and rigorous imprisonment up to 2 years.
(11) When a child is deceived into marriage or parents are coerced or forced into marriage of their child or are forced to sell the child in marriage, or trafficked or used for immoral purposes, such a marriage shall be null and void.
(12) Empowering the courts to issue injunctions prohibiting solemnisation of marriages in contravention of the provisions of the legislation.
(13) Punishments for promoting or permitting solemnisation of child marriage would extend to rigorous imprisonment up to 2 years and fine up to two lakh rupees.
(14) Making the offences under the proposed legislations to be cognisable and non-bailable.
(15) The state government shall appoint child marriage prohibition officer.

Despite this act, in 50 % of marriages in India, girls are married before they are 18 years old.

The Pre-natal Diagnostic Techniques (Regulation and Prevention of Misuse) ACT 1994

The Pre-natal Diagnostic Techniques (Regulation and Prevention of Misuse) Act, 1994 was enacted and brought into operation from 1st January, 1996, in order to check female foeticide. The Act prohibits selection, determination and disclosure of the sex of foetus before and after conception. It also prohibits any advertisements relating to pre-natal determination of sex and prescribes punishment for its contravention. The person who contravenes the provisions of this Act is punishable with imprisonment and fine.

The act permits the use of pre-natal diagnostic techniques for the purpose of determining chromosomal defects, metabolic disorders, congenital malformations and detecting genetic anomalies. This would help parents know the status of the foetus for them to take decisions regarding continuing with pregnancy thereafter. The act states as follows:

(1) No pre-natal diagnostic techniques shall be conducted except for the purposes of detection of any of the following abnormalities, namely:

  (i) Chromosomal abnormalities;
  (ii) Genetic metabolic diseases;
  (iii) Hemoglobinopathies;
  (iv) Sex-linked genetic diseases;
  (v) Congenital anomalies; and
  (vi) Any other abnormalities or diseases as may be specified by the Central Supervisory Board.

(2) No pre-natal diagnostic techniques shall be used or conducted unless the person qualified to do so is satisfied that any of the following conditions are fulfilled, namely:

  (i) Age of the pregnant woman is above 35 years;
  (ii) The pregnant woman has undergone of two or more spontaneous abortions or foetal loss;
  (iii) The pregnant woman had been exposed to potentially teratogenic agents such as drugs, radiation, infection or chemicals;
  (iv) the pregnant woman has a family history of mental retardation or physical deformities such as spasticity or any other genetic disease; and
  (v) Any other condition as may be specified by the Central Supervisory Board.

(3) No person conducting pre-natal diagnostic procedures shall communicate to the pregnant woman concerned or her relatives the sex of the foetus by words, signs or in any other manner.
(4) No person shall open any Genetic Counselling Centre, Genetic Laboratory or Genetic Clinic after the commencement of this Act unless such Centre, Laboratory or Clinic is duly registered separately or jointly under this Act.
(5) Proper records have to be maintained by the clinics of all women who go through pre-natal diagnostic tests in the clinic.
(6) If any person gives advertisement for pre-natal determination of sex of the child, the person can be imprisoned for up to 3 years and fined for an extent of Rs. 10,000.
(7) Any medical geneticist, gynaecologist, registered medical practitioner or any person who owns a Genetic Counselling Centre, a Genetic Laboratory or a

Genetic Clinic or is employed in such a Centre, Laboratory or Clinic and renders his professional or technical services to or at such a Centre, Laboratory or Clinic, whether on an honorary basis or otherwise, and who contravenes any of the provisions of this Act or rules made there under shall be punishable with imprisonment for a term which may extend to 3 years and with fine which may extend to ten thousand rupees and on any subsequent conviction, with imprisonment which may extend to 5 years and with fine which may extend to 50,000 rupees.

(8) Any person or pregnant woman who seeks aid of a genetic counselling centre or gynaecologist etc. for determining the sex of the child shall be liable to be punishable with imprisonment for a term which may extend to 3 years and with fine which may extend to ten thousand rupees and on any subsequent conviction, with imprisonment which may extend to 5 years and with fine which may extend to 50,000 rupees.

7.6 Interventions and Strategies by Non-Government Organisations for Protection from Child Sexual Abuse

TULIR—in Tamil means the first tender leaves of a plant; leaves following a period of adversity…symbolising children and the belief in the resilience and resurgence of the human spirit. TULIR—Centre for the Prevention and Healing of Child Sexual Abuse (CPHCSA) is a registered, nongovernmental, non-profit organisation committed to working against child sexual abuse, with its office in Chennai. It is widely felt that the moral integrity of a society and its worth can be measured by knowing if children are safe and are not sexually abused. TULIR does not believe this. It operates on the premise that every society would have instances of Child Sexual Abuse (CSA). The worth of the society is measured by acceptance of the problem and taking proactive steps to respond to this, provide healing touch to victims and to take measures to reduce CSA. TULIR believes that children have a right to feel safe all the time and should benefit from a caring and thoughtful society.

Preventing and healing CSA requires caring, optimism and pragmatism. We must care deeply for the child, be optimistic that the child would come out of the trauma and be practical and pragmatic in working with children and communities to bring about a positive change and transformation. The approach at TULIR is to convert the vague ideas of prevention in a practical blueprint for action for healing. Prevention has emerged as the most cost effective and prudent way to address CSA. TULIR believes proactivity and timeliness are the essence to an appropriate response. Every child has the resilience to overcome the pain of negative experiences. TULIR works on every child's unique strengths and resilience and helps the child in the healing process, to triumph over abuse and towards normalcy.

The objectives of TULIR are to promote and protect rights of children, raise awareness about CSA, provide direct intervention for victims of CSA and to undertake research. Documentation and dissemination of information on CSA. The services offered include the following:

- Personal Safety Education—It empowers children by teaching them about how to protect them from CSA. The child is informed about 'good touch' and 'bad touch', the self-esteem of the child is worked on so that the child can say 'no' to an adult who is an abuser. Support system for the child is built by preparing the community, family and school to help a child if the child becomes a victim of CSA.
- Training and Consultancy—Tulir-CPHCSA training programs are designed to meet the requirements and needs of various professional and non-professional sectors and include sensitisation and skill building programs for teachers, social workers, doctors, parents and other multi-disciplinary stakeholders crucial to an effective response.
- Healing—Children who have suffered from CSA, TULIR offers holistic care and healing services for them along with legal aid.

Other services include research, advocacy and documentation and publication of resources, booklets, training guides and multi-media resources on CSA for different stakeholders.

Another organisation working for victims of CSA, incest and rape is RAHI foundation. This is a Delhi-based organisation, established in 1996. RAHI (Recovering and Healing from Incest) focuses on women survivors of incest, CSA and rape.

Professionally informed and with deep experience, RAHI is a feminist group that has created a supportive environment for survivors. It goes beyond 'breaking the silence' and has developed a powerful voice that strives to mainstream the discussion about incest/CSA in India and include it in social dialogue. Addressing the long-term impact of incest/CSA on adult women, RAHI not only forms the backbone of work on this issue in India but has also paved the way for incest/CSA to become a 'field' in the country, and inspired other groups working in this area (www.rahifoundation.org). The major services include counselling and support, advocacy, raising awareness and communication, education, training and capacity building and research. Specific programmes include as follows:

- ASAP—Adolescent for Sexual Abuse Prevention. This programme is for school children, teachers, parents and school counsellors. This programme of RAHI is to create awareness, build knowledge, information and skills, all of which allow the adolescents and adults to prevent and handle CSA. The programme ranges from basic orientation, to workshops, to sessions with adolescents.
- PEP—Peer Education Programme aims to build resources within the student community for incest/CSA prevention and healing. The Program is designed to effect change at the individual level—increasing students' knowledge of the subject, modifying their attitudes towards those affected by such abuse, and creating healing resources within the community for student survivors. PEP is also focused on effecting change at the group or societal level, questioning the existing

silence, beliefs and perceptions on incest/CSA in the community and stimulating collective student action for its prevention and healing (www.rahifoundation.org). RAHI selects students from different colleges of Delhi and trains them for 1–3 days on issues related to CSA. Once trained, these students organise debates, workshops, theatre events, stalls and movie events during college festivals. They act as referral sources for friends who have been abused sexually.

- Students also attend workshops for handling disclosure of friends. Students learn the art of listening to a friend talking about her sexual abuse experience.
- The Fireband initiative of RAHI is a unique one. This initiative trains women survivors of CSA/incest to become advocates for the cause. Fireband is a unique combination of healing, training and advocacy. It is based on the belief that social action is a powerful and meaningful way for survivors to transform their trauma into a useful whole.
- RAHI also builds capacity of NGO functionaries of child rights groups, women's groups, youth groups and mental health groups on issue of CSA/incest.

References

Bajpai, A. (2003). *Child rights in India Law policy and practice* (2nd ed.). New Delhi: Oxford University Press.

Mahapatra, D. (2006, December 24) Rape, Sodomy equal before law? *Times of India*. Retrieved From http://timesofindia.indiatimes.com/india/Rape-sodomy-equal-before-law/articleshow/915960.cms.

Ministry of Women and Child Development, Government of India. (2007). *A study on Child Abuse: India 2007*. Retrieved from http://wcd.nic.in/childabuse.pdf.

Ministry of Women and Child Development, Government of India. (n.d.). *A Report of the Working Group on Development of Children for the Eleventh Five Year Plan (2007–2012)*. Retrieved from http://planningcommission.nic.in/aboutus/committee/wrkgrp11/wg11_rpchild.pdf.

Mowli, V. C. (1992). *"Jogin": Girl child labour studies*. New Delhi: Sterling Publications Private Ltd.

National Crime Records Bureau. (2013). *Crime in India 2013*. New Delhi: Ministry of Home Affairs. Retrieved from http://ncrb.gov.in/.

Ray, M., & Iyer, A.N. (2006). *Abuse among child domestic workers: A research study in West Bengal*. West Bengal: Save the Children and Tulir. Retrieved from http://www.humantrafficking.org/uploads/publications/4240_Abuse_amongst_Child_Domestic_Workers_in_India.pdf.

Shweta (2012). *Child rights in India Law, policy and practice*. New Delhi: Arise publishers & distributors.

Suseela, C. (2007). Child abuse in India: The current scenario. In R. Ganga & M. Supputhai (Eds.), *Children's rights as basic human rights*. New Delhi: Reference Press.

Thukral, E. G., Ali. B., & Bild. E. (2008). *Still out of focus. Status of India's children*. New Delhi: HAQ Center for Child Rights.

Tiwari, R. K. (2011). *Child and human rights*. Delhi: Neeraj Publishing House.

World Health Organization. (1999). *Report of the Consultation on Child Abuse Prevention Geneva, 29–31 March 1999, Social Change and Mental Health, Violence and Injury Prevention*. Retrieved from http://www.who.int/violence_injury_prevention/violence/neglect/en/, www.rahifoundation.org.

(Source: Personal collection of author)

UNITED NATIONS CONVENTION ON THE RIGHTS OF THE CHILD

Article 35 (Abduction, sale and trafficking): The government should take all measures possible to make sure that children are not abducted, sold or trafficked. This provision in the Convention is augmented by the Optional Protocol on the sale of children, child prostitution and child pornography

Chapter 8
Child Trafficking: The Victimised Child

Abstract Child Trafficking is the worst form of servitude and India is a source as well as transit country for human trafficking. This chapter discusses the meaning and definition of trafficking, and identifies the vulnerable groups and endemic geographic areas from where children are trafficked the most. Chapter tries to capture the crime mafia and nexuses involved in child trafficking. Child trafficking is not just for prostitution; there are many other purposes for which trafficked children are used. The purposes of child trafficking are identified. The chapter discusses the causes of child trafficking and the extent of trafficking in India. Statistics are taken from National Crime Record Bureau for crimes related to human trafficking. Fundamental principles of any intervention on child trafficking are discussed followed by information on the child tracking system. The laws and schemes addressing the vicious problem of child trafficking are discussed. NGO, Bachpan Bachao Andolan which works like a watch dog and does direct intervention in the states of India with highest child trafficking, is profiled.

Keywords Child trafficking · Bachpan Bachao Andolan

The Indian Constitution prohibits and penalises human trafficking. Article 23 and 39 of the Constitution of India clearly establish every citizen's right to freedom from exploitation of all forms. Article 23 particularly prohibits traffic in human beings, 'beggar' and other forms of forced labour.

8.1 What Is Trafficking?

The dictionary meaning of 'trafficking' is 'illegal trade in a commodity'. Making people commodities, literally, has never before reached the proportions as in the world today, not under slavery, not even in feudal times. There is virtually no difference when one compares people who are trafficked now with the traditional

G. Chopra, *Child Rights in India*, DOI 10.1007/978-81-322-2446-4_8

slaves who were bought and sold in olden times. Although slavery was abolished two centuries ago, slavery is very much alive in full force in today's times as human trafficking. There would be far greater number of persons trafficked today who are virtually slaves and are exploited in all forms than the traditional slaves who were there centuries ago. As per William (2008), trafficking is a growing phenomenon internationally, regionally and nationally considered as a contemporary form of slavery and a gross violation of basic human rights. Trafficking has emerged as a low-risk high return well-organised criminal activity. Human trafficking is the third largest illegal trade. Trafficking in human beings is taking place in almost all countries, only the magnitude differs.

'Trafficking' as a phenomenon has been defined by UN General Assembly in 1994 as the illicit and clandestine movement of persons across national and international borders, largely from developing countries, with the end goal of forcing women and girl children into economically oppressive and exploitative situations for the profit of recruiters, traffickers and crime syndicates as well as other illegal activities such as forced domestic labour, false marriage, clandestine employment and forced adoption (Bajpai 2006).

In the year 2000, the UN Protocol to Prevent, Suppress and Punish Trafficking in Persons, Especially Women and Children (also referred to as the Palermo Protocol on Trafficking) for the first time defined trafficking as an organised crime and a crime against humanity. The Palermo Protocol on trafficking supplements the United Nations Convention against Transnational Organised Crime, 2000, and is hence limited to cross-border trafficking. It does not address trafficking within the countries. It defines trafficking as "the recruitment, transportation, transfer, harbouring or receipt of persons by means of the threat or use of force or other forms of coercion, of abduction, of fraud, of deception, of the abuse of power or of a position of vulnerability or of the giving or receiving of payments or benefits to achieve the consent of a person having control over another person, for the purpose of exploitation. *Exploitation* shall include, at a minimum, the exploitation of the prostitution of others or other forms of sexual exploitation, forced labour or service, slavery or practices similar to slavery, servitude or the removal of organs. *Consent* is considered irrelevant in the case of children. If any of the means stated above are used, consent becomes irrelevant in the case of adults also" (Ali and Thukral 2007).

Working definition of Trafficking by Campaign against Child Trafficking in India (CACT) is "the recruitment, transportation, transfer, harbouring or receipt of persons below the age of 18 years, within or across borders, legally or illegally, by means of threat or use of other forms of coercion, of abduction, of deception, of the abuse of power or of position of vulnerability or, of the giving or receiving of payment or benefits to achieve the consent of such person, with the intention or knowledge that it is likely to cause or lead to exploitation. The words 'legally or illegally' were inserted by CACT to cover all forms and purposes of trafficking in children be it marriage that is valid or adoption that has met all legal procedures and formalities.

Every day men, women and children are trafficked across India and throughout South Asia, with India being a source country as well as transit and destination point. Trafficking is happening not only across international borders, but considerable exchange is happening within the states of India. The Ministry of Home Affairs, GOI, estimates that 90 % of trafficking for sexual exploitation is within the country. The profits from trafficking lead to the practice taking root in a particular community, which is then repeatedly exploited as a ready source from where victims are picked up. People are being trafficked not only for prostitution, but also for labour, entertainment and sports, pornography and sex tourism, begging, organ trade, for sexual exploitation through marriage and for adoption. Many of those trafficked are children, sometimes as young as 8 years old, or even younger (Ministry of Women and Child Development n.d.).

Trafficking is not the same as migration or smuggling. In migration, a person moves from one place to the other at her own will, for a job or for moving residence or any other reason. Smuggling involves illegal import or export of goods or persons from one country to the other with some consideration. The smuggler and the smuggled are both agreeable to a mutually decided figure or consideration for this illegal act. There is no fraud or coercion between them, whereas the following elements put together would constitute child trafficking:

- Involvement of children, i.e. persons under 18 years of age;
- Movement of children from one place to another, either by way of procurement, sale, purchase, recruitment, transportation, transfer or harbouring;
- Use of force, deception, fraud, coercion;
- Exchange of money or goods or a loan waiver in lieu of the child;
- Gain of third party; and
- Exploitation of child while or after trafficking.

Children everywhere are at risk of being abducted/trafficked. But there are groups of children who are more vulnerable than others. These include as follows:

- Children of poor parents,
- Children of unemployed unskilled parents,
- Children who have been affected by disaster or a natural calamity,
- Children from strife and civil unrest prone areas,
- Children living in communities where religious and cultural norms force parents to give children for prostitution,
- Children affected by transitory poverty in families,
- Children of bonded labourers,
- Migrant children, and
- Children of prostitutes.

Traffickers take advantage of the dependency of young pre-pubescent children—for food, shelter and even emotional needs—to persuade the child to do as they are told. The forms of control and coercion used include beating or slaps; rape and sexual abuse; threats of physical punishment; threats to relatives; withholding food and starvation; and confiscation of identity among others (Agarwal 2008).

Child trafficking is about mafias and nexuses. It is also about demand and supply forces. There is a growing demand from people who survive on making profits out of the situation of the child, and on the other hand are the powerless and helpless children that makes their supply easy. 'Child export rackets' or 'child smuggling rackets' are some such organised rackets involved in buying and selling of children for adoption. Then there are 'organ trade rackets', 'drug mafias', 'begging mafias' and so on and so forth. Many children are also kidnapped for trafficking (CACT 2002).

Sinha (2014) states in Times of India that India is now world's slave capital. With over 14.2 million in India being involved in forced labour and being victims of trafficking—for sexual exploitation and forced marriage, the country is home to the largest number of people trapped in modern slavery. Globally, 35.8 million people are enslaved across the world. Of them, 23.5 million people are in Asia, two-thirds of global total in 2014 (65.8 %). The Global Slavery Index 2014 announced on Monday that India and Pakistan alone account for over 45 % of total global enslaved population and have highest prevalence of modern slavery in Asia. The Index said, "Particularly in countries such as India and Pakistan, nationals—often including entire families—are enslaved through bonded labour in construction, agriculture, brick making, garment factories and manufacturing". Modern slavery exists in all 167 countries with five countries accounting for 61 % of the world's population living in modern slavery. It estimates that over 23.5 million people in Asia are living in modern slavery. This is equivalent to almost two-thirds of the global total number of people enslaved. Of these, over 14.2 million are in India and over 2.05 million are in Pakistan, which demonstrate the highest prevalence of modern slavery in Asia (1.141 and 1.13 % of their populations, respectively). Commenting on the report's findings, Andrew Forrest, chairman of Walk Free Foundation, said: "There is an assumption that slavery is an issue from a bygone era. Or that it only exists in countries ravaged by war and poverty. These findings show that modern slavery exists in every country. We are all responsible for the most appalling situations where modern slavery exists and the desperate misery it brings upon our fellow human beings. The first step in eradicating slavery is to measure it. And with that critical information, we must all come together—governments, businesses and civil society—to finally bring an end to the most severe form of exploitation."

8.2 Purposes of Child Trafficking

Clearly, human trafficking is an organised crime, carried out by a nexus of individuals in connivance with or under the patronage of high-ranking government officials and politicians. It is estimated that after drugs and arms trafficking, human trafficking is the third largest illegal business in the world (Ali and Thukral 2007). National Human Rights Commission (2005) reports that 44,000 children go missing in India every year. They are being trafficked for prostitution, marriage or illegal adoption, child labour, begging, recruitment to armed groups and for entertainment (circus or sports). With the opening up of markets and increase in tourism, children have fallen prey to operating paedophiles and sex abusers (Planning Commission 2008).

Although trafficking has been viewed synonymously with child prostitution, but children who are trafficked and sold could be for many purposes. As put by Ali and Thukral (2007), Child trafficking takes various forms. Whether sold or kidnapped or duped or lured, the end result is exploitation. Some known forms and purposes of Child Trafficking are as follows:

- Labour
  - Bonded labour
  - Domestic work
  - Agricultural labour
  - Construction work
  - Carpet industry, garment industry, fish/shrimp export as well as other sites of work in the formal and informal economy
- Illegal Activities
  - Begging
  - Organ trade
  - Drug peddling and smuggling
- Sexual Exploitation
  - Forced prostitution
  - Socially and religiously sanctified forms of prostitution
  - Sex tourism
  - Pornography
- Entertainment and Sports
  - Circus, dance troupes, etc.
  - Camel jockey
- For and through Marriage
- For and through Adoption

Source Ali and Thukral (2007)

The notorious 'child trade' has now replaced the 'silk trade' from district Murshidabad, West Bengal. Girls and boys are sent for begging to Saudi Arabia during the Haj Pilgrimage. Out of a national total of 1000–1500 children flown out each year for Haj, 400 are from district Murshidabad alone. These children 'consent' to their enslavement after rice and chicken meals at Mecca with free Pepsi are given to them. But many children never return home. No trace of many girls who routinely 'disappear' every year into slavery and perhaps to their death (CACT 2002).

Have you noticed the child beggar at the red light signal on the road? Have you ever wondered whose children they are? Where are they from? What do they do with the money that they collect by begging? Are they part of some organised mafia? Where these children trafficked from some remote tribal/rural poor districts of India? Some of them are maimed and disabled. Did someone maim them?

Do these children have any rights? Are the girls, and even boys, sexually abused? Do they become part of organised crime? Which law protects them? Have you ever spoken to them, or you have just shunned them? To be able to survive on the roads of huge metropolis, exposed to all kinds of dangers, mostly without adult protection must be a big challenge for these children.

Focus: the domestic child worker who is ubiquitous in urban homes. It is possible that this child was trafficked by the placement agent and brought to the city? Is the money that he earns reaching his family back in the village? Will the child ever be able to go home?

The acrobats we see on the streets, or the children who are part of a circus. Do we even bat an eye lid when we see them in our midst? Children who have been sent to the middle east for camel jockeying, which could even result in their death. Children as young as 2 years and as small as 4 kg in weight are tied to the camel backs. When the camel moves, the child screams out of fear. This excites the camel and the camel runs faster. This leads to the child falling from the camel, being trampled and even killed. Although the UAE has made using small children as camel jockeys an illegal activity, but it still takes place in the remote desert areas. Children are trafficked for this activity. The younger the children, the more they are in demand!

Children are also trafficked for marriage. Remember a child bride Ameena from Hyderabad, all of 9 years old, was bought for Rs. 10,000 and married to an old Arab sheikh. This news made headlines for a very long time in 1991–92. Ameena was saved. But many such child brides are sexually used in the name of marriage and then left behind in brothels. Children being part of the sex industry in Goa (and of late even Kerala) keeps making news.

The whole racket of trafficking for marriage came to light in August 1980 when the Statesman Weekly carried a news story titled "Marriages Not Made In Heaven". This was about Muslim girls from Hyderabad being married off to Arab nationals for anything between Rs. 5,000 and 10,000, depending on their age and appearance. The story narrated the plight of 25-year old.

Raheema Begum, who managed to escape from the clutches of her 75-year-old Arab husband after she slaved him for over 5 years and bore him two children. Raheema's parents had received Rs. 5,000 from her husband in lieu of their marriage. It further said, "Bride-running from Hyderabad to the Gulf countries has been a lucrative business and on an average 200 girls leave the city every month, according to the regional passport office here.

Marriage brokers have sprung up in the city. Some of the Arabs marry as many as three to four girls on a single trip. Arabs who come to Hyderabad in search of young brides are not the oil-rich sheikhs. They are small time businessmen or petty traders. In a number of cases, these young brides never leave the Indian shores. They are taken to Bombay and when the Arab visitor's tourist visa expires, he leaves the country, promising to send her a ticket on reaching home. The girl never hears from him".

After 10 years from then, in October 1991, the newspapers carried another story of 9-year-old Ameena from Hyderabad. Ameena was married off to 60-year-old Arab Sheikh Yahyah-al-Sageih, who paid Rs. 10,000 to buy her from her parents in the name of marriage. Ameena was Yahyah's fourth victim in the last 6-months (Sinha 1996).

In *State versus Shri Freddie Peats and others case (1992)*, the accused Freddie Peats then 66 years old, claimed to be a man of God (Father Peats), a medical doctor and social worker who ran a 'boarding' or 'orphanage' for boys generally from broken homes and deprived families. Peats used to sexually abuse and assault the boys. On his arrest there were 2305 photographs found in his flat. These photographs recorded different acts of sexual assault, abuse, exploitation and other brute and silent violence against children. These photographs covered a period of 17 years and the boys were from Goa. Apart from photographs there were negatives, syringes, drugs, and other torture paraphernalia. Peats was held guilty by the sessions court and was given life imprisonment and fine (Bajpai 2006).

Few crimes in this county have been marked by such inhumanity as the Nithari killings, a story of abduction, rape, murder, and necrophilia. Several children had gone missing from Sector 31, NOIDA and Nithari village, Gautam Budh Nagar from the year 2005 onwards. The remains of 17 children were found in a home in Noida U.P, in December 2006. These children had been abducted by the domestic help, Koli, who is now waiting to go to the gallows. He also confessed to have slain various woman and children and thrown the body parts in the enclosed gallery at the back of the house and in the drain which flowed in front of the house in which he stayed. The case pointed towards an organ trade racket too and at times even gave indications of Koli having cannibalistic tendencies.

Customs, traditions and religious practices do not spare children. As much as we would hate to accept it, we do follow religious practices and traditions that have for centuries allowed sexual servitude of young girls to temple priests—all in the name of dedicating them to gods and goddess. Examples of these are found in Devadasi, Jogins and Matammas traditions practiced in some parts of India. It is now well established that this dedication is a gateway to trafficking of girls for sex servitude (CACT 2002). The victims of religious prostitution, the Jogins and Devadasis join at a very early age. 95 % of Harijan (Scheduled Caste) families send about 5–10 thousand girls every year in this practice (Sinha 1996).

Over the last few years, there has been an increase in trafficking of girls for and through marriage. In States where there is gender imbalance due to low sex ratio, finding brides for eligible men is becoming difficult. As a result buying brides from other States has become common. In Haryana and Punjab for instance, girls are bought from Assam and other parts of Eastern India for marriage. While trafficking of girls for marriage is a relatively new phenomenon, using marriage as a means to traffic girls into prostitution and farm labour has been an old practice in India.

Organisations working in the Balasore district of Orissa have reported an increasing trend of girls belonging to poor families being lured by middlemen to Eastern Uttar Pradesh with promises of good dowry-less marriage. Inevitably, the aspiring grooms are already married or old. These girls are forced to work as agricultural labourers during the day and cater sexually not only to their husband but to others too at night (Thukral 2005).

Just 350 km from Bhopal, dotted along the Mandsaur–Chittorgarh state highway are girls and women indulging in the sex trade. Nothing unusual, except these women belonging to the Bachda tribe conduct the sex trade in the name of tradition. For them, prostitution is a way of life, passed down generations. No questions asked.

This happens in 35 villages alongside the highway from Mandsaur to Chittorgarh in Rajasthan where pan shops and tea stalls with girl attendants are just a cover up. Asking for a 12-year-old for the night is not considered unusual.

When NDTV reached the highway and asked for a couple of pre-pubescent girls for the night, they were told it could be arranged for.

On the 100 km stretch from Mandsaur to Chittorgarh, the NDTV crew spotted at least 700 girls soliciting customers. Girls who should have ideally been in school or college. They spend their day luring customers who are mainly truck drivers.

And the presence of policemen does not seem to be any deterrent as many women say the police understand and respect 'their tradition'. "The police does not bother us as they know that we have been living here and doing this for generations as part of our tradition", says one such woman on the highway. "There is no particular reason why we are into prostitution. The girls do it of their own free will; we have been doing this from the beginning. There has been no prohibition by the authorities so it has been continuing from generations," she adds.

The police on the other hand say their efforts in curbing this form of prostitution have reaped benefits and fewer girls are now seen on the highway.

But another disturbing reality emerges. While the tribes are now sending their girls to school and colleges, girls from other places and tribes are kidnapped and forced into prostitution. Police say they rescued 62 girls in the last 2 years, 25 of them who were reunited with their biological parents.

What is ironic is that in the early 90s the Madhya Pradesh Government started the Jabali Yojna, a rehabilitation program for the Bachda and other tribes that push women into prostitution as tradition, but one trip down the highway just demonstrates how the programme's implementation remains ineffective (Siddharth 2012).

Infant sale rackets have also always been in the news. A lot of infants sale that continues in hospitals and nursing homes remains unreported. The States of Delhi, Maharashtra, Andhra Pradesh and Tamil Nadu have been in news in this regard. Trafficking of children for adoption is not related only to inter-country adoptions. A large number of cases of sale of infants from local hospitals and nursing homes are of sale to prospective Indian parents (Ministry of Women and Child Development n.d.).

Trafficking for labour is the most under reported crime. If data were to be systematically collected in this regard, children trafficked for labour would far outnumber those trafficked for commercial sexual exploitation. Trafficking for labour or economic exploitation takes various forms. Girls from Orissa, Madhya Pradesh, Chhattisgarh, Jharkhand, Bihar and West Bengal are regularly being trafficked into cities through middlemen who are part of placement agencies that put these girls to work as domestic servants. Besides, it is a well-established fact that boys are trafficked for all kinds of labour, be it labour in the zari units, in gem polishing and diamond cutting units in Surat or, domestic work, work in sweetmeat shops and in small restaurants and dhabas (Ministry of Women and Child Development n.d.).

Hindustan Times reports in an article "Childless families" (2014) that these days child traffickers are getting a new set of clients: Childless families, most of whom want to skip the tedious adoption process. Every year, hundreds of children—all below the age of five—go missing from the city. Most of them end up in the hands of child traffickers. And childless families are willing to pay them anything they want. Most children under 5 years cannot be employed. So traffickers abduct them for selling to childless couples.

8.3 Causes of Child Trafficking

Trafficking is an organised crime. The nexus between traffickers, law enforcement officials and politicians allows very little scope for protecting children from being trafficked. The major causes of trafficking include as follows:

1. Poverty is cited as the major reason for trafficking of children. Parents are unable to afford the basic necessities of life, which forces them to sell their children for paltry sums.
2. The traffickers could be known to the families, someone the family trusts. They could show dreams of a better future for their child to the parent and take the child away.

3. The gangsters and middlemen approach these vulnerable children. In some cases, good-looking girls are taken away by force. It is common for traffickers to even abduct the children.
4. Other factors like low valuation of girls, hence parents who already are considering them a burden, sell them off.
5. Loss of traditional sources of livelihood, leads to hunger and starvation, forcing families to sell children and women.
6. Inadequate legislation and weak law enforcement makes it hard for the traffickers to be caught, so it emboldens them to engage in this.
7. Increasing breakdown of social structures are resulting in loss of family and community support networks, making families, particularly women and children, increasingly vulnerable to traffickers' demands and threats.
8. With increasing globalisation, economic disparities between countries, and porous borders facilitating easy movement of people, there is large-scale illegal migration of women and children into India from the neighbouring countries. Often such situations of illegal migration are exploited by the traffickers to traffic women and children into exploitative situations, including prostitution and labour. Unsafe migration is the best situation to be exploited by the traffickers for their benefit.
9. Some castes and regional groups are more vulnerable to trafficking.
10. Whenever a natural disaster strikes, children and women become highly vulnerable to be trafficked.
11. Children in conflict areas are also more vulnerable to violence, abuse and exploitation of all forms. Due to the extreme conditions in which people are forced to live, they fall prey to various forms of trafficking. The police and civil administration turns its face away from this crime as they feel for them there are larger issues to be handled.
12. There is growing demand for children as they are cheap labour, they can be easily manipulated and they do not pose much threat to the traffickers as compared to adults.
13. Inter-country adoption is another demand for which infants are trafficked. Sometimes the fee charged for handling adoption by foreigners is as high as \$5,000–\$30,000 per child.
14. Commercial sexual exploitation and demand for child prostitutes results in trafficking of young girls. It is believed by many that sex with a pre-pubertal girls would cure AIDS and other STDs.
15. Trafficking is a lucrative trade. Due to poor legislations, it is a safe trade too. Further, the abject poverty and vulnerability of children makes the supply of children easy. All this fuels trafficking.
16. In urban areas, there is a high demand for in-house maids. This becomes a lucrative business for traffickers, who buy these girls from poverty stricken areas for as less as Rs. 2000, sell them to placement agencies for Rs. 4000–7000, who further charge Rs. 25,000–35,000 as one-time payment from employers of domestic help in cities.

17. Victims who are able to return to their communities often find themselves stigmatised or ostracised, and therefore are re-trafficked.
18. Traditional religious practices (Devadasi etc. which pledges young girls into life-long sexual exploitation).
19. Sex—tourism puts a demand for trafficking of young girls and boys for sexual activity, pornography, and entertainment of paedophiles. Children are easy to entice and are easy and cheap source of sexual gratification. Not only is it the perverse psyche which makes adults use them as sex objects, but there is also a belief that having sex with a virgin girl also keeps away the fear of AIDS.

8.4 Extent of Trafficking in India

Although there are no comprehensive and absolutely reliable statistics to this effect, it is a known and acknowledged fact that trafficking women and girls for labour and commercial sexual exploitation is on a rise in India. This includes not merely cross border trafficking but also transportation of victims from less developed rural areas to urban markets where there is a rising demand (Bajpai 2006).

In India, 12.6 million (GOI) to 100 million (unofficial sources) children are reported to be child labour. Over 44,000 children are reported missing annually, of which only about 11,000 get traced. At a conservative estimate, about 200 girls and women enter prostitution daily. 20 % of them are below 15 years of age (Ali and Thukral 2007).

In a startling revelation, an interim report by a government committee has found that a staggering 20,000 women, including minor girls, are sold off in various towns of Telangana and Andhra Pradesh for sex trafficking every year. A high-level committee, constituted by Telangana chief minister K Chandrasekhar Rao, had submitted a series of recommendations on the welfare and safety of women and children in the state last week, highlighting the major issues plaguing them. With respect to human trafficking, the committee pointed out that the modus operandi of traffickers ranged from forced or fake marriage to customary or religious practices like devadasis and joginis to lure women into flesh trade (Sex trafficking: Is there no end? 2014).

The problem of trafficking is acute in Andhra Pradesh, Bihar, Karnataka, Maharashtra, Tamil Nadu, Rajasthan, Uttar Pradesh and West Bengal. While both boys and girls are victims of trafficking, girls are more vulnerable, especially to trafficking for sexual purposes. 60 % of the estimated 2.3 million women and child commercial sex workers in India come from Scheduled Castes/Scheduled Tribes/Other Backward Classes, and according to an ILO estimate, 15 % of them are children. The number of tribal girls, a large number of them under 18 years, migrating from states like Chattisgarh and Jharkhand to Metropolitan Cities every year, runs into thousands. They are lured into leaving homes, and they have no option but to take up petty jobs, ending up at times as sex workers. According to a survey conducted by People's Awakening for Traditional Revival and Advancement (PATRA), there are at least 2500–3000 tribal girls from Jharkhand alone who move to cities every year (Ministry of Women and Child Development n.d.).

> As presented in article, "10,000 children trafficked into NE annually from B'desh, Nepal" (2008) Not less than 10,000 people, mostly children, are trafficked into the Northeast with a good number smuggled in from Bangladesh, Nepal and other South East countries, surveys by NGOs reveal.
>
> Most of those trafficked are then engaged as cheap labour in coal mines of Meghalaya, tea gardens in Assam and prostitution.
>
> "the region besides being a transit point of human trafficking has also emerged as a destination point. It is estimated that Nepalese children constitute 20 % (40,000) of estimated 200,000 Nepalese prostitutes in India."
>
> "it is estimated that some 6,000–10,000 girls are trafficked annually from Nepal to Indian brothels and a similar number are trafficked from Bangladesh. 27,000 bangladeshi women and children have been forced into prostitution in Indian brothels." A Childline foundation report says.
>
> With India sharing 4,222 km border with 28 districts of Bangladesh, most of it open with rivers criss-crossing it, traffickers take advantage of this to smuggle in their hapless human cargo.

Bachpan Bachao Andolan reports one lakh child labourers are in the embroidery and Zari sweatshops in Delhi and nearly the same numbers in Mumbai and elsewhere, trafficked mostly from Bihar, Jharkhand and West Bengal (Thukral et al. 2008).

According to Crimes of India 2013 (National Crime Records Bureau 2014), human trafficking is a group of Crimes involving the exploitation of men, women and children for financial gains which is violation of fundamental human rights. A number of IPC Crimes (Procuration of Minor Girls, Importation of girls, Selling of girls for prostitution, Buying of girls for prostitution), SLL Crimes (Immoral Trafficking Prevention Act—1956, Child marriage restraint Act—1929) and violation of some legislations (Bonded Labour system (Abolition) Act 1976, Juvenile Justice (Care and Protection of Children) Act 2000, Child Labour Prohibition and Regulation Act 1986, Transplantation of Human organs Act 1994) form part of offences under human trafficking as collected by NCRB. The discussions will be based only on a few major crimes of human trafficking for which National Crime Record's Bureau (NCRB) is collecting data.

National Crime Records Bureau (2014) reported a total of 3,940 incidents of crimes related to human trafficking in the years 2013. It has risen steadily from 2848 crimes in 2009, 3422 crimes in 2010, 3517 crimes in 2011 and 3554 crimes in 2012.

A total of 1224 cases of procurement of minor girls were reported. West Bengal alone reported 486 of these cases having 39.7 % national share. 31 cases of importation of girls from foreign country have figured in NCRB statistics. 100 cases of selling of girls for prostitution were reported in 2013 as against 108 cases in 2012. 6 cases of buying of girls for prostitution were reported. Cases under The Immoral Traffic (Prevention) Act, 1956 reported were 2579 in 2013 as compared to 2563 in 2012. Tamil Nadu and Andhra Pradesh together accounted for 489 out of 2579 cases. When total crimes under IPC and SLL were taken, rate of crime under human trafficking in year 2013 was 0.3 %. NCRB does not collect data on missing persons as 'missing persons is not a cognizable crime'.

The rate of conviction of traffickers in India is low. Although increasing number of cases are being filed against traffickers, legal action is slow giving a chance to the traffickers to escape trial and conviction. While the small number of convictions and the inadequate numbers of rescue homes along with the high level of dissatisfaction amongst rescued children regarding the quality of services being provided in these homes, seemingly present a dismal picture, there is evidence of efforts being made at stricter law enforcement and faster justice delivery and to improve the quality of services for care and protection being provided to victims of trafficking (Ministry of Women and Child Development n.d.).

Tiwary (2014) reports a Supreme Court bench, angry over 1.7 lakh missing children and the government's apathy towards the issue, had remarked: "Nobody seems to care about missing children. This is the irony." Close to one and a half years later, government data show over 1.5 lakh more children have gone missing, and the situation remains the same with an average of 45 % of them remaining untraced. Data on missing children put out by the home ministry last month in Parliament show that over 3.25 lakh children went missing between 2011 and 2014 (till June) at an average of nearly 1 lakh children going missing every year.

8.5 Fundamental Principles of Any Intervention on Child Trafficking

As per Ali and Thukral (2007) the following must be kept in mind when intervening in any situation of child trafficking:

- Help the child to the best of one's ability.
- Learn to empathise. A non-discriminatory and unbiased attitude is the best support to offer. We must always remember that it can happen to any child without any fault of theirs.

- The well-being of the child should remain absolute priority under all circumstances. Exclusive priority should not be given to furthering the case to the point of neglecting the well-being, the security and meaningful rehabilitation of the child.
- Right to freedom from all forms of exploitation should be the guiding force for all action.
- Confidentiality of the child and respect for the child's privacy must be maintained.
- It is important to keep in mind that trafficking is often an organised crime with many partners and these syndicates or mafias can be dangerous.
- It is imperative to assess one's capacity before intervening. We must identify people or groups who can be potential partners. We may or may not have the capacity to undertake a legal intervention. In that case certainly, a partner with such expertise will be required. Another organisation could be approached for providing psycho-social counselling to the victimised child and yet another for rescue or rehabilitation, repatriation and follow-up. Linking up to organisations working in the field of securing livelihood options for adults could also be a possibility. This can economically help the unemployed adults and distressed families in the community where the child belongs.

> As reported in The Times of India (Naveen 2014) Madhya Pradesh Police have zeroed in on a village in Chambal region, where over 100 girls, many of whom were abducted, raised and given hormonal injections to push them into prostitution in future. Startling tip-off on the presence of gang using growth hormones to help minors attain early puberty came from a girl, who managed to escape from their den on September 23 in Shivpuri. The girl was sold after kidnapping her from Maxi village in Shajapur district along with three other young girls in 2008. Todipura, the village where she was held captive, is hardly 50 m from Berad police station.

8.6 Child Tracking System

The Ministry of Women and Child Development recognises that at present there is an acute shortage of data and information pertaining to issues related to child protection. Due to this, there is no idea about the dimension of the problem and the extent of services needed for vulnerable children. In order to bridge this gap, National Informatics center has been entrusted to set up a national portal to track missing children and also to monitor the progress of 'found' children who are in various institutes under the JJ act and the ICPS. A nationwide website 'TrackChild' has been developed for tracking missing children and their ultimate repatriation and rehabilitation. The homes, the Child Welfare Committees, JJ boards, police stations etc. are being equipped with computers, staff etc. to facilitate data entry of children under ICPS. The software also provides for mapping of vulnerable locations, i.e., those which have a large number of children reported missing, so that corrective action can be taken in these areas. Monitoring of action taken to trace missing children has been steam lined through this software.

8.7 Combating Trafficking

a. The Immoral Traffic (Prevention) Amendment Bill, 2006

The Immoral Traffic (Prevention) Amendment Bill, 2006 amends the Immoral Traffic (Prevention) Act, 1956 to combat trafficking and sexual exploitation for commercial purposes.

The Bill deletes provisions that penalised prostitutes for soliciting clients. It penalises any person visiting a brothel for the purpose of sexual exploitation of trafficked victims. All offences listed in the Bill would be tried in camera, i.e., the public would be excluded from attending the trial. The term "trafficking in persons" has been defined with a provision for punishing any person who is guilty of the offence of trafficking in persons for the purpose of prostitution. The Bill constitutes authorities at the centre and state level to combat trafficking (www.prsindia.org).

The offences under ITPA include as follows:

1. Detaining a person in a premise where prostitution is being carried out;
2. Seducing or soliciting for purpose of prostitution;
3. Procuring, inducing or taking a person for sake of prostitution; and
4. Seducing a person in custody.

Police personnel entrusted with the implementation of the Act locally (Special Police Officers) as well as at the national level (Trafficking Police Officers) are accorded special powers to raid, rescue and search premises suspected of serving as brothels. Magistrates are authorised to order arrests and removal, direct custody of rescued persons, close down brothels and evict sex workers.

While prostitution is not an offence, practicing it in a brothel or within 200 m of any public place is illegal. There seems to be a lack of clarity on whether prostitution ought to be a legitimate way of earning a living if entered into by choice. Penalising clients who visit prostitutes could drive this sector underground, preventing legal channels of support to victims of trafficking.

The Act provides institutional rehabilitation for "rescued" sex workers. The bill only deals with women and children trafficked for immoral purposes, and fails to address the wider issue of trafficking for other purposes like labour, adoption and marriage. It does not talk about trafficked boys.

Cops Bust Trafficking Racket (2014)—An interstate human trafficking racket was busted in Delhi and four people, including two women, were arrested, police said on Thursday. The gang allegedly trafficked minor girls and young women from West Bengal and Assam and sold them at brothels in GB Road in the Capital. The police rescued a 17-year-old girl from Jharkhand, who was bought to be forced into flesh trade.

Juvenile Justice (Care and Protection of Children) Act, 2000, Amended in 2006 by Amendment Act 33 of 2006

The Juvenile Justice (Care and Protection of Children) Act, 2000 (JJA) is a special legislation for children and defines a 'child' as a person up to 18 years of age. It deals with two categories of children—those in need of care and protection and those in conflict with law.

With amendments to the JJ Act, trafficked children are now meant to be treated as children in need of care and protection under the JJA. The Act recognises certain offences against children as special offences. These clearly address trafficking of children in general as well as for begging and labour. These include as follows:

- Cruelty against a child by a person having charge of such child, including assault, abandonment, exposure, willful neglect or procuration of a child for any of these acts, in a manner that is likely to cause mental or physical suffering to the child;
- Employing, using or causing a child to beg;
- Abetment of the employment or use of a child for begging by a person having charge of such child; and
- Procuring a child for hazardous employment, keeping such child in bondage and withholding the child's earnings for one's own use.

The juvenile justice law provides both institutional and non-institutional measures of rehabilitation of trafficked children, including placement in foster care, adoption and sponsorship.

The Delhi High Court in a recent judgment by Justice Gita Mittal has extended the JJ act to cover minors rescued during anti-trafficking raids as not offenders under the Immoral Trafficking (IT) act, but children in need of care and protection, rather than juvenile in conflict with law as per the JJ act. In essence, the JJ act will prevail over the IT act. This ruling will be binding for police and trial courts at least in Delhi. It was pointed out that a child is incapable of giving consent and any sexual activity involving a child renders the participating adult open to stringent penal action, but 'no penal liability vests on the child for the same'. Children found begging, child labourers or a child likely to be abused or exploited for the purpose of sexual abuse or illegal acts or a child vulnerable to drug abuse or trafficking 'is not to be treated as an offender' but 'as a victim within the means of the expression under the JJ act' (Trafficked kids are not offenders 2014).

b. Ujjawala Scheme

In December 2007, Ministry of Women and Child Development launched a scheme for prevention of trafficking and the rescue and rehabilitation of trafficked women and children called the Ujjawala scheme. The Ujjawala scheme has five components:

1. Prevention, which consists of formation of community vigilance groups/adolescent groups, awareness and sensitisation of important functionaries like police, community leaders and preparation of IEC material;
2. Rescue, safe withdrawal of the victim from the place of exploitation;
3. Rehabilitation, which includes providing safe shelter for victims with basic inputs of food clothing, counselling, medical care, legal aid, vocational training and income generation activities etc.;
4. Reintegration, which includes restoring the victim into the family and community (if she so desires) and the accompanying costs; and
5. Repatriation, to provide support to cross border victims for their safe repatriation to their country of origin (Thukral et al. 2008).

The scheme was initially implemented through 50 projects and 2500 beneficiaries. The shelter component of the scheme houses the women and young girls together. This has raised some questions, considering that the needs and experiences of the two groups can vary greatly, hence a need for separate shelters. This would also be in line with the JJ act.

Another scheme of the government for providing shelter for trafficked women and girls is the SWADHAR scheme. Under this scheme, comprehensive care is provided to victims including education, vocational training and life skill training. It faces the same criticism as far as shelter is concerned. The lost childhood of young girls can never be restored if they stay with women. As per Ministry of Women and Child Development (n.d.), these homes are far few in number in comparison to the magnitude of the problem and many shelters do not have the capacity to provide protection to trafficking victims for more than a few months and for creating the enabling environment to prevent re-trafficking of victims once they leave the shelters. Also, there is no provision to provide adequate protection to victim witnesses to prevent retribution from their traffickers. These shelters are not for boys. Where do the rescued trafficked boys go?

c. Campaign Against Child Trafficking (CACT)

Campaign against Child Trafficking (CACT) has been initiated by Terre des Hommes aiming at developing a national strategy for combating child trafficking using three broad dimensions for addressing the problem: awareness generation, legal intervention, and projects at grass root level creating and strengthening a region specific intervention through data base and building local strategies, and building partnerships with appropriate groups like decision makers, media and citizens to ensure implementation of international conventions, initiating national legislative processes, and aiding in conversion into enforceable laws (Bajpai 2006).

Delhi Police have hit upon a novel idea to check trafficking and prevent children from becoming drug addicts—opening and running schools for them from police stations. The force inaugurated first such school at the Nizamuddin Police station with 20 children—mostly rag pickers—being enrolled in the first batch (Schools at Police Stations 2014).

8.8 Intervention Strategies by Non-Government Organisations Against Child Trafficking

Bachpan Bachao Aandolan (BBA), a ray of hope for many children who are stuck under the burden of slavery and living without human identity and dignity as child labourers, trafficked children and forced labourers. Also known as "Save the Childhood Movement", it is a campaign which was initiated by a Nobel Peace Prize winner, Kailash Satyarthi, in 1980 and has acted to protect the rights of more than 83,000 children from 144 countries. BBA's mission is "to identify, liberate, rehabilitate and educate children in servitude through direct intervention, child and community participation, coalition building, consumer action, promoting ethical trade practices and mass gaming". BBA believes that eradication of poverty and providing children with education can result in lowering the number of child and bonded labours.

BBA follows the three strand strategy: Prevention, Protection and Rehabilitation.

1. Prevention: BBA reaches out to the masses to create awareness about the problems related to child labour through community intervention. It campaigns in the villages and enlightens people about the benefits of education and encourages them to not choose/send off children as employees. Their Bal Mitra Gram program has been a successful model for the elimination of child labour and trafficking. This program acknowledges the villages where all the children have enrolled in school, and villages which are thriving to eliminate the practice of child labour. Some campaigns initiated by BBA against child labour include 'Anti-Firecracker Campaign' which highlights the difficulties of young children involved in the manufacturing of fire crackers. Their 'Fairplay Campaign' was to put light upon the child labour in the manufacture of sports goods in India. At National level, The Child Labour Free India Campaign in 2012 was arranged to demand the blanket ban on Child labour in the country. BBA's Siksha Yatra in 2001, a 6 months long campaign was launched and contributed in making of Right of Children to Free and Compulsory Education Act, which was finally adopted in 2009.
2. Protection: with the help of the Indian legislative provision—BBA yearns to abolish the practice of Child Labour in the country and enforce the fundamental rights of children. It also ensures the implementation of these laws and works to recover fines from employers and traffickers. BBA's Victim Assistance Program ensures the restitution of the rights of children who have been trafficked for bonded or forced labour. Under this program, trafficked victims are identified, rescued and are provided with immediate care and legal assistance. BBA has also worked on the issue of missing children and has focused upon the linkage of missing children with trafficking.
3. Rehabilitation: BBA provides support to the victims of trafficking and protect them from being re-trafficked. They run various programs for the rehabilitation of the children. BBA provides trauma counseling, shelter (in BBA homes), transit rehabilitation centers and also offers legal assistance for access to the provisions provided by the government.

Mukti Ashram is a short-term children home for trafficked and homeless children. BBA provides immediate shelter to the rescued children. They are provided with medical help, food, clothing, non-formal education recreational facilities and psycho-social counseling during their stay until the legal formalities are completed and children are re-united with their parents.

Bal Asharam was established in 1998. It is a long term rehabilitation and training centre for the children who do not have families. Here, children stay for longer duration and are provided with quality education, vocational training and skill development programmes.

Public Interest Litigations: BBA also works for making and enforcing policies in favour of children through the legal route. Some of the recent judgments passed are as follows:

1. Upholding the Constitutional validity of Right to Education;
2. Prohibition of employment of children in Circus;
3. Recovery of fines and cancellation/sealing of establishments employing child labourers; and
4. Protection of girls being trafficked through unregulated placement agencies.

BBA aspires to create a child friendly society which is free from exclusion and exploitation wherein children receive free and quality education. It works at many levels—from direct intervention and community participation on the ground to advocating for policy change at decision-making level. BBA believes in the total elimination of child labour.

References

10,000 children trafficked into NE annually from B'desh, Nepal (2008, September 19). *Press Trust of India.*

Agarwal, I. (2008). *Combating child trafficking*. New Delhi: Adhyayan publishers and distributors.

Ali, B. & Thukral, E. G. (2007). *Combating Child Trafficking. A User's Handbook.* New Delhi: HAQ: Centre for Child Rights and CACT.

Bajpai, A. (2006). *Child rights in India law policy and practice* (2nd ed.). New Delhi: Oxford University Press.

CACT (2002). *Children Bought and Sold. We can STOP it.* NewDelhi: HAQ: Centre for Child Rights. Retrieved from http://www.haqcrc.org/sites/default/files/STOP%20English_0.pdf.

Childless families drive traffickers' business. (2014, October 9). *The Hindustan Times.*

Cops Bust Trafficking Racket; Four arrested. (2014, September 19). *The Hindustan Times.*

Ministry of Women and Child Development, Government of India. (n.d.). *Sub group report child protection in the eleventh five year Plan* (2007–2012). Retrieved from http://wcd.nic.in/wgchilprotection.pdf.

National Crime Records Bureau (2014). *Crime in india 2013.* Ministry of Home Affairs, Government of India. Retrieved from http://ncrb.gov.in/CD-CII2013/home.asp.

National Human Rights Commission. (2005). *Action research on trafficking*. New Delhi: Orient Longman.

Naveen, P. (2014, September 30). Gang injects kidnapped kids with hormones. *The Times of India.*

Planning Commission, Government of India. (2008). *Eleventh five year plan*. New Delhi: Oxford University Press.

Schools at Police Stations to fight trafficking, drug abuse. (2014, November 15). *The Hindustan Times.*

Sex trafficking: Is there no end? (2014, September 28). *Times of India.*

Siddharth, R. D. (2012). *Mandsaur's ugly truth: Sex trade in the name of tradition*. Retrieved November 8, 2014 http://www.ndtv.com/article/india/mandsaur-s-ugly-truth-sex-trade-in-the-name-of-tradition-278629.

Sinha, I. (1996). In *Child prostitution: a discussion*. Jonaki. (Vol. 1, no. 1) *November.*

Sinha, K. (2014, November 18). India is now world's slave capital. *The Times of India.*

Thukral E. G., Ali. B., & Bild. E.(2008). *Still out of focus. Status of India's children 2008.* New Delhi: HAQ Center for Child Rights.
Thukral, E.G. (2005). *Status of Children in India Inc.* New Delhi: HAQ: Centre for Child Rights.
Tiwary, D. (2014, August 7). 1 lakh children go missing in India every year: MHA. *The Times of India.*
Trafficked Kids are not offender. (2014, August 27). *The Times of India.*
William, A. T. (2008). *Child trafficking an unconscious phenomenon.* New Delhi: Kanishka publishers, distributors.

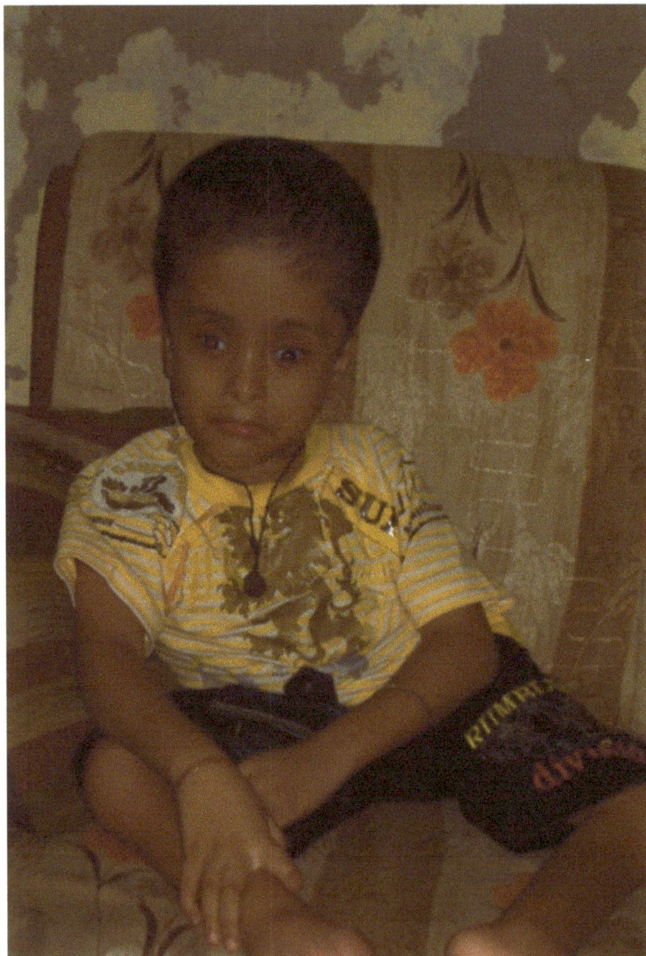

(Source: Personal collection of author)

UNITED NATIONS CONVENTION ON THE RIGHTS OF THE CHILD

Article 23 (Children with disabilities): Children who have any kind of disability have the right to special care and support, as well as all the rights in the Convention, so that they can live full and independent lives

Chapter 9
Children with Disabilities—The Invisible Child

Abstract We must realise that a child with disabilities is not disabled, but is differently abled and hence should be given opportunities to express herself differently. The chapter introduces the concept of disability and traces how this concept has evolved from a charity model, to a bio-centric model, to a social model, to now a human rights model. The chapter gives various definitions of disability, along with the ICF model. It presents the constitutional provisions for Children with disabilities (CWD) in India. The extent of disability as per Census 2011 is discussed. Policies for CWD are presented. CWD and international declarations like UN Standard Rules on The Equalization of Opportunities for Persons With Disabilities (PWD) and The U.N. Convention on the Rights of Persons with Disabilities (UNCRPD) are briefly discussed. The Persons with Disability act 1995 presents specifically the sections covering various concerns related to CWD. National Trust for the Welfare of Persons with Autism, Cerebral Palsy, Mental Retardation and Multiple Disabilities Act (1999) and Rehabilitation Council of India Act (1992) find a place in the chapter. Governmental services and facilities for PWD are outlined. NGOs like Concerned Action Now (CAN), National Association for the Blind (NAB) and National Centre for Promotion of Employment for Disabled People (N.C.P.E.D.P.) working for rehabilitation and advocacy of rights of PWD are briefly profiled.

Keywords Children with disabilities · U.N. Convention on the Rights of Persons with Disabilities

9.1 Introduction

Far from being a mere physical fact, disability is also a normative, cultural and legal construct. What society in a particular time in its history considers as a disabling condition, reflects its conception of a normal and socially functional human beings:

G. Chopra, *Child Rights in India*, DOI 10.1007/978-81-322-2446-4_9

and hence in a way reflects society's self image (National Human Rights Commission 2005).

In the last decade, there has been an increasing discussion about the needs and rights of persons with disabilities and issues that concern their participation in mainstream society. The underlying effort in the past decade has put disability in the centre of debate that focuses on the idea of 'society for all'. There is a new conception of societies that are all inclusive and espouse towards embracing all differences, both social as well as physical. Instead of expecting variously different groups to fit into a common mould of the 'mainstream', there is a marked shift in redefining the construe of social mainstream. There is now a conscious attempt to break the cycle of poverty, disability, segregation, powerlessness and charity, all of which lead to the denial of opportunities for persons with disabilities. Thrust is towards making the persons with disabilities realise their rights. We must realise that child with disabilities is not disabled, but is differently abled and hence should be given opportunities to express herself differently.

Even though it is difficult to have precise figures, it is estimated that more than 10 % of world's total population have some type of disabling physical or mental impairment. These figures are testimony to the enormous size of the problem and highlight the impact of the disability on every society. Disabled people frequently live in deplorable conditions, owing to the presence of physical and social barriers which prevent their integration and full participation in the community. Millions of children and adults worldwide are segregated and deprived of their rights and are, in effect, living on the margins. This is unacceptable (Onsando et al. 2009).

Children with disabilities and their families constantly experience barriers to the enjoyment of their basic human rights and to their inclusion in society. The societal apathy is reflected when their abilities are overlooked and people are over protective or over helpful. Feeling pity for persons with disability is also a form of underestimation of capacities. Many times their capacities are underestimated. Often their needs are given low priority. The barriers they face are more frequently as a result of the environment in which they live than as a result of their impairment.

The Constitution of India ensures equality, freedom, justice and dignity of all individuals and implicitly mandates an inclusive society for all including persons with disabilities. In the recent years, there have been vast and positive changes in the perception of the society towards persons with disabilities. It has been realised that a majority of persons with disabilities can lead a better quality of life if they have equal opportunities and effective access to rehabilitation measures (National Policy for Persons with Disabilities 2006).

There has been an increasing recognition of abilities of persons with disabilities and emphasis on mainstreaming them in the society based on their capabilities. The Government of India has enacted three legislations for persons with disabilities viz. (i) Persons with Disability (Equal Opportunities, Protection of Rights and Full Participation) Act, 1995, which provides for education, employment, creation of barrier free environment, social security, legal redressal of complaints by PWD, etc. (ii) National Trust for Welfare of Persons with Autism, Cerebral Palsy, Mental Retardation and Multiple Disability Act, 1999 has provisions for legal guardianship of the four categories of PWD referred to in the act and creation of enabling environment for as much independent living as possible. (iii) Rehabilitation Council of India Act, 1992 deals with the development of manpower and maintaining standards in it and for providing rehabilitation services.

In addition to the legal framework, extensive infrastructure has been developed. The following seven national Institutes are working for doing research in developing teaching-learning material, assistive devices, documenting researches and development of manpower in different disabilities, namely:

- National Institute of Visually Handicapped, Dehradun.
- National Institute for Orthopaedically Handicapped, Kolkata.
- National Institute for Mentally Handicapped, Secunderabad.
- National Institute for Hearing Handicapped, Mumbai.
- National Institute of Rehabilitation Training and Research, Cuttack.
- National Institute for Empowerment of Persons with Multiple Disabilities, Chennai.
- Institute for the Physically Handicapped, New Delhi.

There are five Composite Rehabilitation Centres, four Regional Rehabilitation Centres and 120 District Disability Rehabilitation Centres (DDRCs) providing various kinds of rehabilitation services to persons with disabilities. Apart from this, National Handicapped and Finance Development Corporation (NHFDC) has been providing loans on concessional terms for undertaking self-employment ventures by the persons with disabilities through state channelizing agencies (National Policy for persons with Disability 2006).

Children grow at different rates and have different character traits unique to them. Even though development follows a broad pattern, there can be variation in speed, sequence and susceptibility to situations among children. In other words, development is differential, with great variation in individual characteristics. When some of these differences are overt and more noticeable than others, and when the deviations go beyond the normal range, they constitute a special need. This special need may arise due to impairment, development delay in a particular domain, or deficit in a particular area (Ramakrishnan and Anandalakshmy 2009).

9.2 The Constitution of India and Persons with Disabilities

The Constitution of India, adopted in 1950, is the country's primary piece of legislation and the foundation of all national laws, rules, and policies. The Constitution embodies the basic concept of 'equality in all spheres of human activity' in its chapter on fundamental rights and prohibits discrimination on the grounds of race, caste, sex, descent and place of birth. However, it does not explicitly mention disability as prohibited grounds for discrimination. The closest it comes to address the concern of disability is in *Article 41* of the Constitution which specifically says that "state shall within the limits of its economic capacity and development make effective provision for securing the right to work, to education and public assistance in cases of unemployment, old age, sickness and *disablement*, and in other cases of undeserved want".

As per The Constitution (Eighty-Sixth Amendment) Act, 2002, *Article 21A* of India's Constitution establishes free and compulsory education for all children aged 6–14 years and *Article 45* of the Constitution provides for early childhood care and education for all children until they reach age six. As an amendment of *Article 51A*, the following clause shall be added, namely:- "... who is a parent or guardian to provide opportunities for education to his child or, as the case may be, ward between the age of 6 and 14 years"; Article 51 fixes the responsibility on parents as well to ensure that their children are attending school.

9.3 Understanding Disability

9.3.1 Concept

Is disability about lack of ability due to impairments in the body or the mind of the individual or is it about a society which is oblivious to diverse needs of persons with disability (PWD) and just expects them to 'fit in' to the mould of the so-called 'normal' people? Or is it about governments and systems which at every step espouse negativity and apathy, hence oppressing and blocking the functionality of PWD? Or is it about a society that has decided to give up on a human resource because it has assumed/formed a stereotype image of PWD as being incapable? These issues will be examined in this section.

For most of the twentieth century in 'western' societies, disability has been equated with 'flawed' mind and bodies. It spans people who are 'crippled', 'confined' to wheelchairs, 'victims' of conditions such as cerebral palsy, or 'suffering' from deafness, blindness, 'mental illness' or 'mental handicap'. The individual's impairment or 'abnormality' necessitates dependence on family, friends and welfare services, with many segregated in specialised institutions. In short, disability amounts to a 'personal tragedy' and a social problem or 'burden' for the rest of the society (Barnes and Mercer 2003). However from 1960s, this orthodoxy in thinking and practice was challenged by disabled people, particularly, those forced to live in residential institutions, who took a lead in calling for policy changes (Hunt 1966). They directed attention to the impact of social and environment barriers, such as inaccessible buildings and transport, discriminatory attitudes and negative cultural stereotypes, in 'disabling' people with impairments (Bowe 1978).

It was largely left to the disabled people to develop their own critique of the conventional approaches to disability. Hunt (1966) in an edited collection challenged the standard preoccupation with the medical and personal 'suffering' experienced by individuals with impairment. Hunt argued that 'the problem of disability lies not only in the impairment of function and its effects on us individually, but also more importantly, in the area of our relationship with 'normal' people.' A sharp dividing line is drawn between the social lives and interests of 'able bodied' and disabled people. The latter are 'set apart from the ordinary' because they pose a direct 'challenge' to commonly held societal values: 'as unfortunate, useless, different, oppressed and sick'. As Darlington et al. (1981) point out, disabled people are viewed as 'unfortunate' because they are unable to enjoy the social and material benefits of contemporary society. These include opportunities for marriage, parenthood and everyday social interaction.

The perception of disabled people as 'useless', flows from their lack of engagement in mainstream economic activities. As a consequence of their failure to conform to 'normality', whether in appearance or in control over their minds and bodies, they are set apart as 'different'. Moreover, people's shocked reactions to obvious 'deviant' stimulate their own deepest fears and difficulties, their failure to accept themselves as they really are and other person simply as 'other' (Hunt 1966).

The emergence of socio-political approaches to disability reflects disabled people's claim that they experience significant and entrenched social oppression. This is evidenced by a highly unequal distribution of material resources and uneven power relations and opportunities to participate in everyday life, compared to those available to non-disabled. Disability is viewed as a form of social oppression akin to sexism and racism. Like sexism and racism, disablism expresses itself in exclusionary and oppressive practices at a wide range of levels: interpersonal, institutional, cultural and societal (Barnes and Mercer 2003).

Iris Marion Young (1990) differentiates five main aspects of oppression: exploitation, marginalisation, powerlessness, cultural imperialism and violence. Marginalisation refers to the systematic removal of a social group from the main stream of everyday life. Powerlessness is when people have little control over what to do with their lives. It is verified by sharp divide between those who exercise authority or power (as in case of professionals) and those who simply 'take orders' and lack authority or status. Exploitation needs no explanation. Cultural imperialism is when 'able bodied normalcy' is embedded in everyday thinking and behaviour as a privileged or desirable state of being. Violence against the disabled people is systematic and wide spread. Irrespective of whether it takes the form of physical or sexual attacks, eugenic policies or verbal ridicule, it is directed at specific individuals because they belong to a particular social category the 'disabled'.

Children are entitled to protection from violence, exploitation and abuse, including from economic exploitation, sexual exploitation and abuse, sale, trafficking and any similar practices prejudicial to the child's welfare. Children and young persons with disabilities have been reported as being significantly more likely to be the victims of physical, sexual and psychological abuse than their peers without disabilities. The powerlessness, social isolation and stigma faced by children with disabilities make them highly vulnerable to violence and exploitation in their own homes, as well as in care centres, institutions or on the street (Baladerian 1991). A child who requires assistance with washing, dressing and other intimate care activities may be particularly vulnerable to sexual abuse. Perpetrators can include caretakers, attendants, family members, peers or anyone who enjoys a position of trust and power. School bullying is also a form of abuse (UNICEF 2007).

CWD is at risk of violence and abuse as not only because they have difficulty in defending themselves, but also because their complaints are often dismissed or not taken seriously.

All too often, however, there is a reluctance to recognise the competence of children with disabilities to contribute effectively to decision-making processes. This can be compounded by attitudes of caretakers, teachers and even parents, who may underestimate the ability of certain children to contribute a valid opinion. Changing such views about the ability of these children to participate—or to benefit from support in participating—in discussion and decision-making concerning their lives is critical. It represents a major challenge to prevailing attitudes and preconceptions in all countries, one that must be addressed through training as well as through wider efforts to shift public beliefs and attitudes (UNICEF 2007).

In summary, people with impairments have been 'isolated, incarcerated, observed, written about, operated upon, instructed, implanted, regulated, treated institutionalised and controlled to a degree probably unequal to that experienced by any other minority group (Davis 1997).

9.3.2 *Historical Understanding*

In Hindu scripture, Mahabharata, Dhritrashatra, the blind prince of the Kaurva dynasty of Hastinapur, was shown as possessor of enormous strength and potency. He excelled in all the sciences and arts, in martial arts like mace-fighting and even in archery. Yet he was deprived of his right to be the king of Hastinapur due to his visual disability (Bagchi 2009). Characters like Shakuni (who had an orthopaedic disability) from Mahabharata, and Manthara (a dwarf) from Ramayana were shown with evil intent and as evil characters due to whom lot of misfortune fell on Pandavas and Lord Rama, resulting in wars, death and destruction.

Histories of disability in western societies start their journey in ancient Greece with its idealisation of body shape and fitness linked to acceptance of infanticide for those born with visible impairments. The dread of impairment is reinforced by examples drawn from the bible suggesting that it is a punishment of past sins. There is also ample evidence that everyday life and popular culture were permeated with views that associated impairment with evil and wrong doings and a source of ridicule, fear and pity (Thomas 1982; Barnes 1997). Darwin also wrote and propagated 'survival of the fittest', making impairment as a kind of threat to social progress. Finkelstein's (1980) primary aim was to explain the development of an ideology of disability that stressed 'personal tragedy, passivity and dependence'. Eugenicists further highlighted links between intellectual and physical deficiency and a range of social evils, including crime, vagrancy, alcoholism, prostitution and unemployment (Kevles 1985).

The nineteenth century and the early twentieth century saw a greater trend towards putting the persons with disability in hospitals and asylums. Here, they were not just excluded, but were controlled by medical practitioners. The image of helplessness and dependence was further perpetuated. Medical monopoly of health care was legitimated by the state. Also emerged, segregated schools for disabled children. So, there were special schools for 'cripples', 'blind', 'deaf and mute', 'morons' and so on. The training provided to children in these institutions further ensured their minimal participation in mainstream society and in economic participation, leading to further exclusion. Further, the concept of 'social hygiene' gained grounds, where persons with disability were not just put in institutions, but were sterilised so that they could not procreate 'more of their kind'.

Finkelstein's (1980) accounts emergence of post- industrial society in the second-half of twentieth century, with the new computerised, information technology identified as harbinger of significant social and economic changes. He interprets this as bringing together more positive opportunities for the inclusion of persons with disability in paid employment, so allowing 'the most severely physically impaired people…to live independently in community'.

The twentieth century has been marked by a host of social movements, one of the most recent ones being the disability movement. The philosophical foundations of disability studies are rooted in the activism and experiences of the disabled people themselves. The disability rights movement and the narration of the experiences of the disabled people challenged the traditional meaning assigned to impairment based on medical approach. This is contrast to the new meaning assigned to 'disability' under the disability studies perspective, which interprets it in social and contextual terms (Chander 2013). The activism began with the impairment specific groups like the blind and the deaf who started demanding equal rights in the twentieth century. The movement spread to include all disabilities and many groups joined the movement.

With increasing consciousness about their identities, the leaders of the new born movement of the disabled people identified themselves as those who were deemed and rendered by society as 'disabled'. Their slogans reflected this newfound consciousness: slogans like 'you gave us your dimes, give us our rights now' became well known (Scotch 2001). Today one of the most popular slogan at the international level of the disability movement is 'Nothing about us without us', speaking clearly of a need to take control of decisions affecting their lives, and that persons with disability are not handing over the reins to anyone. Disabled people have come to take greater pride in their identities and begun to demand their rights just like the other minority groups. Hence, the focus has shifted from medical or welfare approach towards social-and right-based approach. The disabled people are not subjects of pity or charity, but have equal right to be counted in for all amenities and opportunities in education, participation, decision making, recreation, just like their non-disabled counterparts.

9.3.3 *Models of Disability*

Disability has been defined differently in terms of medical, social and human rights aspects. The definitions associated with disability have changed over time with new perspectives evolving at a global level as a result of continuous research and discussion among the stakeholders involved in the process of empowering all individuals to be productive members of society.

The diverse approaches to disability can be traced in various definitions of disability. Law, policy, programmes and rights instruments also reflect these different approaches and associated discourses that treat disability either as an individual pathology or as a social pathology. Within these two over riding paradigms- (a) individual pathology and (b) social pathology- the five major identifiable formulations of disability are: the charity model, the bio-centric or medical model, the functional model, the social model and the human rights model. The first two are chronologically prior and reflect the ways disability has been framed historically in many cultures around the world. The latter three view disability as a social pathology and have emerged in recent decades through interventions by disability and human rights activists (National Human Rights Commission 2005). It is worth noting that all the five approaches are still at play in contemporary laws, social practices and the way programmes are designed for persons with disability.

Charity Model The natural elements, demonology, past life, karma, curse and religious beliefs are the primary basis of this definition. This model treats people with disabilities as helpless victims, needing care and protection. Provisions are made for children and people with disabilities as a matter of charity and not as judicial or human rights (Kitchlu 1991). As the term 'handicap' implies, derived as it is from the image of a beggar with a cap in his hand, this model relies largely on the goodwill of benevolent humanitarians for 'custodial care' of the disabled (Tomlinson 1982). The model rests on benevolence received form 'normal' people rather than the principle of equality and justice for PWD.

The charity model has its roots in English Poor laws, according to which claims to rights is valid on certain grounds and invalid on certain others. Disability was perceived as a disqualification and perhaps for this very reason, the expression 'invalid' became synonymous with PWD. The charity model engineered stringent criteria for groups declared invalid ensuring their exclusion from social arrangements and services in public domain. The charity model-driven interventions, which are intended to be beneficial can actually compromise the beneficiaries' rights. Since entitlement to rights is often substituted by relief measures, over which the groups declared invalid have little control or power to bargain, the charity model creates an army of powerless individuals dependent on either state sponsored charities or arrangements maintained by individuals (National Human Rights Commission 2005).

Bio-centric or Medical Model This approach emphasises the biological origin of the disabling condition which may be prevented or ameliorated through medical intervention. Persons with disabilities are positioned as abnormal deviations from accepted norms of physical, cognitive and mental and emotional standards for normal human beings and given custodial care. On one extreme of this paradigm, is considering the deviant person as being undeserving and dangerous and therefore placed in prison like institutional environments (Kavoori 2002).

In the medical model, individuals with certain physical, intellectual, psychological and mental impairments are taken as disabled. According to this, the disability lies in the individual as it is equated with restrictions of activity with the burden of adjusting with environment through cures, treatment and rehabilitation (Ministry of Statistics and Programme Implementation 2012).

The contemporary bio-centric model of disability regards disability as a medical or genetic condition. The implication remains that disabled persons and their families should strive for "normalisation", through medical cures and miracles. Although, biology is no longer the only lens through which disability is viewed in law and policy, it continues to play a prominent role in determining programme eligibility, entitlement to benefits, and it also influences access to rights and full social participation (Mohit 2003). The aims of intervention of this model are twofold; one to prevent disability, and second to bring the individuals' embodied experience in line with conventional standards of normalcy. PWD are positioned as 'abnormal' in comparison to the established norms of a normal human being. The limitations of the medical model are evident as it aspires to address problems of inequality by preventing or minimizing the existence of differences by imposing the majority norm of behaviour on inherently different minorities (National Human Rights Commission 2005).

The medical model of disability views people with a disability as having a deficiency or impairment that needs to be "fixed." Therefore, the person with a disability is the problem, and not the (sometimes) inaccessible society in which that person lives. As a result, "everything is done to help the person by trying to make them more 'normal', believing that this alone will lead to a better quality of life." The ideologies that the medical model is built upon are integral to the segregated model of education. Both see the person and their disability as the problem, and both seek to "fix" the disability, bringing the person as close to "normal" as possible. As put by Ramakrishnan and Anandalakshmy (2009), disability tends to be mystified by the medical model and, as a result, children with special needs are marginalised.

Under the medical approach to disability, disability is the direct consequence of the individual impairment. Therefore, medical cure or rehabilitation is the natural solution for disabled people from the view point of scientific authenticity. Disability activists themselves established the social approach of disability that challenged the very assumption of 'normality' and redefined disability as social oppression. In other words, the problems are not within the individual disabled person but within society. Human rights approach conceptualises disability as violation of human rights. This approach challenges the fundamental inequality (Onsando et al. 2009).

A critical analysis of the development of the charity and bio-centric models suggests that they have grown out of the "vested interests" of professionals and the elite to keep the disabled "not educable" or declare them mentally retarded (MR) children and keep them out of the mainstream school system, thus using the special schools as a "safety valve" for mainstream schools (Tomlinson 1982).

Till the nineteenth century, the above two models dictated the care of persons with disabilities. This was mainly considered a charitable act and special organisations run by missionaries, religious and philanthropic organisations established segregated institutions designed to provide care for persons with disabilities; education was not the primary aim of these institutions (Byrnes 1990).

Functional Model In this model, the difficulties experienced by a person are seen as arising from a mismatch between the individual's biological condition and functional capacities on the one hand and environmental and situational factors on the other (National Human Rights Commission 2005). In comparison to the medical model which tries to prevent or cure the impairment, the functional model tends to treat perceived incapacity of the disabled individual through services and supports which are aimed at making the individual as functional as possible. This involves compensation rather than cure, in order for people to live lives that are as 'normal' as possible (Meyer et al. 1990).

The positive contribution of the model has been in the development of assistive technologies and specialised services. Its failure, however, lies in linking the entitlement to rights with the ability of the disabled person to negotiate diverse environments, with the use of compensatory skills and assistive technologies. The onus is on the individual to fit within the system, not on the system to include the individual. Moreover, in the functional model, the professionals remain in the centre of defining and addressing needs by virtue of their position. In many instances, the key problem with the professionals' decisions taken in the 'best interest' of the disabled person may actually be in contradiction to that persons own goals and life choices (Rioux 2001). Hence, the functional model fails to address the short comings of the environment and social arrangements, and encourages continuous control over the lives of people with disabilities by various state mechanisms and professionals (National Human Rights Commission 2005). Segregated or special schools are hence considered appropriate environments to develop the individual's functional abilities to cope with the normal, physical and social environment (Alur 2002).

Social Model A very recent and a radical new development is the intervention of disabled people themselves in the social construction of disability. This perhaps is happening for the first time in the human history. It has contributed to a process away from negative definition of disability as indicating abnormality and impairment to a positive definition that first and foremost asserts essential humaneness, understood around notions of human rights and community life, of the disabled that they share with others, and then within this shared framework identifies special features that make disabled people different from others (National Human Rights Commission 2005).

The social model of disability acknowledges that obstacles to participation in society and its institutions reside in the environment rather than in the individual, and that such barriers can and must be prevented, reduced or eliminated. Environmental obstacles come in many guises and are found at all levels of society. They are reflected in policies and regulations created by governments. Such obstacles may be physical—for example barriers in public buildings, transportation and recreational facilities. They may also be attitudinal—widespread underestimation of the abilities and potential of children with disabilities creates a vicious cycle of under-expectation, under-achievement and low priority in the allocation of resources (UNICEF 2007).

In the social model, the focus is on the society, which imposes undue restrictions on the behaviour of persons with impairment. In this, disability does not lie in individuals, but in the interaction between individuals and society. It advocates that persons with disabilities are right holders and are entitled to strive for the removal of institutional, physical, informational and attitudinal barriers in society (Ministry of Statistics and Programme Implementation 2012). The social model of disability doesn't find the deficiency within the person.

This approach to disability has led to a shift in focus from *a child's limitations* arising from impairments, to the *barriers within society* that prevent the child from having access to basic social services, developing to the fullest potential and from enjoying her or his rights. This is the essence of the social model of disability (UNICEF 2007).

This model rejects the long-established idea that obstacles to the participation of disabled people arise primarily from their impairment and focuses instead on environmental barriers. These include:

- prevailing attitudes and preconceptions, leading to underestimation;
- the policies, practices and procedures of local and national government;
- the structure of health, welfare and education systems;
- lack of access to buildings, transport and to the whole range of community resources available to the rest of the population;
- the impact of poverty and deprivation on the community as a whole and more specifically on persons with disabilities and their families (UNICEF 2007).

Social model views disability as a form of social oppression like sexism and racism. It is viewed like this since the PWD are deprived of opportunities in day-to-day life either due to under-expectation of 'normal' people or due to seclusion due to lack of understanding/fear of the 'deviant disabled' or due to desire to control lives by taking decisions for PWD and hence rendering them powerless. The sense of 'cultural imperialism' is predominant in the discourse of 'normal lives' where a nuanced assumption is of the normal way of living being superior and desirable, leaving the disabled oppressed, weak and with a poor self and social esteem.

Emphasizing the social construction of disability in no way implies rejecting medical and professional services and supports. Nor does it mean denying the potential of intervention in reducing or alleviating an impairment or in providing rehabilitation or training. Provision of technical aids, medical intervention and professional support are all important ways of promoting empowerment and independence and are an integral part of the social model. For example, a simple medical procedure may be all that is required to help a child with eye or ear infections to benefit from classroom learning (UNICEF 2007).

Human Rights Model This affirms that all human beings irrespective of their disabilities are equally entitled to rights as others in all respects of education, employment and opportunities to live with dignity. This places the onus on the legal and social environment to provide all the necessary support to accommodate the different needs of the individual. In this model, the environment has the compulsion to change to meet individual needs rather than requiring the individual to somehow fit into standard norms. This has resulted in a major shift in paradigm which has caused the entire world community and all stakeholders to reframe the policies and guidelines for the education and care of people with disabilities as matter of their fundamental human right to enjoying equal opportunities in all respects (National Human Rights Commission 2005).

The human rights model positions disability as an important dimension of human culture, and it affirms that all humans irrespective of their disabilities have certain rights which are inalienable. This model build upon the spirit of Universal Declaration of Human Rights, 1948, according to which all human beings are born free and equal in rights and dignity (National Human Rights Commission 2005).

At the heart of this mission lies respect for variation in human cultures and the recognition that people are different on several considerations such as gender, race, language, religion and other aspects. We have to respect diversity. Yet at the same time, it is important to remember that all individuals cannot be put in a single mould. Another important dimension is equality and non-discrimination. Yet at the same time, equality has to have with it reasonable differentiation or else we would disrespect individual variations. It does not have to be blind non-discrimination, but a reasonable differentiation which accounts for diversity. Accessibility is an important component of human rights achievement. Accessibility is not just at physical level, but also of social and cultural structures.

9.3.4 Definitions of Disability

The World Health Organisation (WHO) in 1976, provided a three fold definition of impairment, disability and handicap, explaining that, 'an impairment is any loss or abnormality of psychological, physiological or anatomical structure or function; a disability is any restriction or lack (resulting from an impairment) of ability to perform an activity in the manner or within the range considered normal for the individual'; handicap is a disadvantage for a given individual, resulting from an impairment or a disability, that prevents fulfillment of a role that is considered normal (depending on age, sex, social and cultural factors) for that individual. The disability sector around the world found the description of impairment, disability and handicap very confusing. The WHO redefined and said 'impairment' refers to organ level functions or structures, 'disability' refers to person level limitations in physical and psycho-cognitive activities, and 'handicap' to social abilities or relation between the individual and society (National Human Rights Commission 2005).

As per the *World Health Organisation; Disability* is an umbrella term, covering impairments, activity limitations, and participation restrictions. Impairment is a problem in body function or structure; an activity limitation is a difficulty encountered by an individual in executing a task or action; while a participation restriction is a problem experienced by an individual in involvement in life situations. Thus disability is a complex phenomenon, reflecting an interaction between features of a person's body and features of the society in which he or she lives (Ministry of Statistics and Programme Implementation 2012).

The Convention on the Rights of Persons with Disabilities (2006), the first legally binding disability specific human rights convention, adopted by the United Nations gives two descriptions of disability. The Preamble to the Convention states that "Disability results from the interaction between persons with impairments and attitudinal and environmental barriers that hinder their full and effective participation in society on an equal basis with others." Again it emphasises that "Persons with disabilities include those who have long-term physical, mental, intellectual or sensory impairments which in interaction with various barriers may hinder their full and effective participation in society on an equal basis with others." Both the expressions reflect a shift from a medical model to social model of disability (Ministry of Statistics and Programme Implementation 2012).

Medical definition of disability considers disability as individual pathology- a condition grounded in physiological, biological and intellectual impairment of an individual. Social definition of disability is well put by UN Standard Rules on the Equalization of opportunities for persons with disability, 1993 from a perspective that emphasises social conditions which disable a group of individuals by ignoring their needs of accessing opportunities in a manner conducive to their circumstances. British Council defines disability from human rights perspective as 'disability is the disadvantage or restriction of activity caused by a society which takes little or no account of people who have impairments and thus excludes them from mainstream activities'. Therefore, like racism or sexism, disability is described as a consequence of discrimination and disregard to the unique circumstances of people with disabilities (National Human Rights Commission 2005).

In India, different definitions of disability conditions have been introduced for various purposes, essentially following the medical model and, as such, they have been based on various criteria of ascertaining abnormality or pathologic conditions of persons. In absence of a conceptual framework based on the social model in the Indian context, no standardisation for evaluating disability across methods has been achieved. In common parlance, different terms such as disabled, handicapped, crippled, physically challenged, are used inter-changeably, indicating noticeably the emphasis on pathologic conditions (Ministry of Statistics and Programme Implementation 2012).

National Human Rights Commission (NHRC), in Disability Manual, 2005 outlines the definitions as given by the Rehabilitation Council of India Act, (RCI) 1992 and the People with Disability Act, (PWD) 1995. These are adopted by all current Indian

Government regulations. The definitions given by the World Health Organisation (WHO) in 1976 are also taken as guidelines by many Indian institutions (Table 9.1).

Table 9.1 Definitions of Disability

Source	Terminology	Definition
RCI Act, 1992 PWD Act, 1995	Person with Disability	A person suffering from not less than 40 % of any disability as certified by a medical authority
WHO 1976	Impairment	This is a disturbance at the organ level, identified by a process of pathological or medical diagnosis
WHO 1976	Disability	This is the consequence of impairment in terms of functional performance and activity by the individual
RCI Act, 1992	Handicap/ Disability used as synonyms	
WHO, 1976	Handicap	This is the disadvantage experienced by the individual as a result of impairments and disabilities, thus reflects interaction with and adaptation to the individual surroundings
PWD Act, 1995	Disability	'Means': Blindness, Low vision, Leprosy-cured, Hearing impairment, Locomotor disability, Mental retardation and Mental illness
RCI Act, 1992 PWD Act, 1995	Person with Low Vision	A person with impairment of visual functioning even after treatment or standard refractive correction, who is potentially incapable of using normal vision for the planning or execution of normal movement or work even with appropriate assistive device
RCI Act, 1992	Visual Disability/handicap	Refers to a condition where a person suffers from any of the following conditions: Total absence of sight or Visual acuity not exceeding 6/60 or 20/200 (Snellen) in the better eye with correcting lenses; or Limitation of the field of vision subtending an angle of 20 degree or worse
PWD Act, 1995	Blindness	
PWD Act, 1995	Leprosy cured person	Any person who has been cured of leprosy but is suffering from loss of sensation in hands or feet as well as loss of sensation and paresis in the eye and eye-lid but with no manifest deformity; He may manifest deformity and paresis, but has sufficient mobility in hands and feet to engage in normal economic activity; Extreme physical deformity as well as advanced age which prevents him from undertaking any gainful occupation, so the expression "leprosy cured" shall be construed accordingly
RCI Act, 1992	Hearing disability/deafness	Hearing impairment of seventy (70) decibels and above in the better ear or total loss of hearing in both ears. On the extreme spectrum would be those in whom the sense of hearing is non-functional for ordinary purposes in life. They do not hear sound at all even with amplified speech

(continued)

Table 9.1 (continued)

Source	Terminology	Definition
PWD Act, 1995	Hearing impairment	Loss of sixty(60) decibels or more in the better ear in the conversational range of frequencies
RCI Act, 1992 PWD Act, 1995	Loco motor disability	A person unable to execute distinctive activities associated with moving, both himself/ herself and objects, from place to place, and such inability resulting from affliction of either bones, joints, muscles or nerves
RCI Act, 1992 PWD Act, 1995	Mental retardation	A condition of arrested or incomplete development of mind of a person which is specially characterised by sub-normality of intelligence. Mental retardation is divisible into the following four categories Mild retardation IQ 50–70 Moderate retardation IQ 35–49 Severe retardation IQ 20–34 Profound retardation IQ under 20
RCI Act, 1992 PWD Act, 1995	Mental illness	Any mental disorder other than mental retardation
PWD Act, 1995	Cerebral palsy	A group of non-progressive conditions of a person characterised by abnormal motor control posture resulting from brain insult or injuries occurring in the pre-natal, peri-natal or infant period of development;
RCI Act, 1992	Orthopaedic or neurological disorder	A person shall be deemed to be orthopaedically or neurologically disabled if he/she has having disability of bones, joints or muscles leading to substantial restriction of the movement of the limbs or if he/she has any form of Cerebral palsy

Source National Human Rights Commission (2005)

The ICF is a classification of health and health-related conditions for children and adults that was developed by World Health Organisation (WHO) and published in 2001. The International Classification of Functioning Disability and Health (ICF) defines disability as functioning in a number of life areas like walking, talking, taking a bath, socializing accessing social services and many such domains are included in the definition. Disability is seen as a result of an interaction between *a person* (with a health condition) and that person's *contextual factors* (environmental factors and personal factors). Simply, disability is not seen as an individual's intrinsic feature but a result of interaction in an environment. The interaction of the same person with the health condition may yield different functioning level in different environments. Disability covers a spectrum of various levels of functioning at body level, person level and societal level. Disability denotes all of the following:

(A) impairments in body functions and structures
(B) limitations in activity
(C) restriction in participation

Simply, Disability = A + B + C

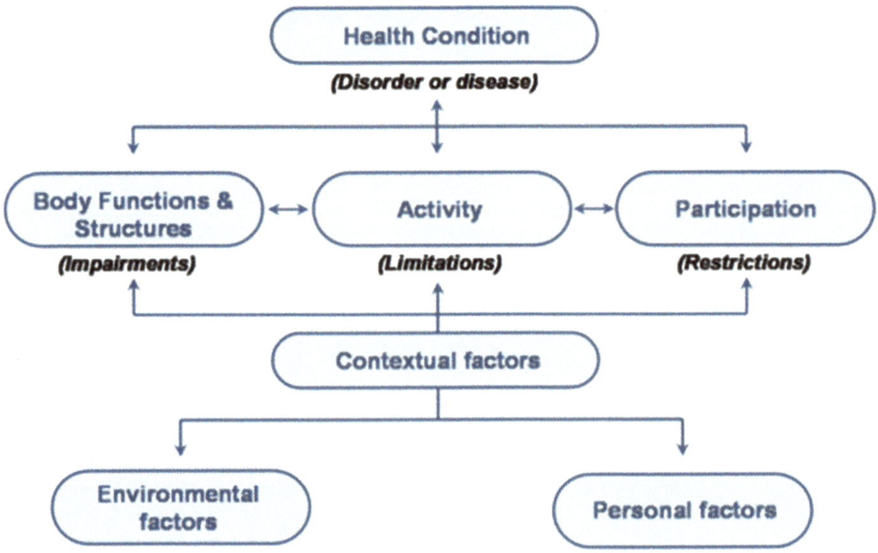

(*Source* http://www.rehab-scales.org/international-classification-of-functioning-disability-and-health.html).

Disability covers all impairments, activity limitations, and participation restrictions. This comprehensive approach is useful for prevention, rehabilitation, social policies and other interventions. ICF has been ratified in the World Health Assembly by 192 countries, legally binding as an information standard.

India continues to use the medical model of defining disability. Nearly, all definitions in the Indian context of government publications identify an individual as disabled based on medically determined physical or mental impairment that limits the person's ability to perform an activity. It is important to note that the complementary possibility that the individual is limited by a barrier in society or the environment is never considered. Reliance upon defining disabilities in purely medical terms, or as a functional deficit is a major problem with Indian policy design and implementation.

9.4 Magnitude of Disability in India

In Census 2011, information on 8 disabilities was collected which were, seeing, hearing, speech, movement, mental retardation, mental illness, any other, multiple disability. India's disability population was put at 26.8 million (2.21 % of population) of which 15 million were males and 11.8 millions were females. An overall increase of 4.8 million in absolute numbers has been recorded compared to Census 2001. Looking at the type of disability, 5 million seeing, 5 million hearing, 1.9 million speech, 5.4 million movement, 1.5 million mental retardation, 0.72 million mental illness, 2.1 million multiple disability, 4.9 million any others.

The first national level survey to enumerate the magnitude of disability was done only in 2001 in the census survey which is a decennial exercise. According to the 2001 Census findings, India's disability population was 21.9 million, or 2.13 % of the total population. Of the total population, 1.03 % were people with visual disabilities, 0.16 % were people with speech disabilities, 0.12 % were people with hearing disabilities, 0.59 % were people with locomotor disabilities, and 0.22 % were people with mental disabilities. People with visual and mental disabilities were slightly more concentrated in urban areas, while people with speech, hearing and locomotor disabilities were reported to be somewhat more concentrated in rural areas (Census 2001).

In its 58th round, the NSSO conducted its third comprehensive sample survey of the disabled population (July to December 2002). The survey included persons with mental disability, visual disability, hearing disability, speech disability and locomotor disability, and gathered data on the incidence and prevalence of the different types of disability, the causes of disability, and the marital status, educational level, living arrangements and activity status of individuals with disabilities. According to the survey, the disabled population is estimated at 18.49 million, or 1.8 % of the total population, which is slightly less than the 2001 Census findings. In rural areas, 1.85 % of the population has a disability, and in urban areas, 1.5 % of the population has a disability. About 8.4 % of rural households and 6.1 % of urban households report having at least one member with a disability (NSSO 2002). The NSSO survey found locomotor disability to be the most prevalent type of disability, affecting about 1,046 in 100,000 people in rural areas and 901 in 100,000 people in urban areas. The majority of people with disabilities acquired their disability during their lifetime, with only about 69 people in 100,000 who were either born with a disability or had become disabled during the previous 365 days. About 84 % of people with mental retardation and 82 % of people with a speech disability were born with their disability.

The NSSO results suggest that the number of people with disabilities in the country has declined in the last 10 years. However, the substantial difference between the Census 2001 and NSSO 2002 findings suggests that methodological issues, rather than any real shift in population numbers, may account for any noticeable change in disability statistics.

Table 9.2 Comparative Figures of Persons with Disabilities

Categories	Census (2011) Lakh	Census estimate (2001) (Lakh)
Locomotor	54	61.05
Visual	50	106.35
Hearing	50	12.62
Speech	19	16.41
Mental disability	–	22.64
Mental illness	7.2	–
Mental retardation	15	–
Multiple disabilities	21	–
Any other	49	–

The difference between the disability figures obtained from the three sources is due to different sampling designs as well as disability definitions. The Census and the NSS have different sampling design. The Census is an enumeration of the entire population of India while the NSS has a nationally representative stratified sample. The difference between the two census is because 8 disabilities were enumerated in Census 2011, while five disabilities were enumerated in Census 2001. There were changes in the definitions too. For example, one eyed persons were treated as disabled at Census 2001. At the Census 2011 such persons have not been treated as disabled in seeing. So, we see a decline in the numbers of persons with visual disability coming down to half from 106 million to 50 million in Census 2001 and 2011, respectively. Mental Retardation and Mental illness were covered under mental disability in Census 2001, but were put as separate categories of Mental Retardation and Mental Illness in Census 2011 (Table 9.2).

If we accept the census estimates 26.8 million people with disabilities, this certainly is a large number. Yet, it arguably is a gross underestimation especially, when one considers that WHO estimates a global prevalence rate of 10 %. This figure also falls considerably short when one compares these rates with those of more developed countries, such as USA (20 %) and UK (12 %), and indeed more recently, with other developing countries such as Brazil (14.5 %), Turkey (12.3 %) and Nicaragua (10.1 %). In India different authorities use various estimates, a leading India disability NGO, the National Center for Promotion of Employment for Disabled People (NCPEDP) argue that 5–6 of the population has a disability (Laha 2009). According to World Bank (2007), it is estimated that people with disabilities comprise between 4 and 8 % of the Indian population (around 40–90 million individuals).

9.5 Polices for Children with Disabilities

9.5.1 At the National Level

The two polices pertaining to children with disabilities that will be discussed here are National Policy for Persons with Disability (2006) and National Plan of Action for Children.

The government has adopted *National Policy for Disabled People in 2006*. The policy specifically says this for Children with Disabilities: Children with disabilities are the most vulnerable group and need special attention. The Government would strive to:—(a) Ensure right to care, protection and security for children with disabilities; (b) Ensure the right to development with dignity and equality creating an enabling environment where children can exercise their rights, enjoy equal opportunities and full participation in accordance with various statutes. (c) Ensure inclusion and effective access to education, health, vocational training along with specialised rehabilitation services to children with disabilities. (d) Ensure the right to development as well as recognition of special needs and of care, and protection of children with severe disabilities.

The core intervention areas included in the policy are on Prevention and Early Detection of disabilities where the government would target public health initiatives (like immunisation), functionaries would be trained for early detection of disabilities, rehabilitation staff like physiotherapists, occupational therapists, audiologists, speech pathologists would be made available. Training modules and facilities in disability prevention, early detection and intervention will be developed for medical and para-medical health functionaries and Anganwadi workers; Medical, educational and social rehabilitation programmes will be developed with the assistance of medical and rehabilitation professionals and with the participation of persons with disabilities and their families, legal guardians and communities; manpower development for health care and for inclusive education at preschool as well as primary and elementary school level; to ensure that all children with disabilities have access to preschool, primary and secondary school by 2020. For achieving this, effort will be made to make schools barrier free and accessible for CWD. Teaching learning aids (like Braille) will be made available for education of CWD. In case of children who can't be part of inclusive schools but are attending special schools, efforts will be directed to re-model these schools based on latest technology.

The National Policy for Persons with Disability includes extending rehabilitation services to rural areas, increasing trained personnel to meet needs; emphasizing education and training; increasing employment opportunities; focusing on gender equality; improving access to public services; encouraging state governments to develop a comprehensive social security policy; ensuring equal opportunities in sports, recreation and cultural activities; increasing the role of civil society organisations as service-providers to persons with disability and their families.

The National Plan of Action for Children (2005) has devoted a complete section to *Children with Disabilities*. The goals for CWD according to NPAC (Department of Women and Child Development, n.d.) are

- To ensure right to survival, care, protection and security for all children with disability.
- To ensure the right to development with dignity and equality creating an enabling environment where children can exercise their rights, enjoy equal opportunities and full participation in accordance with the UN Convention on

the Rights of the Child, the Persons with Disability Act, National Trust Act and other laws dealing with child rights in India.
- To ensure inclusion and effective access to education, health, vocational training along with specialised rehabilitation services to children.
- To ensure the right to development as well as a recognition of special needs and of care and protection to children with disabilities who are vulnerable, such as, children with severe multiple disabilities, children with mental illnesses, severe mental impairment, children with disabilities from poor families, girl children with disabilities and others.

The above goals will be achieved through the following *objectives* (Department of Women and Child Development, n.d.):

- Primary prevention of disabling conditions in children through timely immunisation, dietary corrections and supplementation of nutrients to children, prevention of accidents, proper maternal care during pregnancy and at the time of child birth.
- To prevent secondary level of disability through early detection and timely intervention and effective provision of information to families.
- To provide early identification and integrated early childhood services and opportunities to ensure optimum development of children with disabilities up to the age of 6 years.
- To provide early intervention services to prepare infants and pre-school children by integrating them into the general educational system.
- To ensure continued rehabilitation services to all children with disabilities, whoever requires them.
- To ensure inclusive and accessible education and life skill training for all children with disabilities beyond the stage of early interventions to enable them to develop their personality and abilities to their fullest potential.
- To ensure the safety, security and freedom of children with disabilities with focus on children with severe disability, mental disability and mental health difficulties, from abuse, exploitation, neglect and maltreatment.
- To enable all children with disabilities to participate fully in all areas of the family, community and society.

9.5.2 CWD and International Declarations

UN Standard Rules on the Equalization of Opportunities for Persons with Disabilities (PWD) Recalling the Convention on the Rights of the Child which prohibits discrimination on the basis of disability and requires special measures to ensure the rights of children with disabilities, and having regard to the Declaration on the Rights of disabled persons adopted by the UN General Assembly, UN Standard Rules on The Equalization of Opportunities for PWDs was adopted.

The Standard Rules express a political commitment on the part of States to adapt society to individuals with functional impairments. The Rules address all aspects of the lives of persons with disabilities and indicate how governments can make social, political and legal changes to ensure that persons with disabilities are treated as full citizens of their country. The Rules cover four main areas:

1. Preconditions for equal participation (awareness raising, medical care, rehabilitation, support services and accessibility).
2. Target areas for equal participation (accessibility, education, employment, income maintenance and social security, family life and personal integrity, culture, recreation and sports, religion).
3. Implementation measures (information and re-search, policy-making and planning, legislation, economic policies, coordination of work, organisations of disabled persons, personnel training national monitoring and evaluation of disability programmes in the implementation of the Rules, technical and economic cooperation and international cooperation).
4. Monitoring mechanisms. The implementation of the Rules is monitored by the Special Rapporteur on Disability, assisted by a committee of experts drawn from the main international NGOs concerned with disability (UNICEF 2007).

The *U.N. Convention on the Rights of Persons with Disabilities* (UNCRPD) was signed by India on March 30, 2007. Subsequently, India was also among the first countries to ratify the Convention on October 1, 2007 and with the 20th ratification happening on April 3, 2008, the Convention came into force 1 month later. In so doing, India reaffirmed its commitment towards the International Policy Framework in respect of the persons with disabilities.

The UNCRPD is a human rights instrument with an explicit social development dimension. It adopts a broad categorisation of persons with disabilities and reaffirms that all persons with all types of disabilities must enjoy all human rights and fundamental freedoms. It clarifies and describes how all categories of rights apply to persons with disabilities and identifies areas where adaptations have to be made for persons with disabilities to effectively exercise their rights and areas where the protection of their rights must be reinforced (UNICEF 2007).

The Convention reflects a 'paradigm shift' in attitudes and approaches to persons with disabilities, in the direction of the social model of disability described above. It represents the culmination of the process initiated over two decades ago by the United Nations of moving from the treatment of persons with disabilities as 'objects' of charity, medical treatment and social protection towards viewing persons with disabilities as 'subjects' with rights who are capable of claiming those rights and making decisions for their lives based on their free and informed consent, as well as being active members of society (UNICEF 2007).

The purpose of the UNCRPD is to promote protect and ensure the full and equal enjoyment of all human rights and fundamental freedom by all persons with disabilities and to promote respect for their inherent dignity. PWD include those who have long-term physical, mental, intellectual or sensory impairments which in interaction with various barriers may hinder their full and effective participation in society on an equal basis with others. The principles of the UNCRPD are:

a. Respect for inherent dignity, individual autonomy including freedom to make one's choices
b. Non-discrimination
c. Full and effective participation and inclusion in society
d. Respect for differences and acceptance of disability as part of human diversity
e. Equality of opportunity
f. Accessibility
g. Equality between men and women
h. Respect for evolving capacities of children with disabilities and respect for CWD to preserve their identity (Alkazi, n.d)

The UNCRPD has 50 articles in all covering various aspects like accessibility, employment, health, participation, dignity, opportunities, education, habitation etc. The articles especially for children are:

Article 7 enjoins all countries to ensure that CWD enjoy all human rights and fundamental freedoms that other children enjoy. All decisions relating to children have to be in their best interest.
Article 16 recognises high level of violence and abuse against children.
Article 23 reiterates the right of children with disability to retain their fertility. It also emphasises the right of the child to live within home and family.
Article 25 emphasises the need for disability specific health services such as early identification and early intervention services designed to minimise and prevent further disabilities, including among children and elderly.
Article 30 ensures that children have equal access to play, recreation and leisure and sporting activities including those in school system (Alkazi, n.d).

9.6 Major Legislations for PWD in India

9.6.1 The Persons with Disabilities (Equal Opportunities, Protection of Rights and Full Participation) Act, 1995

The PWD act is a land mark legislations and policy framework for PWD in India. The objectives of the act are

- Promoting and ensuring equality and full participation of PWD, and

- Protecting and promoting their economic and social rights (National Human Rights Commission, n.d.).

The criteria for classification of each disability are embodied in the bio-medical model. In Section 2(t), a person with disability means 'a person suffering from not less than 40 % of any disability as certified by a medical authority'. The act covers 7 disabilities listed in Section 2, viz. blindness, low vision, leprosy-cured, hearing impairment, locomotor disability, mental retardation and mental illness.

The act spells out responsibilities of the government at all levels including establishments under its control. It lays down specific measures for the development of services and programmes for equalizing opportunities for the enjoyment of right to education, work, housing, mobility and public assistance in case of severe disability and unemployment (National Human Rights Commission 2005). It envisages a Central Coordination committee and state coordination committees representing major ministries, members of parliament, disability NGOs and women with disabilities to execute the mandated responsibilities. It redresses individual grievances, monitors implementation of disability laws, rules and regulations. It oversees budget allocated on disability concerns (National Human Rights Commission, n.d.). It is a quasi judicial body vested with the powers of a civil court. This historic legislation is the cornerstone of evolution of jurisprudence on the rights of persons with disabilities in India.

It has XIV chapters in all, which include two chapters devoted to establishment of Central Coordination committee and State Coordination Committees, two chapters on guidelines for setting up the offices of Chief Commissioner and Commissioners for PWD, prevention and early detection of disabilities, education, employment, affirmative action, research and development of manpower, non-discrimination and Social security. Some of the chapters of the PWD act are summarised as under

Chapter IV: Prevention and Early Detection of Disabilities (http://ccdisabilities.nic.in/Prevention.htm)

Within the limits of their economic capacity and development, the appropriate Governments and the local authorities, with a view to preventing the occurrence of disabilities, shall:

- Undertake or cause to be undertaken surveys, investigations and research concerning the cause of occurrence of disabilities;
- Promote various methods of preventing disabilities;
- Screen all the children at least once in a year for the purpose of identifying "at-risk" cases;
- Provide facilities for training to the staff at the primary health centres;
- Sponsor or cause to be sponsored awareness campaigns and is disseminated or cause to be disseminated information for general hygiene. Health and sanitation,
- Take measures for pre-natal, parental and post-natal care of mother and child;
- Educate the public through the pre-schools, schools, primary health Centres, village level workers and anganwadi workers;

- Create awareness amongst the masses through television, radio and other mass media on the causes of disabilities and the preventive measures to be adopted;

Chapter V: Education (http://ccdisabilities.nic.in/Education.htm)

- Entitles every child with Disability to have access to free education till the age of 18 in an appropriate environment
- Promotes the integration of students with disability in the normal schools
- Endeavours to equip special schools for children with disabilities with vocational training facilities
- Encourage non-formal education for child with disability
- Recommends the establishment of teacher's training institutions to develop requisite manpower
- Provide for appropriate transportation, removal of architectural barriers and restructuring of curriculum for the benefit of child with disability
- Entitles the child with disability to free books, uniform and other learning materials

Throwing more light on Chapter V of the PWD act, it extends from Section 26 to 31.

- Section 26 of the act, apart from making access to education free and compulsory for CWD till they attain the age of 18 years, it endeavours to promote integrated education of CWD in normal schools, and setting up of special schools in such a manner that CWD living in any part of the country have access to education. Section 26 also states for providing of vocational training opportunities for CWD.
- Section 27 of the act enunciates part time classes for CWD who have not been able to avail full time education. It also proposes functional literacy for children above 16 years of age. It recommends imparting education through open schooling system, distance learning and open universities. It is worth noting that the act also asks for providing special books and equipments necessary for his education, free of cost to CWD.
- Section 28 recommends development of teaching aids, assistive devices, special teaching material and any such items that are necessary to equip the child to have equal access to education opportunities. Section 29 brings to the fore teachers training as a core concern wherein it suggest setting up of teachers training institutes and developing teachers training programmes so that requisite manpower is available for special schools and integrated schools for CWD.
- Section 30 recognises the need to provide for transport for the travel of CWD from home to school, removal of architectural barriers, supply of books and uniforms, grant of scholarships etc. It also suggest the setting up of an appropriate agency for attending to the grievances of parents with respect to education of CWD. Recognizing exceptional educational needs of CWD, Section 30 also recommends modification of curriculum and examination system for the benefit of CWD.

- As per Section 31, all institutions are expected to provide amanuensis to blind students and to students with low vision.

There are 74 sections ion all in the PWD act, spread over XIV chapters. Activists have pointed out that the Persons With Disabilities Act, 1995 is not very comprehensive as it leaves out several disabilities like other mental disorders and those with learning problems like dyslexia.

Most legal action related to employment of PWD is on identification and reservations of posts in the organisations for PWD. Litigations are also on benefits of invalidity pension and continuation of service in case of employees who become disabled while in service. Legislative measures have been taken to prevent arbitrary dismissal and retrenchment of an employee and courts have vindicated the right of employees with disabilities.

The PWD Act 1995 is now almost 20 years old. It has been crafted on the medical model of disability. There is a pending bill in the parliament to replace The Persons with Disabilities (Equal Opportunities, Protection of Rights and Full Participation) Act, 1995 with a new legislation which is right based. The new legislation is going to be harmonised with the provisions of United Nations Convention on the Rights for Persons with Disabilities (UNCRPD) and provisions of other legislations on the subject.

9.6.2 National Trust for the Welfare of Persons with Autism, Cerebral Palsy, Mental Retardation and Multiple Disabilities Act (1999)

A landmark legislation to protect and promote the rights of persons with Autism, Cerebral Palsy, Mental Retardation and Multiple Disabilities, spread over IX chapters

- enables and empowers persons with disabilities to live as independently and as fully as possible within and close to the community to which they belong (http://socialjustice.nic.in/pdf/ntact1999.pdf)
- promotes measures for the care and protection of persons with disabilities in the event of death of their parents or guardians (http://socialjustice.nic.in/pdf/ntact1999.pdf)
- Strengthens families in crisis
- Provides for legal guardianship
- extends support to registered organisations to provide need based services during the period of crisis to the families of disabled persons covered under the Trust Act.

The government has contributed a one-time amount of rupees one hundred crore to the trust with which a corpus has been formed. The interest earned from the corpus is used to undertake the activities mandated by the trust. The activities that are supported by the trust are

- counseling and training of family members,
- setting up of adult training units, individual and group homes
- any programme which promotes respite care, foster care, day care for PWD
- development of self help groups
- setting up of local committees whose major role is granting of guardianship of PWD to other individuals. This would be more true in cases where the PWD has movable and non-movable assets which need to be protected for him

The overall supervision of the act is vested with the National Trust Board.

9.6.3 Rehabilitation Council of India Act (1992)

The *Rehabilitation Council of India* was set up in 1986 and by the act of parliament, acquired the status of a statutory body in 1992. Basic object of Rehabilitation Council of India is to standardise and regulate the training courses for rehabilitation personnel. The specific aims are:

- to standardise the training courses for professionals dealing with PWD
- to prescribe minimum standards of education and training of various categories of professionals dealing with PWD
- to regulate standards in all institutions uniformly throughout the country
- Accreditation to training centres, institutions, universities running degree/ diploma/ certificate courses
- To promote research in rehabilitation and special education
- To maintain central rehabilitation register for registration of professionals

RCI regulates training standards of 16 categories of rehabilitation workers. The council promotes training and research initiatives utilizing the experience of specialised as well as mainstream educational institutions (National Human Rights Commission, n.d.). As per the act, 'rehabilitation professional' means:

- Audiologists and speech therapists; clinical psychologists;
- Hearing aids and ear mould technicians;
- Rehabilitation engineers and technicians;
- Special teachers for educating and training the handicapped;
- Vocational counselors, employment officers and placement officers dealing with the handicapped;
- Multipurpose rehabilitation therapist, technicians.

9.7 Government Facilities and Services for Persons with Disabilities

A. Education (Chopra 2012)

1. Under a special scheme, children with disabilities are entitled to receive 100 % financial help for their education (Integrated Education for Disabled Children, Department of Education, Ministry of Human Resource Development). Under this scheme, children would receive.

   Rs. 600/- per annum for books and stationery
   Rs. 300/- per month for transport
   Rs. 200/- per annum for uniform
   Rs. 150/- per month reader allowance for children with visual impairment
   Rs. 600/- per month escort allowance for children with severe disability
   Maximum of up to Rs. 3000/- per student for 5 years allowance for aids
   Rs. 500/- per annum for purchase/development of instructional material

2. *Fellowships*: Junior and Post Doctoral fellowships are awarded by U.G.C. Post Doctoral fellowship is of Rs. 2100 per month while junior fellowship is Rs. 1800 per month. The duration of Post Doctoral fellowship is 2 years and that of Junior fellowship is 4 years.
3. Scheme of National Scholarship for PWD. Under this scheme, every year 500 new scholarship are awarded for pursuing post matric professional and technical courses of duration more than 1 year. However, in respect of students with CP, MR, multiple disabilities profound or severe hearing impairment, scholarship is awarded for pursuing studies from IX Std. onwards. Students with 40 % or more disability whose monthly family income does not exceed Rs. 15,000/- are eligible for scholarship.

B. Financial Assistance for Vocational Rehabilitation (Chopra 2012)

1. A bank (National Handicapped Finance and Development Corporation) has been set up with the main aim of providing a bank to the handicapped persons. Financial assistance is provided to handicapped adults for self-employment, professional training, assistance in agricultural activities, starting/augmenting income generation activities, artisan activities, cottage industry etc. Parent Associations for persons with mental retardation can also take a loan to set-up for them income generating activities. Assistance from Rs. 5,000 to Rs. 50 lakh is available under this bank.
2. Under another scheme (Integrated Rural Development Programme, Ministry of Rural Development and Employment), 3 % of the total subsidy budget has been

earmarked for providing assistance of Rs. 25,000/each to self-help groups of the rural poor person with disability for carrying out suitable economic activities of their choice.

C. Reservation in Jobs and Training (Chopra 2012)

1. 3 % reservation in government jobs for the persons with disability has been made for jobs of A and B category and 5 % reservation is for jobs of C and D category. Government has also identified different kinds of jobs that are suitable for PWD.
2. 3 % seats are reserved for training in all ITI's for persons with disabilities.
3. *Self Employment* Govt. of India has introduced several other schemes to promote employment/self employment among disabled population. Govt. provides assistance to voluntary organisation for training and sheltered workshops. Banks provide loans at low interest rates to promote self employment. Certain categories of disabilities are allotted public telephone booths and other types of shops such as tea stalls.

D. Travel Concessions (Chopra 2012)

1. Transport facilities have been made barrier-free (Ministry of Surface Transport) by incorporating and enforcing handicapped-friendly features in the vehicles, both in the production as well as at the operation stage in all State Transport Undertakings. In addition, handicapped persons are given a concession of 50–100 % on the fares in the state-run buses.
2. Another Ministry (The Railway Ministry), has been providing facilities for barrier-free entry for persons with disabilities into railway offices and railway stations. The following concessions are also provided on production of a certificate from a government doctor/RMP for travel in the Indian Railways:

	1st class	2nd class	Sleeper
Concession (%)	75	75	75

3. The Ministry of Civil Aviation gives 50 % discount on fares to visually impaired persons for air travel. There are no fare concessions for the physically handicapped but they are allowed to carry their wheel chairs, crutches, calipers etc. free of cost.
4. Persons having their own vehicles are exempted from paying road tax and petrol is provided on concessional rates.

E. Provision of Aids and Appliances (Chopra 2012)

1. Under a scheme (Assistance to Disabled Persons for Purchase/Fitting of Aids/Appliances), assistance is provided to needy persons in procuring durable, sophisticated, and scientifically manufactured standard aids to facilitate their rehabilitation and integration in the mainstream.
2. Aids and appliances like wheel chairs, hearing aids, crutches, calipers, Braille slates etc. up to the value of Rs. 3600/- are given free of cost if monthly income of the disabled individual is up to Rs. 6500/- and 50 % assistance is given if income is between Rs. 6500–10,000/- per month.

F. Other Concessions (Chopra 2012)

1. There is a 7 % reservation in allotment of dealership agencies/retail outlets for Kerosene and LPG for physically disabled persons/widows of personnel (Ministry of Petroleum and Natural Gas).
2. Educated and unemployed disabled persons get preference in allotment of STD/ISD booths. To avail this benefit, the person must be educated up to at least Class VIII in rural areas and be a matriculate/high school pass in urban areas.
3. The Postal Department provides free postage for 'Blind Literature Packets'.
4. Residential houses are allotted to the handicapped persons who are in govt. service on priority basis. The DDA has reserved 5 % of shops, 10 % residential plots and 1 % flats in each housing scheme for PWD.

9.8 Interventions and Strategies by Non-government Organisations in Disability

CAN (Concerned Action Now) was established in Delhi in 1982. CAN works for the welfare of Persons with disabilities (particularly physically and mentally disabled) and people cured of leprosy. It focuses mainly on advocacy, action and research on all issues concerning disability. CAN uses 'Action Learning approach' to work with disabled persons and their families, professionals, service providers, scholars and other agencies. The 'Action learning' approach is based on the belief that people learn new ways of doing things most efficiently when they acquire them by tackling a real life problem. CAN strives to bring forth the disabled people into the mainstream by making them aware of their rights, empowering and educating them. It also creates awareness and sensitivity amongst people regarding the issues related to disability.

Since its inception, CAN has undertaken several projects and programmes for the welfare of disabled in collaboration with the Indian government as well as several national and international organisations such as OXFAM, Action Aid, Leprosy Mission India, UNHCR, University of Newcastle, IGNOU, ICSSR and others. In collaboration with the University of Newcastle (UK) and CSIR (South Africa), CAN has conducted a study on the accessibility and utilisation of specialised services by the lower income disabled people. CAN has also done intensive case studies on UN refugees with disabilities in Delhi and also accessed the nutritional status of refugee children at the behest of United Nations High Commissioner for Refugees (UNHCR). CAN has successfully implemented SAVERA Project in 36 villages of Thikri block of Badwani District in MP. Under the project, training workshops were conducted for PWDs and field workers; awareness and sensitisation camps were organised and community groups were formed in the villages. This project was highly appreciated by the Ministry of Social Justice and Empowerment, GOI. For the Leprosy Mission, India, CAN prepared a research report containing guidelines and a prototype day care centre for the disabled on paper. CAN has recently completed a report based on fieldwork carried out to evaluate National Trust's "Supported Guardianship Scheme". CAN has successfully compiled a comprehensive database on disability in collaboration with the District Rehabilitation Center, Government of India. It has also compiled a Delhi Disability Directory in the year 2000.

CAN is currently running Vocational Training Centres in two slum areas of South Delhi to empower the poor disabled people. The handcrafted products, such as greeting cards, kantha work bags in cotton and silk cloth, glass paintings, wall hangings, papier-mâché and hand-made paper and jute items etc., are made by disabled people and their family members and then are sold under the brand name of CAN CRAFTS.

CAN maintains a data bank on prevention of disabilities and rehabilitation and equalisation of opportunities for the disabled. It also collects and disseminates information about the safeguards created by the Disability Act. It publishes books and pamphlets and also conducts workshops, seminar and media interactions on disability issues and organises Ribbon Campaign for the disabled every year on 3rd December (the International Day for Persons with Disabilities).

The **National Association for the Blind, NAB** was established in 1952. The major mission of NAB is to integrate all visually impaired individuals into the mainstream of society. It strives to empower the visually impaired persons with education, training and employment. NAB has 19 state branches (in Delhi, Uttar Pradesh, Uttaranchal, Himachal Pradesh, Haryana, Chandigarh, Madhya Pradesh, Jharkhand, Gujarat, Maharashtra, Orissa, Assam, Sikkim, Chhattisgarh, Tamil Nadu, Karnataka, Kerala, Andhra Pradesh, Union Territory of Daman, Diu and Dadra Nagar Haveli and Goa) and 65 district level branches across India.

NAB provides for integrated education of visually impaired children in regular schools. Presently, about 270 blind students of the NAB, Delhi branch study are studying in app. 32 regular schools in integration with the sighted students. NAB, Delhi organises regular weekly Eye Camps in rural and slum areas and provide free medicines and spectacles to the visually impaired. Cataract Surgery is also done in these camps. NAB has also established a home for the elderly blind people in Delhi.

The NAB branch, Delhi provides for various specialised services at the centre. It has a Preparatory School where 5–9 years old blind children are admitted and are trained in mobility, daily living skills, perceptual skills, functional literacy (reading and writing), physical exercises and recreation. The Visually Impaired Multi Handicapped Centre in NAB looks after the needs of blind children with additional disabilities like hearing impairment, intellectual disability or cerebral palsy etc. It focuses on the overall development, education and rehabilitation needs of such children. The Deaf-blind Unit takes care of deaf-blind children and runs various Centre Based and Community-Based Programmes for them. In the training centre at NAB, students undergo Computer training in Windows, Word Processing and Internet etc. To facilitate computer learning by the visually impaired individuals, Speech Synthesizer is attached to each computer. NAB also has a talking book library where Audio recording of the Text books is done and then these Audio cassettes and CDs of the text books are made available to the visually impaired students. Braille Books are also made and given to students to facilitate their studies. NAB also has hostel facility for blind students both boys and girls.

The *National Centre for Promotion of Employment for Disabled People (N.C.P. E.D.P.)* was established in 1996. The Board of Management of NCPEDP comprises of people from all spheres, i.e. industry, N.G.Os, disabled people and international agencies. The main objectives of NCPEDP are better educational and employment opportunities and appropriate legislation for the empowerment of the disabled, the easy and convenient access of the disabled to all public places and increasing public awareness on disability issues.

Ever since its inception, the major mission of *N.C.P.E.D.P.* has been to improve the situation of employment of the disabled in corporate sector of India. It has raised the issue of the dismal employment of disabled people in the corporate sector of India at various forums. Due to its efforts, the Confederation of Indian Industry has constituted a core group to promote employment of the disabled in the private sector. This core group increases awareness about the abilities of disabled people and provides guidelines for creating a disabled friendly infrastructure to its top hundred member companies. It also works to train disabled people in various skills and competencies to work in companies. It also advocates for new policies for education and legal rights of the disabled.

In partnership with the British High Commission, N.C.P.E.D.P. is currently running a 3-year project "Mainstreaming of Disability in the National Agenda—Policy to Practice". Under this project, it has conducted studies on the existing policies and schemes, physical infrastructure facilities for the disabled and has given recommendations for the future policies for the disabled.

NCPEDP has put together lists of employment exchanges, placement centres and vocational rehabilitation centres for the disabled. It also compiles and disseminates information about various government employment and self-employment schemes for the disabled people.

It was due to NCPEDP tireless efforts that disability got included in the Population Census of 2001. N.C.P.E.D.P. has also served on the social sector committee of the Planning Commission and is a member of the disability core group with the National Human Rights Commission. NCPEDP is creating a detailed plan for disabled friendly railways and airlines and disabled friendly bus transport in at least all four metropolitan cities of India. NCPEDP is also persuading the Government of India for including disability in the Central and State building by-laws so that new public buildings are constructed disabled friendly. NCPEDP is also developing a joint action plan with apex bodies such as the National Institute of Design and the Council of Architecture, to establish a National Access Institute. It has also partnered with the Council of Architecture for inclusion of disability in the curriculum of Architecture.

N.C.P.E.D.P. instituted Shell Helen Keller awards in 1999 to honour individuals and organisations doing exemplary in the field of disability. Every year it honours 10 role models who have done distinguished work to integrate disabled people into the national mainstream.

References

Alkazi, R.M. (n.d). *Understanding the UNCRPD a toolkit*. New Delhi: Aarth Astha.

Alur, M. (2002). Special needs policy in India. In S. Hegarty % M. Alur (Eds.) *Education & children with special needs: From segregation to inclusion*. New Delhi: Sage Publication.

Bagchi, A. (2009). Disability and human rights: A socio-historical dichotomy. In A. Bhuimali (Ed.), *Rights of disabled women and children in India*. New Delhi: Serials publications.

Baladerian, N.J. (1991). Sexual abuse of people with developmental disabilities. *Sexuality and Disability*, *9*(4), 323–335.

Barnes, C., & Mercer, G. (2003). *Disability*. Malden, MA: Polity Press and Blackwell Publishers.

Barnes, C. (1997). A legacy of oppression: A history of disability in western culture. In L. Barton & M. Oliver (Eds.), *Disability studies: Past, present and future*. Leeds: Disability Press.

Byrnes, M. (1990). The regular education debate: A view from the field. *Exceptional Children, 56* (4), 345–349.

Bowe, F. (1978). *Handicapping America*. New York: Harper and Row.

Census India. (2001). Retrieved January 12, 2009 from www.censusindia.net.

Census India. (2011). Retrieved from http://censusindia.gov.in/.

Chander, J. (2013). Disability rights and disability studies. In R. Addlakha (Ed.), *Disability studies in India*. New Delhi: Routledge.

Chopra, G. (2012). *Early detection of disabilities and persons with disabilities in the community*. New Delhi: Engage Publications.

Darlington, T., Miller, E. J., & Gwynne, G. (1981). *A life together*. London: Tavistock.

Davis, L. J. (1997). The need for disability studies. In L. J. Davis (Ed.), *The disability studies reader*. London: Routledge.

Department of Women and Child Development. (n.d.). *National plan of action for children, 2005*. New Delhi: Government of India. Retrieved from http://www.wcd.nic.in/NAPAug16A.pdf.

Finkelstein, V. (1980). *Attitudes and disabled people*. New York: World Rehabilitation Fund.

Retrieved April 20, 2015 from http://www.rehab-scales.org/international-classification-of-functioning-disability-and-health.html.
Hunt, P. (ed). (1966). *Stigma: The experience of disability*. London: Geoffrey Chapman.
Kavoori, P. (2002). Inclusive education experiences. In S. Hegarty & M. Alur (Eds.), Education and children with special needs. From segregation to inclusion. New Delhi: Sage Publication.
Kevles, D. J. (1985). *In the name of eugenics: Genetics and the uses of human hereditary*. New York: Alfred A. Knopf.
Kitchlu, T. N. (Ed.). (1991). *A century of blind welfare in India*. Delhi: Penman Publishers.
Laha, S. S. (2009). Work participation rate among disabled population of India. In A. Bhuimali (Ed.), *Rights of disabled women and children in India*. New Delhi: Serial Publications.
Meyer, L. H. et. al. (1990). *Critical issues in the lives of people with severe disabilities*. Baltimore: Paul. H. Brookes.
Ministry of Statistics and Programme Implementation. (2012). *Manual on disability statistics*. New Delhi: Government of India. CSO-MDS-2012.
Mohit, A. (2003). Human rights model and access. *International Journal of Human Rights*.
National Human Rights Commission. (2005). *Disability manual 2005*. New Delhi: NHRC.
National Human Rights Commission. (n.d.). *Know your rights–rights of persons with disabilities*. New Delhi: NHRC.
National Policy for Persons with Disabilities. (2006). Retrieved from http://www.disabilityindia.org/nationalpolicyfordisable.cfm.
NSSO 58th Round (July–December 2002). *Report No.485 (58/26/1), Disabled Persons*. Retrieved from http://mospi.nic.in/mospi_nsso_rept_pubn.htm.
Onsando, M., Nanjunda, D. C., & Venugopal, P. N. (2009). Human rights approach for disabled persons: Issues and prospects. In A. Bhuimali (Ed.), *Rights of disabled women and children in India*. New Delhi: Serials Publications.
Ramakrishnan, U., & Anandalakshmy, S. (2009). Presenting and inclusive tool understanding diversity. In M. Alur & V. Timmons (Eds.), *Inclusive education across cultures crossing boundaries, sharing ideas*. New Delhi: Sage Publications.
Rioux, M. (2001). Bending towards justice. In L. Barton (Ed.), *Disability, politics and struggle for change*. London: David Fulton.
Scotch, R. K. (2001). *From goodwill to civil rights: Transforming federal disability policy*. Philadelphia: Temple University Press.
Thomas, D. (1982). *The experience of handicap*. London: Methuen.
Tomlinson, S. (1982). *A sociology of special education*. London: Routledge.
UNICEF Innocenti Research Centre (2007). *Promoting the rights of children with disabilities*. Florence Italy: Innocenti Digest no.3. ISBN: 978-88-89129-60-9 & ISSN: 1028-3528.
World Bank (2007). *People with disabilities in India from commitments to outcomes*: South Asia Region.
Young, I. M. (1990). *Justice and the politics of difference*. Princeton: Princeton University Press.

FSC
www.fsc.org
MIX
Papier | Fördert gute Waldnutzung
FSC® C083411

Kolibri 360 GmbH
Ferdinand-Jühlke-Straße 7
99095 Erfurt, Deutschland
produktsicherheit@kolibri360.de